Spirit
rescue

About the Author

Born in Paisley, Scotland, Wilma Davidson has lived in the South of England for forty years. She has worked in the field of spiritual contact and psychic development for many years, and has studied feng shui and geopathic stress. She is a Reiki master as well as a healer and spirit rescuer, has organized healing circles, and is a member of several such groups. She teaches and lectures on these topics, and frequently appears on radio and television programs to discuss them.

Spirit
rescue

A Simple Guide to

Talking with Ghosts

and Freeing

Earthbound

Spirits

Wilma Davidson

Llewellyn Publications
Woodbury, Minnesota

First Edition
First Printing, 2006

Cover art © Photodisc
Editing by Connie Hill
Llewellyn is a registered trademark of Llewellyn Worldwide, Ltd.

Library of Congress Cataloging-in-Publication Data
Davidson, Wilma
    Spirit rescue : a simple guide to talking with ghosts and freeing earthbound spirits
   / Wilma Davidson. — 1st ed.
      p. cm.
    Includes bibliographical references and index.
    ISBN 13: 978-0-7387-0907-9
    ISBN 10: 0-7387-0907-7
    1. Ghosts. 2. Spirits. 3. Parapsychology. 4. Death. I. Title.
BF1444.D38   2006
133.9'1—dc22   2006046721

Llewellyn Publications
A Division of Llewellyn Worldwide, Ltd.
2143 Wooddale Drive, Dept. 0-7387-0907-7
Woodbury, Minnesota 55125-2989, U.S.A.
www.llewellyn.com

Printed in the United States of America

Contents

Introduction

———————————————— ● ————————————————

Do you ever wonder why certain events happened to you, and then you begin to realise that the lessons you learned from them enable you to pass on advice and information to others? Perhaps if you sit down and think back over the years, you will, like me, realise that many of the crisis or events you experienced have given you the knowledge you need in your life.

People often ask me how I became a healer. And how did I know that I had these abilities? The answer is "I didn't know." It all happened by accident, although we all know there is no such thing as an accident. My marriage had broken up unexpectedly after nearly thirty years, and as I had known my husband since I was three years of age, you can understand my confusion. I visited an astrologer who told me I would become a healer and work in the spiritual field. This I found hard to believe as I had never been interested in this way of life.

Further confirmation was given to me some time later when on holiday in France, by a clairvoyant also on holiday. This lady assured me that I would be a healer. Again, I did not take her words seriously, but perhaps it was at the back of my mind, as a few weeks later I was invited by a friend to join a six-week basic healing course.

Normally I would have discarded the idea of attending a healing course, but something inside my brain stirred and encouraged me to go along to the class. There were ten of us gathered in the room, all beginners and all a little apprehensive.

When I had learned the basics of healing, I knew it was time to join a development circle, which I attended for several years. There I learned all sorts of valuable lessons including absent healing, spirit rescue work, psychometry, dowsing, and psychic development, which gave me the confidence to explore these subjects further.

When you start on this spiritual pathway, you soon find that each time you think you have a reasonable knowledge about healing or other spiritual work, you realise that you know very little, that there is so much to learn, and that learning is continuous.

It is so important for all of us to pass on our knowledge of these subjects to others, and so I am passing on some of my experiences to you in the hope that you will find a few of these facts helpful, and it will give you the confidence to heal, dowse, or rescue any trapped soul you meet. Perhaps there is one spirit living in your home or workplace.

When we die, we are offered help to join our loved ones. Those who are earthbound have, for some personal reason, refused or ignored the help, and are drifting. You cannot make a spirit move on unless he or she is ready to go home.

As well as telling you about earthbound spirits, and how you can help them on their journey, I have covered a range of subjects including spiritual healing, as our world today needs many healers. Also included is a chapter on the art of dowsing, some tips on learning to dowse, and some of the many uses of this invaluable tool. The pendulum can be used to find the sex of a spirit or the number of years it has been trapped. It can also be used to establish the presence of geopathic stress in a building, as this negative energy affects health and attracts earthbound spirits.

Whether you are doing spiritual work or are in the presence of a negative person, it is essential that you don protection so that you'll feel secure and can avoid being drained of energy. Protection is invaluable and should never be underrated. I have explained a few basic forms of protection—the choice is yours.

I have included some facts about reincarnation, astral travel, near-death experiences, electronic voice phenomena, psychic surgery, and other fascinating subjects that are all part of psychic development, which is a never-ending learning.

Once you become in tune with the world of spirit, you will find that all methods of healing and other spiritual work are interrelated, and you can extend your skills to other areas. The secret of success in all spiritual work is to be relaxed, and to enjoy it, secure in the knowledge that you are never alone—your spirit guides and helpers are always there waiting to help when asked.

Each of us has a guardian angel who is constantly around us. We also have a main spirit guide and many spiritual helpers. By meditating regularly, joining a development circle, or becoming an astral traveler, you will build up a relationship with these wonderful, invisible spirit beings and learn to communicate with them.

Before telling you about the spirit world and how you can recognise and help earthbound spirits, I want first to tell you about the wonders of exploring the universe by astral travel, and how past life regression can enable you to visit scenes from some of your past lives and give answers to any of the unexplained feelings, fears, or dislikes you experience in this life.

Other than the few facts quoted from books or magazines, all the information is drawn from my own experiences or is my understanding of the subject. I hope you will find some of the information in this book helpful, and that it will enable you to progress even further on your spiritual pathway.

Death is not the end. Life is like a never-ending cycle, so I want to begin this book by talking about reincarnation and near death experiences before telling you about earthbound spirits and psychic development.

chapter one

Reincarnation— Are You a Believer?

———————————•———————————

Like earthbound spirits or near-death experiences, reincarnation is another conversation stopper! It's a subject guaranteed to get people arguing about proof, or lack of it. Sceptics have a great time with this subject, while others are firm believers because they have received positive proof that they have lived many lives before their present life on Earth.

The big questions are "Is there such a thing as reincarnation?" "Does it really occur?" "How does it happen?" and "Is there life after death on Earth or on any other planets?" These questions are regularly debated, but until we pass to spirit, we will never know the answers.

Déjà Vu

Many of us have experienced déjà vu. This is that inexplicable flash of insight when you know instinctively that you have been in a place before, but your common sense tells you that you have never in your life been within a hundred miles of the place. Have you ever turned a corner and known instinctively what you are going to see? How can you explain that you know what the street scene and the houses will look like?

You know their shape and they feel familiar, but how do you explain this strange phenomena?

When you comment to anyone about this strange experience, they will often say "Oh, that's déjà vu," but what is the real explanation? Is it perhaps linked to a past life experience? Often what is called déjà vu is in actual fact a past life recall, and yes, you could have been in that place in a previous life, either as an adult or a child. When this situation is a glimpse of a past life, you will receive confirmation, as you will feel some emotion—whether warmth, sadness, or even fear—which will confirm you have been there before.

It is a different situation when you see something almost immediately before it happens, but you don't feel these familiar emotions, as this is not a past life. In fact, it is the opposite, as you are experiencing a timeslip, when you are going forward, instead of backward.

Some therapists report it is possible to go forward in time, and this would certainly account for the occasion when you are talking to a person and seem to have heard the conversation before, as you know what words you are about to hear. It is possible to be regressed forward in time, as well as back in time. Since we are meant to learn from our experiences, seeing what's ahead may sound great, but we are not going to learn from it as human nature will encourage us to take evasive action to avoid anything that does not please us. So, yes, you can go forward in time, but I would not recommend attempting to do this except in unusual circumstances.

Déjà vu can occur when you happen to meet a person for the first time. You feel as though you know them intimately and they seem so familiar to you, in that you seem to know their every facial expression and movement, and yet you know you have never before met this person.

This is almost certainly someone you have known in a past life—the only explanation that can account for feeling a strong bond of friendship with them. Some folks describe it as a wonderful surge of "love energy, like a bombshell" that hits them in their heart, and it is confusing and difficult to handle.

It is also possible to meet a stranger who makes you feel ill at ease; your stomach starts to churn, and your legs tremble for no apparent reason. It is almost certainly a past life contact, and if you have a session of regression therapy, you will be able to establish why you feel ill at ease with one person, or why you feel an inexplicably great attraction to another.

Scientists and sceptics will give us all sorts of technical and scientific explanations why these situations occur, but are you convinced? I'm not. How do they explain why we are drawn with an almost unnatural craving to visit certain countries, or buildings? When you get there, you feel you know the area so well, and yet you know you have no link with the area—but your gut feeling is telling you a different story.

I have had some interesting experiences over the past twenty years that have convinced me that reincarnation is a perfectly normal part of the soul's development.

Time Slip or Déjà Vu?

I recently had a very unexpected, and powerful emotional experience that added to my conviction that there's life after life. Although I did not realise it at the time, it all started last year when, walking down some steps to the beach near my home, to my astonishment I experienced a time slip. For a split second, I saw this amazing sight of a group of Viking ships sailing toward the shore, and although they appeared to be only a hundred yards away from where I was standing, much to my surprise I did not feel the least bit afraid. A very warm and calm feeling came over me; I was aware of being part of a familiar scene and knew instinctively that the Vikings had been fishing and were coming home, and that I was waiting for their arrival.

This overwhelming experience was pushed to the back of my mind and did not surface again until this week when something out of character happened to me. As my home is in the process of being sold to enable me to move back to the mainland, I decided to plan a holiday in Scotland during the time when my furniture was in storage and my life in limbo. After requesting several brochures on tours of Scotland, they duly arrived and I enthusiastically opened them to see what was available.

Included in the mail was a brochure for the Shetland Isles, the Viking country, and to my utter astonishment, when looking at the pictures of the beautiful golden sandy beaches and lovely scenery of this area, I became totally overcome with emotion. This feeling was completely out of character as I am normally a very calm person who finds it difficult to cry, so you can imagine my astonishment when I began to shake like a leaf. My stomach was churning round and round like a toy top, and I was shaking from head to foot. Was I being confronted by a past life?

When I sat down to digest this strange reaction, the pieces began to fit together. I remembered the strange experience when I saw the Viking boats during the time slip, and also the fact that I have for several years been drawn to learn the Viking Runes. Had I, in the past, had a life in the Shetland Isles? So far, I have purchased four books on the runes, but not yet had time to learn the secrets of these mystical signs. My enthusiasm for the runes drove me to collect a number of stones and make a complete set of runes.

Confirmation that I had indeed lived in the Shetland Isles many years ago came when I least expected it, and from an unusual source. The proof arrived with an Australian lady who visited me for healing to reduce jet lag. To my delight, when I was giving the healing, this lady told me she was a medium, and then proceeded to tell me of my own fascinating past life.

She told me that I had a past life in Shetland. As a child I had lived on this beautiful wild coast, and, with many other children, had been taken away by a group of invading Vikings to grow up in their community. She explained that the fear I felt when I viewed the brochure appeared to have been a repeat of the terror I experienced when being dragged away from my home and my helpless parents.

There's now absolutely no doubt in my mind that I must visit the Shetland Isles to find the root of this powerful affinity to the Vikings, which I believe is a link from a previous life.

Regression Can Track Down Past Lives

Past life therapy is a wonderful way to find answers to unexplained feelings, and helps to fit the missing pieces to the jigsaw. This therapy is very useful if you are concerned that you have a negative attachment, or are possessed by an earthbound spirit, as this therapy will expose these problems. A regression session will show your age when the attachment joined you, and any link you may have with this attachment.

Having a past life regression is a fascinating experience, as it gives you answers to all sorts of little mysteries in your life, and you will know instinctively that the answers are correct. Those who have been regressed can tell of many lives in different parts of the world, of being male in some of these lives, and female in others. The fact that you are male or female in this life does not mean that you are the same sex in each life time. Your hair, skin colour, and build can also be very different in each life.

Don't worry if you don't expect to learn any true facts during a session, as you don't have to believe in regression for it to work. Simply by relaxing and trusting the therapist, one of your many lives will almost certainly be revealed.

If you have a specific problem in your life—perhaps you can't stand the company of a certain person, and the slightest thing they do, however inoffensive, irritates you—mentally asking if this particular personality clash is linked to a past life will sometimes provide the explanation. You may find that the person let you down badly in a previous life, or perhaps even injured or killed you—it is quite amazing what may be revealed.

There are several different ways to be regressed, but if you are not experienced in meditation, I would advise going to a hypnotherapist or past life therapist. Here are the most common methods of being taken into a past life regression:

1. Hypnotherapy, when you are taken into a very light trance.
2. Meditation group, when all the sitters go into a deep meditative state and mentally ask to be shown a past life.
3. Self-induced, altered state of consciousness.

When you visit a hypnotherapist or past life therapist, you are asked to sit down and relax, and usually the therapist will help you to relax by having soft music playing in the background, and may ask you to visualise a nice country or riverside scene. When you are relaxed, they will talk you down a flight of stairs, counting each one, until they think you are on the right vibration. You do not need to worry about being unconscious, as in some countries it is illegal for a hypnotherapist to take a patient to the level used by stage hypnotherapists, who have people doing all sorts of ridiculous, undignified tricks.

Once you see the past life you can ask questions, or allow the therapist to ask the questions, and you will feel that the scene makes a lot of sense, and will probably throw some light on the reason for certain likes or dislikes in your life.

Past Lives in Meditation

Another option is to sit in a meditation circle each week, learning how to meditate and contact your spirit guides and helpers, and be shown past lives. Some circle leaders will do an exercise of taking you down fifteen steps. At the bottom of the steps there will be a large hall with six doors, each a different color. Each door represents a past life, and you will be asked to open the door of your choice, and have a look inside the room. There you will see a past life scene—if you do not like this scene you will be told to close the door, come back into the hall, and choose another door to open. Having the knowledge that you can walk away if you do not like what you see eliminates apprehension.

On a spiritual level, past life therapy done during meditation can reveal information that will help you to progress on your spiritual pathway. We each have a soul that is on it's own journey, and regression can often show our pathway ahead. Seeing details of your spiritual progress can help to give confidence and reassurance that you are doing the right spiritual work—at times we all have doubts.

Group Regression Therapy

Group regression is an ideal way to dip your toe in the water if you feel a little apprehensive about having a one-on-one treatment, as it gives you an insight into what it is all about and helps you to decide whether you would like to learn more about this form of therapy. Group therapy is a good starting point, but it is not the best place to resolve emotional issues, as that is a job for an experienced therapist.

Souls travel in groups, so folks you met in a past life will appear in this life. Don't be surprised if you see friends or members of your family from your therapy in a past life. The person who is your mother in this life may have been your brother in a past life, or the person who was your father in your past life may be your mother in this life.

Regressed by Telephone

I mentioned to an acquaintance one day several years ago that I had some personal problems, whereupon this kind soul said that she could take me back to a past life to find the cause of the problem. As the regression was going to be carried out during a telephone conversation, I felt rather sceptical, but having nothing to loose by accepting this kind offer, I was prepared to go along with the idea, and awaited the experience with interest.

It was a very uncomplicated regression as she took me straight into a past life where my husband was behaving badly. Because this lady was psychic, she was able to see everything that I could see, and she was able to give me answers to my questions. It was a quick and effective way to have a regression, but I would not recommend it to anyone who is not very experienced in this field.

Regression for a Shoulder Injury

I had a regression to find the cause of a shoulder injury that refused to heal, and opened the door for a fascinating story to unfold. The therapist asked me to lie on a couch and relax, then to visualise myself lying on a magic carpet that was going to take me on a magical trip. As I saw myself lying on this magic carpet, she told me that it was going to float into the beautiful, clear blue sky, moving forward for a few minutes. She then told me that the carpet was going to stop, turn around, and move backward in time, and that I would be able to look down and see all the past times in history, and that I would know when it was time to get off the magic carpet.

Lying back and enjoying this magical history tour was an amazing experience, and I can remember looking down at different countries and times, and suddenly I knew it was time to land. I found myself in the wilds of Africa, probably one of the last places I would have expected to find the answer to the cause of my shoulder injury, but what was revealed was a fascinating story, and one that I don't think I could ever have made up.

I was the chief warrior in an African village, and I led my warriors to fight the enemy tribes. I could very clearly see this battle in place—my warriors were throwing their spears at the invaders, and then turning to run away. As I also turned to run away, disaster struck. I could see a spear flying through the air toward me. As it hit me, it dug deep into the back of my right shoulder. Needless to say, I was then unable to throw a spear. On returning to the village, the tribal chief banished me to the wilderness to die, as I was no longer any use as a warrior.

I left my wife and children and went off to the wilderness, but being a very determined person, I did not simply wait to die. Instead I healed my wound with plants and taught myself to throw the spear with my left hand. I practised continuously until I was again an expert, and then marched back to the village and demanded my old job back as chief warrior.

Perhaps I would have taken this story as a load of absolute nonsense had it not been for the fact that I am a keen golfer and my shoulder injury was upsetting my game—during the previous year, before my trip on the magic carpet, I had decided to learn to play left-handed! Was it just a coincidence?

Being regressed can be a very serious experience, but it can also be great fun and quite exciting, as it is an opportunity to see the different lives you've led. It feels a bit like sitting back in the theatre and watching a play unfold, with yourself as the star performer. You may have had a life at sea, so could see yourself on a sailing ship, as a deckhand or the captain of the ship, and in another life you could see a scene of yourself as a servant girl, or as a fine lady in a beautiful ball gown.

As well as past life therapy being fun and helping to explain likes and dislikes, it is also an excellent tool to get to the root of unexplained emotional fears or a specific illness. Once the cause and the history of the problem have been revealed, it is then possible to have the right treatment, but until the cause is found, no amount of drugs or therapy treatment will give a permanent cure.

Many people still think of past life therapy as an airy-fairy, New Age thing, but how wrong can they be? Regression is an excellent method of finding the cause of any behavioural problems, relationship turbulence, or personality clashes, as well as fears and unexplained phobias, so if you have any puzzling problems, think regression. You'll be glad you took this step to open the door, which can hold the key to many of your life's problems.

A past life therapy session allows you to access your subconscious mind and, if the time is right, it will show you a traumatic experience or other unresolved issues. But don't worry as you will never be shown anything which is too painful, or horrible, for your emotions to handle. After release of past life baggage, you will most likely find you have turned a corner, and that you feel lighter, as the issues that were shown in regression have been lifted out of your life so that you can move onward. Because this therapy allows you to access your subconscious mind, it enables you to tie up the ends of unfinished business with others, and to heal old scars.

Regression Can Solve Marriage Problems

A good therapist will be guided to assist you to release both physical and emotional energy blockages, and balance your energy. Marriage problems can be many and varied—often it is the little things your partner does that drive you mad, or perhaps they seem to get a feeling of power from trying to lower your self-esteem.

This is a surprisingly common problem. Many people describe how their partner seems to get a sadistic satisfaction from lowering their self-worth. The situation is often revealed in regression—the problem could be an unresolved issue in a previous life, so before your self-worth gets any lower, consider regression, as it will possibly help you to turn the tables around and find balance in your marriage.

Reincarnation cannot yet be proved by science, but people who have experienced it are in no doubt that we all have had many lives in different places. It is important to have past life issues cleared up in this lifetime, as if they are not resolved in this life, then they will appear in future lives until the issue has been resolved.

Past Lives on Other Planets

Yes, there does seem to be life on other planets, and many people living today on planet Earth have incarnated on another planet in at least one past life. If you are able to dowse, you can ask your pendulum if you have had a past life on another planet. If you receive a "Yes" answer, you can then ask if you have had more than one life on other planets. Don't be too surprised if your pendulum confirms that you have indeed lived on other planets, perhaps not looking exactly the same as humans on Earth, but similar. Remember, your soul does not change each time you incarnate, even if your appearance or shape changes!

Releasing Emotional Baggage

Sometimes an event of a past life can have a very harmful effect on this life, perhaps causing a stressful phobia. Regression will resolve the issue and help you to let go of the traumatic memory, whether physical or emotional, so that once this baggage has been released, your body can heal itself.

This is often a very good time to have spiritual healing and use an alternative therapy to rebalance the body's energy, as releasing painful memories can be exhausting and leave your body out of balance.

Good Bye to Phobias

Although most people who suffer from a phobia seldom mention their problem, phobias are very common. When you raise the subject of phobias in a group of friends, it is quite amazing how many people will admit they have a phobia about something, but have never found a reason for this violent reaction. If you suffer from a phobia that causes stress in your life, please don't feel self-conscious about it, as this seldom talked about fear is more common than you realise.

A phobia is an unexplained fear that can be so powerful that it can make your tummy muscles contract and your heart beat so fast that you can hear it thumping and vibrating.

Are you terrified of being in water so have never learned to swim, and cannot even bring yourself to go for a sail on a boat or a cruise on a large ship? Then it's time to be regressed, as this phobia can disrupt your quality of life, and also affect the family. This type of phobia is often cleared quickly, as invariably regression will show a past life when you were a passenger on a ship that sank and you were drowned at sea. Or perhaps you fell into a river as a child and were carried away by a rapid current. The explanation is often simple—when you realise the root cause of your phobia, you are then able to let go of the fear and get on with your life.

Whether your phobia is a terror of water, heights, or sleeping in a dark bedroom, help is at hand. After a regression session when a phobia has been revealed, it is important to rest, to allow your mind and body to recover from the shock of the revelation. Give yourself a little space and enjoy a short relaxation period before going back to normal chores.

Birthmarks from Past Lives

Those taking part in a birthmark research study by scientist Professor Ian Stevenson reported their birthmarks were caused by injury in a past life. Children involved could give details of relatives, and how they had died.[1] These results confirm reports from other folks who have had the explanation of a birthmark revealed during a past life.

There are so many factors about life on earth that are unknown to us, and we will probably never know the answers until we pass on to the next dimension.

Children's Past Lives

Sceptics can say this subject is a load of nonsense, but how do they explain the enormous number of plausible stories of children and adults who can relate accurate information about people and places, which they could not possibly have known if they had not experienced that life? In the last two decades, many of the children being born are very "old souls," so it is hardly surprising that many parents are staggered by knowledgeable comments made by their young child, who had absolutely no way of knowing the facts he or she has quoted.

A fine example is Rabih, a little Lebanese boy born in 1985, who remembers clearly his previous life as a famous football player. Yes, it's almost every little boy's dream to be a famous football player, but this little lad could give amazing details of his death, where he had lived, and facts about his family that had never been made public. So how could this child give such accurate information about the life of this footballer, who had died before the child was born?[2]

Past Lives Will Answer Some Questions

Shirley MacLaine, the colourful actress, film star, and prolific author, has written many books referring to her previous incarnations, and describes a past life when she was a dancer in an Egyptian harem—not difficult to visualise! She also claims in her book *Camino, A Journey of the Spirit*, that she was the lover of Charlemagne, who lived from 768 to AD 814, and that she bore three children to him.[3] It looks as though Shirley has brought many of her talents learned from these previous lives with her to this life, and has used them in her career.

Regression Fills in the Blanks

Another interesting case is a three-year-old boy in Northern India who said that in a previous life he had robbed many people, and hidden the spoils forty years ago. He identified the woman in a nearby village who had been his wife in that life, and found the buried treasure. The accuracy of these facts has been confirmed by the Department of Clinical Psychology at the National Institute of Mental Health and Neuroscience in Bangalore, India.[4]

Monica, a forty-seven-year-old housewife, was terrified of water, so could not visit the beach. Regression showed that, as a young girl, she had drowned on the *Titanic*. She told her name and the village where she had lived, and local records confirmed the facts.[5] Regression is a fascinating subject—most people who have been regressed have amazing tales to tell.

A colourful past life is remembered by the man from Gravesend, Kent, who can give details of his life at sea, beginning as a cabin boy when he visited many countries as a crew member on Nelson's ship, *The Victory*. He tells how he saw a French battleship, the *Courageux*, draw alongside *The Victory*, and describes how Nelson was shot. Sceptics will say he read the story, but if so, how can they explain the accurate details—it could just be a good imagination, but is it?[6]

If you are fascinated by the subject of past lives, then I recommend the website of the magazine *Life and Soul*, which is full of interesting examples of reincarnation and other paranormal experiences.

In certain circles of Christianity, the subject of life after death is taboo—it is a great unmentionable subject, which almost falls into the same attitude category as that toward the subject of sex fifty years ago. In my childhood, I desperately nagged my mother to tell me how women had babies. The question was sidestepped for a long time, until one day in exasperation, she gave me the only answer I ever received: "Exactly the same way as cats have kittens," and it was years before I discovered the answer to that mystery.

The same frustration I experienced when my mother constantly evaded my question is being experienced by many children who know instinctively that they have been in a place or situation before, but come up against a stone wall when they ask about a past life.

Times are changing, and today the subject of sex is widely discussed in the media, so can we expect the subject of reincarnation to follow suit, and to see the same change in attitude toward reincarnation? Although in many non-Christian countries the belief in reincarnation is part of the culture, the subject is only now bubbling to the surface in the West. So many people are hungry for more information and answers to their questions about life after life.

Many mediums believe reincarnation is an essential part of evolution, as mankind would cease to exist without this traffic of spirits moving back and forth from one dimension to another. We reincarnate to experience situations and gain more knowledge. We may forget most of it, but there are times when we know a fact instinctively, but cannot explain how we know it. There is a strong possibility that we gained the knowledge in a previous incarnation and brought it with us from that previous life.

It's all about cause and effect, and creating balance. By reincarnating in another life we are given the opportunity to correct any mistakes we made in a previous life, and balance outstanding karma. Please don't be fooled by airy-fairy folk who bandy the word "karma" about in a theatrical fashion. Karma is simply about creating balance in our every intention, thought, and everyday behaviour. It involves reaction for all past ill deeds or debts, rewards or punishments, depending on whether you owe a karmic debt to someone, or perhaps they owe it to you!

Have you had any experiences that convince you that we reincarnate? The subject will remain a mystery unless science unearths some secrets, but in the meantime, I believe in reincarnation until it is proved that death is final.

Summary

I have given you some proof of reincarnation. If it has stirred up a desire to be regressed, and you feel the time is right to investigate any of your past lives, either to answer a question surrounding the mystery of a specific situation or to satisfy your curiosity, then a visit to a qualified hypnotherapist will give you the opportunity to experience past life regression. The real difference between regressing backward and fast-forwarding in time is that in a past life regression you will experience feelings and an inner knowing of the place and people, whereas with a time slip forward, it will feel as though you are looking at a scene in a shop window, without being involved. You will feel you know exactly what will happen next, but you do not experience any feelings of warmth, longing, fear, or anger, so it is easy to tell the difference between the two experiences.

When being regressed, remember that if you do not like the past life that is revealed, you can come out of it at any time, as the hypnotherapist has only taken you down to a very light trance. You can walk out of the room, and never need to feel trapped there.

Regression is an excellent tool to reveal the answer to an unexplained problem, so if the answer is eluding you, then try regression. Some of your past lives are very nice places to visit, but you certainly don't want to live there, as you have learned many lessons from these lives, and it is time to move on.

Proof that public interest and popularity in spiritual subjects is growing is confirmed by the fact that nine universities in the UK now include this category in their list of subjects—this fact would have been hard to believe a decade ago.

Notes

1. Prof. Ian Stevenson. "Regression & Biology" Vol. 1. *Birthmarks*. Vol. 2. "Birth Defects & Other Anomalies." Pragar, 1997. "The Future of an Illusion, 1927." Standard Edition. Vol. 21 (Hogarth Press. London, 1961).

2. *Reincarnation International* No. 15. June 98. "Druze Children Who Remember Past Lives, True or False?"

3. *Life and Soul*. No. 19. July 99. Roy Stemman. "Shirley MacLaine Claims She Was Charlemagne's Lover." Karma Publishing Ltd.

4. *Life and Soul*. No. 17. "Psychic Research Enjoying a Revival at Nine UK Universities." "Boy Reminds his Widow of Buried Treasure."

5. *Reincarnation International*. No. 2. April 94. "I Died on the Titanic."

6. Ibid. "I Saw Nelson Die."

chapter two

Do You Astral Travel?

———————————————————●———————————————————

We hear people talking confidently about astral travel, and it is easy to be impressed, but can anyone use this new form of travel? It sounds like something from a modern-day, space-age programme! This subject regularly crops up, and most people are intrigued, and a little envious, to hear friends describe their trips. Astral travel is an out of body experience (OBE). This is surprisingly common amongst the enormous number of people who meditate or practise a form of yoga. Some people are so relaxed, yet in control of their body, that they can leave their body at will, while other people experience this phenomena but don't realise it is an OBE.

It's still a bit of an unknown quantity as very little research has been done on the subject, but the Institute of Projectiology and Conscienciology (IPC) carried out a worldwide online survey on astral travel. The Institute has sixty-four offices in different countries, including the United States, Brazil, Canada, Spain, Portugal, Argentina, and Great Britain, and is recognised as the expert in this field. This non-profit educational and research institution is the largest organisation studying OBEs.[1]

The IPC is an international research organisation. It's non-religious, non-political, and non-mystical, so is acceptable to most people. They organise excellent courses for those who want to learn more about out of body experiences, produced a video, "A Glimpse of Immortality," and the quarterly *Journal of Conscientiology*.

This specialist organisation works hard to research OBEs, to create a deeper understanding of consciousness evolution, and to spread awareness of the broad spectrum of human abilities in this field. They aim to clarify the amazing multidimensional nature of life on Earth, to enable those who desire it to advance their self-awareness, a truly fascinating subject.

Astral Travel—It's Free!

How does an out of body experience happen? It occurs when your centre of consciousness is out of your body. It sounds very far-fetched, but it is quite natural for this energy to go off on a trip to distant places, instead of being sited in its normal place in your body.

Where in the body is the natural place for this centre? Believe it or not, it's smack between the eyebrows. When it takes you off on a magic carpet, you will experience different perceptions, but unfortunately some of us do not remember much about our visit and are often only aware of the violent thud or jerk as we return to our body.

How common is this phenomena? More common than most people realise, as the Medical and Scientific Network reports that between eight and nineteen million people in the USA have admitted experiencing OBEs.[2] When interviewed, they explained it was a combination of information relating to daily life and new experiences. Some travelers felt they acquired extrasensory perception while experiencing these viewings.

To most of us, an OBE is something special that happens when we least expect it, and very seldom, so it is an event to remember and to report to friends. These OBEs usually make an impact on the person, but as most people are completely unaware of the enormous potential and endless possibilities of OBEs, they don't consider exploring the subject further.

Would you like to become part of the group of people around the world who take OBEs very seriously, and spend a lot of time organising their astral travel trips?

A Real Out of Body Experience

Sometimes a person will go on their journey alone, while others work with a companion helper whose job is to ensure they are fully protected while they depart from their physical body. Is one of the attractions the fact that this trip is free and you don't need a passport? And you can go anywhere you choose when you feel like getting away from it all?

Various techniques are used by experienced travelers. All that's necessary is common sense and an ability to visualise and relax, as most techniques involve powerful visualisation. Some travelers use basic tools to help them get into the right frame of mind . . . beads, crystals, a simple mantra, or affirmation are favourites. Tools are used only as a prop or gimmick, and are not necessary for those who are really in tune with their body and the energy of the universe.

Travelers who have complete peace within are able to regularly enjoy OBEs, almost like an extension of themselves.

It's difficult to imagine being so relaxed and at peace with yourself that you can go off to another energy plane at will and be able to control the experience. One of the secrets of success seems to be the ability to blank out all the unimportant everyday events that clutter our mind—by blanking them out, the mind is still. It's all about mind over matter.

Are you one of the millions of people who astral travel, but can't remember much about your trip, except that you felt really good or absolutely great? It's a bit frustrating when you can't remember the details, nor repeat it at will, and only know for certain that it was a wonderfully relaxing and uplifting experience.

A Way to Visit Your Loved Ones

A friend related how, when she visited her sick mother in a hospital, her mother was suffering excruciating pain and the doctors refused to believe her suffering, so did not prescribe pain killers.

The lady died the following day. As you can imagine, my friend was very upset and extremely angry. In fact, she was so angry and disillusioned that she blamed the spirit world. The poor soul was devastated and lost her faith in her Creator, as she felt her mother had been badly let down by God.

For six months, she felt bitter and continued to shut off from spirit, until one night when she left her body on an astral travel trip. She was taken on a wondrous journey to see her mother, who had an enormous smile lighting up her gentle face, and confirmed she was happy, pain free, and at peace. The relief my friend experienced was so tremendous that she instantly shed the bitter frustration and anger that had haunted her since her mother's death. This experience was necessary for her to release all the negative energy she had bottled up over the months, and she was then able to again establish her relationship with her Creator, and progress on her spiritual pathway.

There are other people who've also found that astral travel flight has changed their lives for the better by releasing fear and anger, and proving death is not the end. This also confirms that when we pass to the world of spirit, all our aches, pains, and deformities are repaired, so there's no need to worry that a loved one may still be suffering pain, as they are now free from all pain and have found peace.

Choosing Your Destination

Astral travel seems to be one of the most wonderful natural experiences available to us, and those who are regular travelers report amazing visits to the halls of learning in the spirit world, with their magnificent libraries and opportunities to study with great teachers.

Many people report traveling to visit a loved one, or to meet guides and helpers, or spiritual beings who do special spiritual work. Without exception, almost everyone you speak to who has experienced an out of body journey reports it is a wonderful experience that they would hate to have missed. A great many travelers will say that they have learned from the trip, or that it has changed their attitude or strengthened their spiritual beliefs.

Astral traveling is often described as similar to near death experiences, as the spirit experiences the presence of nonphysical beings, and seems to be able to see all that is happening around them very clearly, through closed eyes. Most out of body experiences (OBEs) involve the same beautiful, floating feeling and sense of exhilaration as described by the NDEs. Some people are very aware of being lifted from their body, and the trips are quite lucid, not the imagination playing tricks.

"Spiritual sleepwalkers" is a good description of those who leave their bodies and wander off to visit relatives or others. The regularity of astral travel varies, as there seems to be no obvious pattern to the trips, other than with those enthusiasts who induce them at will.

Research on Out of Body Experiences

The early Egyptians have many ancient writings describing OBEs, and *The Tibetan Book of the Dead* contains descriptions of a duplicate physical body, which has been seen lifting out of the physical body.

This is known as a *Bardo body,* which the Egyptians call a "BA." This amazing phenomena is regularly seen by shaman, and also by many Chinese, who experience the trip after meditation.

Early missionaries in Africa and America discovered that native tribes used OBE skills to obtain knowledge of surrounding villages within a 100-mile radius.[3]

In research by Dr. Dean Sheils that involved over 1,000 studies of OBEs, results showed no variation in different continents.[4]

Famous authors, including D. H. Lawrence, Virginia Woolf, Ernest Hemingway, Tolstoy, Tennyson, Edgar Alan Poe, and many others, all claimed to have had at least one OBE.[5]

Research has shown conclusively that people of all ages, nationalities, cultures, and walks of life can have an out of body trip, and that level of intelligence is not a deciding factor. A complete contrast to the peace of an OBE is the panic of sleep paralysis. For more information on this amazing subject, have a look at Victor Zammit's wonderfully informative website.

Sleep Paralysis—The Worst Nightmare

Have you ever experienced sleep paralysis (SP)? You certainly won't forget it in a hurry, as it is a terrifying—you are trying desperately to move and every muscle is frozen still. People who experience deep paralysis will often report the feeling of someone leaning heavily on their body, feeling as if they were being held down on the bed.

Recently, I received a phone call from someone asking advice, as this person was convinced he was being held in his bed. He described feeling petrified, which was hardly surprising, as he could not move one inch, although he was aware of everything going on in the room. The poor man was convinced an invisible spirit was holding him down, which is much more frightening than when you can see the enemy.

This form of paralysis seems to becoming more prevalent, although there's no obvious medical reason. Seep paralysis is often blamed on either an alien presence or black magic, but this is not always the case, as the phenomena can strike anyone, either as they're about to go to sleep, or when they've had a night's sleep, and awakened in the morning.

The symptoms of this nightmare situation, in addition to being unable to move your body, which is weighted down on the bed, include being aware of your breathing and an ability to move your eyes, which is an indescribable feeling. Most cases of SP occur when a person is about to drift into a sleep state.

Once you become aware of sleep paralysis, you are better able to cope with it, as your brain tells you this nightmare experience will pass in a few minutes, helping to control the panic. The people who have the biggest problem are those who have absolutely no knowledge of this situation, and so this frightening scenario goes from bad to worse.

Some people let their imaginations (OBE) run riot. They panic and become convinced there is someone or something present in the room, usually of the negative variety. Being unable to move your head or body an inch means that, although you are convinced there's someone nearby, you are unable to turn your head to see who, if anyone, is in the room. A patient described to me how he felt a desperate urge to fight off this unseen enemy, which was in fact an hallucination, but, to him seemed so real.

Do any members of your family experience sleep paralysis? You can reassure them it is a common occurrence, and they are not being bombarded by evil spirits. Should you feel that the person's behavior suggests they have a negative attachment, then it is time to enlist the help of a spirit release therapist.

I received a vivid description from a patient of a nightmare experience when, on two separate occasions, she awakened in the middle of the night being raped by a demon spirit. She related how she had been unable to move or cry for help and was trapped in this nightmare scenario until the spirit decided to move. This woman was a practical person, not given to flights of fancy or imagination, so I knew instinctively that she was telling the truth. When her body was scanned for the presence of any entities, sure enough, there was a very nasty and powerful entity. It was a great pleasure to capture him and ensure he would not rejoin my patient. This type of case is fortunately not very common, but it does happen, so don't dismiss it if you hear this tale of woe!

Have a look on the Internet under sleep paralysis, astral travel, or out of body experiences, and you'll find more information on this unusual experience.

All the subjects lumped under paranormal or parapsychology have for many years been studied by the Society for Psychical Research, and a lot of interesting research on paranormal subjects has been carried out.

Attitudes toward these subjects are changing rapidly, as parapsychology is now a subject on the menu at several universities where grants have been available to study both mental and physical phenomena. A related subject is near death experiences—there is a lot of reliable proof from hospitals that these experiences do occur.

Near Death Experiences Do Happen

Near death experiences (NDEs) have become such an accepted phenomena that several people have taken a PhD on this subject, so it will be interesting to learn the results of their research on this ever-controversial subject and read what they have to say about the existence of supernatural powers, invisible energy, and reincarnation.[6]

What is a near death experience, and why are they so common? When you mention near death experiences, it is surprising how many people have either experienced an NDE, or known a family member or friend who's had one. In 1982, a Gallup study found eight million people in the United States had experienced NDEs, but the figure is now estimated at thirteen million adults in the US,[7] and when you add the numbers in Europe and other countries, we are talking about a lot of people who have experienced this trip.

Studying Near Death Experiences

Two major studies have indicated that of all the people who come close to death, between 35 and 40 percent will later report an NDE. What about the other 55 to 60 percent of folks? Have they experienced a similar NDE, but do not remember their journey?[8]

Most people who have had an NDE have experienced it when on a hospital operating table, or in a serious accident or disaster. There are wide variations in the symptoms; but both adults and young children describe the unforgettable experience of traveling down a tunnel and the warm White Light, also the feeling of safety and unconditional, overpowering love, and the disappointment of having to force themselves to come back to their bodies. Theories abound about why everyone who dies and is resuscitated doesn't experience an NDE. There doesn't seem to be any common denominator, such as religion, lifestyle, good or bad behaviour, nationality, or age group.

Some describe having been fortunate to experience events, which had the effect of making them decide to immediately change their outlook or improve their behaviour toward other people. They report that it has increased their understanding of life, and totally changed their attitude to life. An NDE is one of the most powerful spiritual experiences any of us could ever hope to experience in our lifetime.

Many people report having been shown a startling review of their life, with emphasis on their wrong doings, inspiring them to completely change their behaviour and become loving people. They were helped to realise they needed to change their ways. Others say their mind was working faster than normal, and they seemed to think more clearly due to the change in energy vibration.

There is much controversy and discussion about the cause of NDEs, but no one knows why some patients describe being completely free from pain, and seldom does anyone report an unpleasant experience.

Dead on the Operating Table

Perhaps the most convincing category of near death experiences are those people who are certified dead on the operating table and then return to life, able to give information about the event. How have they been able to relate exactly what happened, the reaction of family and friends and of the medical staff present, after they were pronounced dead? One thing that convinces people it is not a figment of their imagination is that some of these patients can tell what activities were going on in nearby rooms or in the next ward.

Sceptics will say that the hearing is the last body function to go, so the patient could have heard voices, but this does not explain how they could describe what they had seen, even through curtains or walls. One commonly described feeling is of floating ten to fifteen feet above their bodies, watch activities below, while feeling detached. This can also be experienced by patients who are very seriously ill and near death. The one fact which keeps coming through loud and clear from almost everyone who has had an NDE is that, in their short journey, they felt absolute peace and love, and were completely at one with the Light.

Some describe in great detail how they felt the Light seemed to communicate with them, and although they could not hear voices, they knew the message was beautiful and peaceful, radiating love and joy. This Light seems to be the most transformative part of their vision, for young children as well as adults

What Is a Near Death Experience?

Medical science and technology are advancing at an enormous rate, and new cures are regularly discovered, yet no explanation is offered for this simple biologically based experience that occurs in all parts of the world. Science can't explain why patients can describe how and when all the negative thoughts in the body have been removed in a split second. They then discover the most indescribable feeling of total love, which seems to envelop their entire being. Ironically, this total love energy is all around us all of the time, but we shut it out from our consciousness as our minds build up a barrier. We can find it by pushing away the dense frequency that surrounds most of us and moving on to a lighter vibration, one of the joys of meditation.

Surviving an NDE

The fact that so many people who have survived an NDE tell of a complete transformation in their outlook on life is confirmation to all of us that there is nothing to fear about death. Many people, quite independently, tell similar stories of becoming nicer characters, their priorities changing to such an extent that people comment on the difference in them. Men who, during their lifetimes, were generally difficult, violent, or argumentative become pleasant and loving, while women who were constantly nagging and complaining about everything become serene and content. Many folks feel they no longer need material things, and their attitudes to others changes for the better.

The Dalai Lama Sums It Up

The Dalai Lama describes life after a near death experience as a change of energy to a clearer Light, a most sensible description of this phenomena. He says the body's energy rises again after death, and at the moment of death, our body is at its most sensitive, due to the change of energy. I agree with his explanation, as we are all energy, and upon death we move to a different energy vibration

The lesson learned by those who have returned from the tunnel is the realisation that life is very precious, and what you do with it is all important. This monumental experience opens new doors, which show momentarily what life on Earth could be like, if we could let go of all life's aggravations. A real bonus is that it gets rid of any fear of death.

The more child-like we become, the easier it will be to find this illusive peace. Children of all ages have, over a period of time, told of near death experiences. Many of these children were far too young to have any real concept of death, and could not have known about the wonderful White Light or the tunnel.

American pediatrician Dr. Melvin Morse has studied this subject and the reaction of young children in an intensive care unit, many of whom were critically ill. These children reported similar near death experiences—some were as young as three or four years of age.[9]

The Blind Can See During NDEs

How do scientists explain the fact that doctors have reported cases of blind people, or those with very little sight, who have been able to give details of the experience, which they have seen clearly. Many have reported accurate details of the ward and what clothes their relatives wore. These were facts they would not have known when blind. It's as though their eyesight had miraculously returned. Perhaps the most astonishing fact is that they are able to describe, in detail, medical equipment in the area that had not been invented until long after they lost their sight.

This is a real puzzle for doctors as it is not an isolated incident—many of these patients were able to describe in great detail what they had seen during this time. When the facts were checked out, they proved to be correct, and all details were accurate. Some people reported that they were able to see all that was behind them, as well as the view in front of them. Even stranger and more difficult to explain is the fact that some patients could tell the nurse they had seen the number on the top side of the overhead light in the room, when the staff were not aware that there was a number on the shade. These are the sort of facts that confirm without question that these experiences do occur.

Patients who experience NDEs after being pronounced clinically dead seem to be much more common today. Is it simply that people are more open minded now, so patients are not afraid to tell their family or medical staff of their experiences? A few decades ago, eyebrows would have been raised when such experiences were described.

History Tells of NDEs

Near death experiences are not solely a modern day occurrence, as literature over the centuries has recorded historical accounts of these situations. In Plato's *Republic* there are details of a soldier, badly injured in battle, who describes his journey through the dark area into the Light, and the wonderful angels who accompanied him on his journey.[10]

Near death experiences over the past few centuries have proved that the mind operates outside of time and space, and lives on after death. People who have been pronounced clinically dead when their brains ceased to function have been miraculously revived and lived for years. Modern science has proved conclusively that the mind is the driver of the soul, and the brain is purely the engine of the body. The mind never dies, it moves on with the spirit.

Perhaps the most upsetting fact about these experiences is that many people report being devastated when they find themselves back on Earth after this experience, and in exactly the same situation as before. These poor souls find life completely intolerable, and coping with the situation they thought they'd left for good is a disappointment. When outside of their bodies, they were free from all pain, unhappiness, and negativity, so it's a real blow to find they have to leave this wonderful place where they found peace and joy and come back to their troubles. It's not difficult to understand they feel cheated when they are told, "You must go back, it's not your time yet!"

Film Stars Who've NDE'd

Film star Elizabeth Taylor told a television show interviewer that she had died on the operating table and gone through the tunnel to the Light. She described how her beloved deceased husband, Mike Todd, came to her and said "Go back, honey, it's not your time."

Another Hollywood film star, Sharon Stone, recently told the press she had experienced a near death experience when she suffered a brain hemorrhage.

The late Christopher Reeve, famed for his role as Superman, tells in his autobiography *Still Me* how he had a near death experience after suffering the riding accident that left him paralyzed. He describes floating out of his body and hovering up at the ceiling. These stories confirm that strange things do happen on the operating table.[11]

Traditionally accepted thinking restricts our belief in NDEs. We've all been taught that humans are usually born with five senses. This is wrong—we're all born with other senses, but most of us go through life without discovering or using them.

We are all born with an invisible energy link to our Creator, and this link can be used to channel healing energy to people and animals. It can also be used to help us link with our Creator to find peace and love, and is often described in detail by people who regularly meditate.

Contacting Others Who've Had an NDE

Would you like to contact other folks who have also experienced an NDE? The International Association for Near Death Studies (IANDS) is a worldwide organisation with groups in many countries. This specialist association offers information and networking in the field of near death studies and is the world's first organisation devoted to exploring this subject. You'll find groups in America, Canada, Europe, Australia, and Asia. IANDS has an excellent website where you'll find useful information and contacts.[12]

Deathbed Visions Are Real

Have any of your relatives told you of their deathbed visions? Hospital staff often share reports from patients who say that shortly before their death they saw their deceased husband, wife, or parent standing at the end of their bed, smiling at them. These visions can occur a few hours or days before death, and an interesting piece of the jigsaw is that the patient will describe seeing a person at the bedside whom they did not know had died, perhaps a relative or friend who had completely lost touch, but was now standing there smiling and waiting to take them to the Light. Others tell of seeing a wonderfully compassionate Being of Light standing beside or above their bed. Not much is written about Beings of Light, but these almost luminous spirits, who give out so much love, are often seen near the time of death.

Perhaps the most common sight related to a nurse or caregiver is the amazingly clear view of the patient's life, which has passed in an instant. They explain they have been shown their complete life on Earth, but as it's shown at the speed of light, it's over almost before they realised it was happening; others tell of hearing lovely heavenly music.

American medical student Raymond Moody, in 1975, wrote an excellent book called *Life After Life*, which contained details of interviews with 150 people of all ages.

They had all come close to death, and survived, so had interesting tales to tell, but most of them reported very similar experiences. Those interviews were done over thirty years ago—isn't it ironic that science today has not acquired more knowledge of this mysterious subject?

Nearly half a century ago Dr. Karlis Otis of the American Society of Physical Research carried out a study on deathbed visions. The results were very thoroughly checked, and verified in several different cultures. They proved conclusively that you don't have to believe in life after death to have a death-bed vision, as patients who did not believe in any form of afterlife reported seeing friends or beautiful places. This experience removed fears of death, and in turn gave comfort to the family of the dying person.

Research into Deathbed Visions

Dr. Otis and his colleague Dr. Erlenddur Haraldsson published a fascinating little book, *At the Hour of Death*, which was an extension of the work done seventeen years previously. The chapters contain reports from more than a thousand doctors and nurses in the United States and India on deathbed visions from over one hundred thousand patients.[13]

The universe truly works in wonderful and mysterious ways, but sceptics often state categorically that these unexplained visions are due entirely to the hallucinatory effects of drugs taken by the patient. This argument is squashed by the fact that most of the patients involved in Dr. Otis' study had not received any of these drugs, so they will have to find another explanation. Scientists are able to land men on the moon and inventing tiny mobile phones, yet we have very little more knowledge of the human mind today than half a century ago.

Medical Research into Near Death Experiences

Why is there so much opposition to NDEs? Literally thousands of these experiences have been documented, mostly by normal, well-balanced, very ordinary people with no prior knowledge of NDEs. Why do doctors and scientists wave it off as mere hysteria, delusions, and some real sceptics blame schizophrenic hallucinations? Others state that NDEs are linked to lack of oxygen to the brain, but this has been disproved by research at Southampton General Hospital in England.

Anyone reading the work of Elisabeth Kübler-Ross cannot fail to be convinced that NDEs are a fact of life. Kübler-Ross dedicated many years to working with patients who had all been on the verge of death. Sixty-one percent had experienced typical NDE signs, and could all describe details of the operating theatre and ward activities accurately.[14]

In other words, the NDE patients retained a clear picture in their minds of what happened, whereas the other group questioned did not have a clear picture of the situation, proving the NDE patients had hovered around the room, having a detailed look at what was going on.

Hospital Research

A very comprehensive research programme to study near death experiences is being carried out by the Horizon Research Foundation at Southampton General Hospital. This foundation has been set up by doctors to support research to further understanding of the human mind during near death experiences and on the point of death.

Based at Southampton, the research foundation is raising funding for a large scale study, as there is an urgent need for more research on this subject. Two studies have already been carried out in Britain and The Netherlands on patients who survived cardiac arrest, and results confirm that there is absolutely no evidence to support the sceptics' theory that the experiences are related to lack of oxygen, an increase in carbon dioxide, or the use of drugs.

Research on a much larger scale, involving cardiac arrest patients, commenced in the UK during 2002, and will be watched with interest by the medical profession around the world. The work involved interviewing 1,500 patients in twenty-five hospitals across the UK. Research results will be supervised by Dr. Sam Parnia and a team of four research specialist nurses, who are each responsible for six or seven hospitals, during the entire period of the programme. This is no half-hearted effort, as Dr. Parnia is determined that near death experiences should be thoroughly and fairly researched.

A very interesting previous study was carried out over a two-year period in The Netherlands by cardiologist Dr. Pim Van Lommel. The study involved 343 patients in ten different hospitals who had all survived cardiac arrest. These patients were followed up for eight years, and all reported feeling "Less fear of dying, and a more positive attitude to life." The study results are being reported in *The Lancet.*[15]

Results of this research showed sixty-two of the 343 patients were identified as having experienced a near death experience, which were recognised as genuine by the patient's ability to recall any of ten common elements. This group of patients had lots to say about their experiences—most mentioned more than one type of feeling, and the majority of their comments were very similar to those recorded over the years from patients of all ages. More than 50 percent of the group stated they had feelings of very positive emotions, and 50 percent admitted they had a half awareness of being dead.

Traveling through a tunnel, an experience described over the years by many NDE subjects, was experienced by 31 percent, while some described what they had seen. Thirty-two percent of the group described meeting deceased persons, and others described seeing a celestial landscape. Other patients in the group told of communications with the Light, or seeing color, while others described an out of body experience where they had observed doctors working hard to save their life.

This research, done at the Hospital Rijnstate in Arnham, Holland, and reported in the medical journal *The Lancet*, confirms the evidence of other near death experiences, but why do NDEs occur? We still don't know the answer; all we know is that they do happen.

It seems fairly logical that if thousands of people who have been pronounced clinically dead by experienced doctors have near death stories to tell, these doctors cannot possibly all have made a mistake with their diagnosis of death. There has to be a strong foundation for these near death stories being true, as these patients were all unconscious, and showed no sign of pulse, breathing, or brain activity.

We may never know why the human mind maintains a very lucid process, allowing people to form crystal-clear memories that last forever. Those who have experienced NDEs know it was real—the rest of us have to wait for proof from further results of the research.

Religion and NDEs

Near death experiences have over the centuries been described in many countries around the world, including the Middle and Far East. It is interesting to note that, although the basic experience is similar in both West and East, the religious aspect may differ. Christians will often report seeing Jesus during an out of body or near death experience, whereas other people will report seeing Buddha, Sai Babba, Allah, or a Hindu figure, depending on their religious beliefs.

You won't ever have control over a near death experience, but you can arrange your own astral travel, so if you would like to learn how to open the door to this opportunity to leave your body and travel, then have a look at Dr. Joe H. Slate's book *Psychic Vampires*, which gives step-by-step instructions on how to become an astral traveler. Good luck!

Summary

We have examined both near death experiences and astral travel, and have looked at examples of these situations and at research being carried out to give positive scientific proof that we humans are able to leave our bodies and return none the worse for our trip.

Astral travel, sometimes called soul travel or astral projection, is an out of body experience that can either occur naturally or can be self-induced, and occurs completely outside of the human body. Don't worry that you will not be able to return to your body if you find yourself in an out of body situation. That nightmare won't happen while you are alive and living on Earth, as you have an invisible Earth connection that is only severed upon death. That connection, sometimes described as a silver cord, comes from the Creator, down through your body and into the ground, so you are always linked, and when you go outside of your body, you still maintain your own personal connection with your body.

Astral travel is possible for everyone, and gives you the opportunity to explore the universe or meet your spirit guides and helpers, but before you take a trip, remember to place a cloak of protection around your aura. You are unlikely to meet any earthbound spirits as they are on a lower vibration, but protection is always a good investment.

The near death experience is also an out of body trip, but you do not usually have control over this, as NDEs are often events we must experience to learn an important lesson or be reminded of our faults.

An out of body experience is an opportunity to learn more about your life and about the universe, so if your gut feeling is that you would like to explore this subject, then be assured it is probably right for you.

Notes

1. IIPC. The International Institute of Projectiology & Conscientiology.
2. Scientific & Medical Network. Isle of Wight UK. March 2001. www.scimednet.org.
3. Victor Zammit. "Out of Body Experiences." *A Lawyer Presents the Case for the After Life.* Inglis: 1977: 30–35. www.victorzammit.com.
4. Ibid. Lazarus 1993:166–167.
5. Ibid. Inglis: 1977: 30–35.
6. Roy Stemman. "Shirley MacLaine Claims She Was Charlemagne's Lover." *Life and Soul,* No. 19. July 99. Karma Publishing Ltd.
7. Zammit. Inglis: 1977:131.
8. IANDS. The International Association for Near Death Studies, Inc. http://www.iands.org.
9. Horizon Research Foundation. Southampton General Hospital. Southampton. UK. http://www.horizon-research.co.uk.
10. Zammit. Book 20. "Deathbed Visions."
11. *Reincarnation International.* No. 15. June 98. "Superman Tells of Out of Body Experiences."
12. IANDS.
13. Zammit. Book 20. "Deathbed Visions."
14. Elisabeth Kübler-Ross, *The Truth Campaign.* "Beyond Death's Doors" by John Clamp. March 1997.
15. Horizon Research Fouundation.

chapter three

What Are Earthbound Spirits?

———————————————●———————————————

Do you ever experience the chilling feeling that you're not alone in a room, that someone is watching you, while your head is telling you to stop thinking ridiculous thoughts? So why is your gut telling you a different story, and why are your legs shaking? You just know there is someone else in the room, and although you cannot see them, you can feel their presence. These feelings suggest the presence of an earthbound spirit who can be either a resident or a visitor.

Many people refer to earthbound spirits as ghosts, but a ghost is only a memory imprint, often played over and over again, like the headless horseman, or the lady in a ball gown crossing the lawn every day.

An earthbound spirit is a deceased spirit whose mind and surviving consciousness have moved on to a different energy wavelength from us, but broken their journey at the half-way point. In other words, they have become lost on the way home and have not moved to the next stage after death, so need redirecting to find the Light.

Death and birth are by far the two most awesome events we experience during our lifetime, but death is not the end, simply a new beginning. Most of us assume that when we die, we will automatically move on to heaven, or the next phase of our life—but in fact, because we have free will, we have three choices of what happens next:

1. The first, most sensible choice is to move on to the welcoming Light.

2. The second choice is staying earthbound in the same place for any one of a variety of reasons. Understandably, some spirits linger as they are concerned that their will is honoured, or to see that the funeral is organised as they requested, or they want to know what the family is doing to their property, so they remain on the site after death until they are happy everything has been carried out to their satisfaction.

3. The third choice available to the spirit is to attach to any living person who showed compassion at the scene of death, whether a relative, nurse, or policeman. When a person shows compassion, they open their chakras, which allows the spirit to enter their body and remain there, often causing problems.

There are two very separate categories of spirits you may meet. One is a human spirit who is earthbound, and the other is a nonhuman spirit. The latter entity can be demonic, and a dark force, but is seldom seen. It's fairly easy for a medium, or anyone who is sensitive to energies, to tell the difference, but you are unlikely to see the nonhuman variety.

We are all spirits with a body, and not a body with a spirit, as the spirit never dies. It lives on and is always there in both life and death, and in all previous lives and future ones. An earthbound spirit is a spirit in limbo, until it is helped to move on in its journey home. The spirits you are most likely to meet are the earthbound human spirits, as these are the ones who try frantically to attract attention by turning lights off, or switching on printer or radios.

> *There is no death.*
> *Tell out the mighty message,*
> *There is no death.*
> *Go tell it far and wide.* (Lytton)

These lines from an old Spiritualist hymn[1] are a message to all earthbound spirits. If only they had heard and believed these words during their life, they would have avoided their present plight. Trapped spirits are usually friendly and keen to make contact.

Sensing a spirit presence or seeing a ghost is a shock to most people, as it's usually unexpected and unexplained. When they have recovered from the shock of seeing the spirit, the person will often say "I wish I had spoken to them, taken a photograph as proof, or tried to touch them." For most people, the experience is not repeated, so it's difficult to prove to family and friends that you have actually seen a ghost.

Anyone can see a ghost, and a great many nonbelievers have seen at least one of these earthbound spirits, so there's no special talent or gift required to be able to see a ghost. If the ghost wants to be seen, it will appear at the right moment and circumstances. Even if you don't feel you could ever become involved in rescue work, it's an act of kindness to try to help lost souls, so if you sense a presence or see a spirit, mentally say "Hello" and ask them to go to the Light where their family and friends are waiting to welcome them.

Talk to Lost Spirits

Whether you talk mentally or speak aloud to a spirit, they can hear what you are saying to them. You won't hear an answer, as usually they have gone before you could get into conversation. Don't worry if they don't go away, as you cannot force a spirit to move on until they are ready to do so, but it's always worth offering assistance. After all, if you saw a frail old lady or a blind man trying to cross the road, you would automatically offer help. It's a very similar situation, as the trapped spirit needs guidance. They are often confused and can't see clearly where they are going.

There is normally nothing unpleasant about a ghostly spirit, as every spirit has at one time led a normal life on Earth. He or she has probably been a parent and had a responsible job, so has experienced all the ups and downs of living, and has known fear, sadness, joy, and happiness.

That wise old Indian, Silver Birch, taught us that death is inevitable to the physical body, whatever our nationality. When we have served our time on planet Earth, it's time to move on to the next stage of our development. Unfortunately, most of those trapped spirits have not heard the words of Silver Birch.

There are many reasons why spirits get stuck in limbo, but a few of these lost spirits are known to stay in this grey area for many decades. Some of these unhappy souls will stay close to their home or workplace, and will be confused as they can see everyone and all that's going on. They speak to people, but nobody answers. It's difficult to imagine the frustration and agony some of them must experience when they are ignored by loved ones. The hurt and confusion is usually the reason a spirit will move objects and give other clues of their presence. If that doesn't work, they may give a person a hard push or cause them to trip. They do not mean any harm, it's simply that they are exasperated at being ignored. These spirits often don't accept they have died.

Can you imagine how it must feel to hear the voices of your family but be unable to communicate? It must be a nightmare similar to the experience of someone who has suffered a stroke and has lost the power of speech, so cannot communicate.

The mind lives on forever with the soul, remaining crystal-clear, although the brain has died. Hearing is the last function to switch off after death. If a person is pronounced brain dead after an accident, illness, or natural death, they can still hear conversations for a short time after death. Doctors can no longer deny the evidence that certain people have had near death experiences because, when resuscitated, they have been able to relate accurately conversations that took place after they were pronounced dead.

Ghosts Come in Many Shapes and Sizes

Descriptions of earthbound spirits vary enormously, as some people will describe seeing a spirit in solid form. The spirits look alive and, at first glance, are alive, yet observers know that the person had already died some time ago, so they realise in astonishment that they are seeing a spirit. Others describe seeing a shadow, a ball of light, or a wispy cloud, or feeling a cool draught.

Roads with an unexplained number of traffic accidents are often called "black spots." Some are linked to bad driving, but some of these accidents are linked to the presence of a ghostly memory imprint that has been trapped in time. Drivers have many times reported swerving to avoid the figure of a young woman in a long dress who ran in front of their car, or a highwayman on horseback who rode across the road, forcing a quick reaction. Kindly looking monks are often seen walking across the grounds of an abbey or old churchyard, going about their daily or nightly business.

Many drivers have seen a figure appear from a hedgerow and taken drastic action to avoid killing them, only to discover it was a well-known local ghost.

Spirits are renowned for staying in the vicinity of the area where they were killed, but do not show themselves at the same time or in exactly the same place. Scenes when the person is a creature of habit are memory imprints and cannot harm you.

Probably the most frightening sighting of a ghost is the one who appears as part of a body, such as a headless horseman, a knight in armour, or even worse, a head without a body. When these sights are reported by a number of people who have all seen the same sight at exactly the same place, this is confirmation that it is a memory imprint caught in time, and not an earthbound spirit in need of rescue.

These imprints come in a variety of scenes. Some people report seeing the figure of a sad-looking woman at the window of an old house or castle; others see a lady who glides across a lawn.

Earthbound Spirits Can Be Seen Anywhere

A trapped spirit can appear absolutely anywhere, so don't associate them solely with buildings standing today, as they can be seen on a piece of vacant ground that had once been the site of a large house or a small cottage, before a German bomb demolished the building and killed the occupants. Spirits often remain on the site of their death, even though another building has been built on that site. Unless you know the history of the area, it is sometimes difficult to find out facts about the spirit—it could have been there for a couple of centuries.

People often report seeing a *spirit light* that seems to dart about. It's a very bright ball of light and feels very friendly. Rather than being earthbound spirits, these lights, known as *orbs*, are often angels hovering around to offer protection.

There is seldom any pattern to spirit behaviour so this makes it very difficult to photograph them, and it is sometimes a hard job to convince the family you saw a ghost in an open space. It is impossible to make a ghost or departed relative appear on request, as they will only appear when the energy conditions are right, and when they want to appear.

People visiting a medium will often ask to speak to a deceased husband or relative, but the medium cannot make the connection. All they can do is send out the invitation, as they have to wait until the spirit chooses to make contact.

Free Will Is the Problem

We have all been given the gift of free will. It is with us when we are born, and it stays with us when we die. This gift from our Creator is in the mind, so it lives on.

A big question that confuses many people is: "Why don't relatives or guardian angels come down to Earth and rescue the lost spirits?" Surely this would eliminate the problems of earthbound spirits and ghosts forever.

Some relatives already in spirit will often come down to lead a person to the Light, but if the person does not want to go, or perhaps remembers a family feud and did not like the relatives, then the spirit of the newly deceased may on Earth, each one of us has free will over all our actions. In other words, we are free to choose whether to stay between planes, or move to the Light, just as we can choose a career, a partner, or how we behave, and how we look after our health and our body.

Exactly the same principle works after death, so all human spirits have a free will to choose whether to remain close to loved ones and be earthbound or move on to the Light, and find peace in the Summerland (as it is known in the Spiritualist church). This is the reason why guides, helpers, or relatives in spirit don't ever influence the choice a person makes regarding their transition—it is their own decision.

A patient's pale face will sometimes become alive and radiant for no apparent reason, and family members get the impression this dying person has seen a long-lost friend. The explanation is simple! A spirit rescuer or relative will often come down to a dying person's bedside so that person can follow them to the Light. Trouble comes when family disputes have occurred in the past—people may have lost contact with their family, or haven't spoken for many years since a family row erupted over some very minor matter.

If this unforgiven spirit comes for them, no way will the dying person listen to the spirit, and they certainly will not follow them anywhere—in fact, it can make obstinate people do the opposite. That old saying, "biting off your nose to spite your face," is sometimes applicable to earthbound spirits.

How to Find the Identity of a Spirit

Are you curious about the identity of an earthbound spirit who visits your home or office? Would you like to do a little bit of detective work to establish his or her name? This is not such an impossible task as local records offices hold copies of past censuses. As well as having data about recent residents, a census will give you an insight into what was on the site before your home was built. Although some trapped spirits can be traced to a previous owner or tenant of a property, others can be victims of an accident or battle that occurred on the site decades ago, so the spirit may not have been a previous resident of the site.

In the UK, the electoral register is a useful starting point, giving details of previous tenants or owners of the property; also servants and other staff who lived on the site. The register dates back over 200 years, so it is a useful starting point. The family records centre in London can direct you to information on wills in England and Wales as far back as the fourteenth century, and birth records from the early 1800s. This is a free service. Other countries offer various helpful services.

If you have actually seen the spirit, and have a description of age, height, and colour of hair, type of dress, or perhaps they appeared in a military uniform, then it is easier to identify the spirit. An elderly neighbour may recognise the description of the spirit. Another option is doing genea-logical research on the Internet, which could provide clues.

Proof Eludes the Scientists

Sceptical scientists have a difficult task finding ghostly experiences to research, as most sightings are singular events that cannot be repeated at will. Reported viewings of earthbound spirits and other paranormal situations cannot be tested or measured in laboratories with scientific equipment, so scientific proof is as illusive as the spirit.

The scientific mind needs to see and touch before accepting the existence of a spirit. This state will continue until the day when they can dissect a spirit in a laboratory or examine one under their microscope! Seeing a spirit certainly denies scientific or even normal explanation, so modern science will continue to be frustrated, as spirit phenomena continues to contradict scientific viewpoint. The world of spirit is an important part of creation that we must simply accept as a fact of life.

Those who feel the need to prove its existence on a scientific level had better be patient, as they will have a long wait for the answer. Scientists have not yet unearthed a scientific explanation for ghosts, but it's time now for "Man who is alive, to learn a lot more about man who is dead."

Are they missing the truth by looking for technical information, instead of looking at simple facts? There are plenty of books available on the subject that offer a selection of interesting theories, but we would all like firm confirmation of life after death. You'll find a wide selection of books on ghost and spirits at your local library and at all good book-sellers, but it would be nice to have proof.

Although science has not traveled far down the psychical research path, there are paranormal researcher groups all around the world. Their members take ghost hunting and UFO viewing very seriously, and methodical preparation is done before a pre-arranged meeting. When a ghost sighting has been reported, a group of members will arrange to visit the scene, complete with equipment, with a view to recording any unusual noises and taking photographs or sound recordings of any happenings.

Paranormal researchers also take their interest very seriously, as is evident by the amount of equipment used. As well as the video camera, still camera, and audio recorder, they use an anemometer that is able to record accurately both the speed and direction of the wind, which could be the cause of strange noises. They also use a barometer to register changes in atmospheric pressure and air pressure, which could be caused by a spirit presence.

The favoured barometer is the mercury model, as it gives the highest accuracy for important readings, rather than the old barometer from the hall wall, which you'd give a tap as you passed.

Also popular is the hygrometer, a nifty gadget capable of measuring output signals in proportion to surrounding humidity in the atmosphere. In other words, nothing is left to chance! I have been on the receiving end of science, as I have been wired-up by two scientists in experiments to measure the levels of my psychic energy and the healing energy I channel, and more experiments are planned.

Perhaps the best-known paranormal research groups are the Society for Psychical Research, which has members in both the UK and the US. These groups are regularly quoted in articles about psychic phenomena. Another group is the Association for the Scientific Study of Anomalous Phenomena, which is steadily growing in numbers. Researchers belonging to these well-established and respected groups seem to take along everything but the kitchen sink when doing an overnight watch. As well as the equipment I mentioned, there are the basic requirements for comforts: a flask of coffee to keep you awake, a sandwich to maintain your energy levels, and warm jumpers or a blanket.

Members take the search seriously and many are sceptics, so ironically, although these researchers may be fortunate enough to see or hear the poor spirit, they can only prove their presence, just as they can prove whether a squeaking door hinge is caused by a draft or a presence. They are unable to do the all-important job of rescuing the earthbound spirit, and so making their visit really worthwhile, as many are only interested in the technical details. Two excellent American websites crammed full of information on ghosts are maintained by the American Ghost Society and the Ghost Research Society. Simply type in the name on a search engine and sit back to learn about ghosts and trapped spirits.

There will always be a number of forward-thinking scientists who are the exception to tradition and open to this unexplained phenomena. Sir Oliver Lodge and a few of his friends were some of those exceptions. One hundred and eighteen years ago, this man was making his first paranormal investigations in telepathy, which led him to the paranormal. A professor at the University College, London, and knighted in 1902, he was always "certain we all survive life." He is quoted as saying, "Everything material is temporary, but the forces of the world of the mind are permanent. The forces of the mind are very superior to anything material." These are the words of a brilliant scientist. Author Raymond Smith has written several channeled books on the work of Sir Oliver Lodge, including *Nobody Wants to Listen Yet* and *Why I Believe in Personal Immortality.*[2]

Another scientific genius was Albert Einstein, who gave the world great theories, and told us "Great spirits have always encountered violent opposition from mediocre minds." Was he talking about the scientific community? It appears the situation is much the same today as in yesteryear.[3] It took many centuries to convince man the world is round, so the big question is: "How many more centuries before it becomes generally accepted that death is not the end?" Perhaps during the next ten years we will receive the proof we so desperately need to give us factual proof beyond doubt that there is life after death.

Stories have been handed down from generation to generation of the haunting sight of the grim reaper standing at the end of the bed, as he waits to take the deceased to some mysterious place. It's time to say a final good bye to this ghostly figure and banish his image forever from modern-day life. In today's fast-moving world of technology and genetic changes, it does seem a bit ironic that this important subject is still veiled in mystery.

When it becomes accepted that death is more than simply dying and being buried, rescue therapists will become redundant!

More people today are becoming interested in earthbound spirits, and accept the idea of life after death. In the United States, John Edwards, the famous host of the television programme "Crossing Over" has an enormous following of viewers. This controversial, popular programme has increased the channel's rating, as five days each week, thousands of families watch this fascinating medium at work.

Many mediums are doing media work in both sides of the ocean, and are doing a great job of spreading awareness that life continues after death. The more people who view these programmes, the more they will be comfortable with the thought of death, and so will not become earthbound.

Arthur Findlay, in his fascinating book *Looking Back,* recounted stories of séances held in the Vatican in Rome.[4] This is a surprise as the Vatican is not the place you expect to find a séance being held! This amazing man addressed large audiences of people there, including high dignitaries of the Catholic church. Ironically, Findlay was told by a friendly cardinal that Pope Pius XI was not a good sitter!

Much is written about famous people who have used mediums and received accurate messages, but this does not make media headlines. There are many reasons spirits remain earthbound—and most of these could be avoided if the subject received more publicity.

Reasons for Remaining Earthbound

There are a number of reasons that spirits remain earthbound, instead of moving on to the next stage of development. Some people have no religious beliefs, and so no expectations of any life after death. They have no comprehension of the process of dying and have never heard of the White Light, so don't realise it will guide them home. The spirit simply expects to die, and that's the end of the cycle, so they drift around for years, completely oblivious to it, not realising there is love and peace waiting for them at the Light.

We've all, at one time in our lives, known people who proudly claim to be an atheist, or agnostic, and state firmly there is no God in Heaven, no Creator, so it's not too difficult to accept that these people would have a serious problem when they die, as our temperament does not change on death.

How many people fall into this category? Often they are individuals who have never been told or don't believe there is love waiting on the other side of the veil. Many of these spirit refugees find it hard to believe, when a rescuer tells them there is more to life than this colourless dimension where they float around without purpose.

During their lifetime, they never read or were told about the energy plane next to Planet Earth, which is a passing-through zone, not a permanent home. What is needed is an enormous "NO WAITING" sign in this grey area to discourage lost spirits from lingering here. This uninspiring, emotionless area totally lacks warmth and comfort for lost souls. It is a timeless area, and it is only fear, guilt, or ignorance that holds spirits in this between-world state. Spirits who believe this grey mist is the end are usually easily rescued, as they are so pleasantly surprised to make contact and learn there is more to death than they realised. As children we are taught that when we die, we go to Heaven, but as we become adults, many people forget these childhood stories. With no expectations of life after life, we may have a weight on our conscience.

Strong Feelings of Guilt

Spirits can be held earthbound by a strong feeling of guilt that binds them to a specific place. This can be home, place of work, or scene of an accident, so they stay in No Man's Land. Some may choose to stay in this unpleasant dimension to repent for the inconsiderate or violent way they may have treated their family or friends. These poor souls often try to make amends, not realising they are not helping either themselves or their families by remaining in limbo.

Perhaps they feel the burden of a failed marriage or business. Others are in this predicament because, although they saw the Light, they did not see any point in going there, as they would not be welcome. This can apply to some spirits who have very negative energy or have low self-esteem—lack of self-worth encourages them to stay in this sad situation.

Fear of Death and Dying

Other earthbounds are the group of people who, in their lifetime, always had a strong fear of death and dying, so easily became trapped in their fear. These sad souls have often been indoctrinated that there is no life after death, only Heaven and Hell.

A guilty conscience can block their progress and, however minor their sin, they are so brainwashed and conditioned that they don't consider themselves good enough for Heaven, so remain in this self-inflicted state rather than risk moving on for fear of the fire, which they believe will pass judgment on them. You can understand just how easily this situation arises, and how these poor, frightened souls need to be rescued.

Are some of these confused spirits who suffer such guilt trapped by the past teachings of the Roman Catholic church, which says that upon death the spirit has to go through purgatory to be purified before going to Heaven? I have rescued spirits who told me they were waiting for purgatory, as they were confused, and had minor wrongdoings on their conscience. Fortunately, there are only a small number of people caught in this situation, but there are a few others floating about out there who lack self-worth.

Lack of Self-Worth

Some spirits are earthbound by their lack of self-worth. They've gone through life rejected by society, never receiving respect, support, or reassurance, and so can't believe they will ever find love and security in the next life. It is so important to help these souls to realise that by going to the Light they will find peace. Most of us know someone who fits this description, someone who lacks confidence. Be a good Samaritan and offer them support during their life, as this will give them confidence to go to the Light when their time comes.

The Obstinate Spirits

One group of earthbound spirits are trapped by their obstinate nature. They were obstinate in life and have not changed in death, as our temperament does not change when we die. These spirits need gentle but firm handling, as they are confused at being in the grey mist. When you make contact, they will experience great relief. It is difficult to comprehend the love they receive from the healing energy sent to them, as it must feel like someone throwing you a lifebelt. Never underestimate the importance of rescue work, as the benefits are indescribable.

Although earthbound spirits are trapped between worlds, it is important never to tell them they have died, as many do not realise they are dead. For this reason, I always talk to them as though they are still alive—it's important to avoid upsetting them. Occasionally, people who have been involved in an accident that caused a quick and violent death are understandably confused, and don't realise they are dead.

These spirits will often tell a medium that they can see the car or aeroplane crash and see bodies, but don't realise they are one of the corpses, even though the accident may have occurred several decades ago.

Held Back by Love

Some of the saddest groups of trapped spirits are those held by love. There is such a thing as being too loving and not allowing the deceased to pass to spirit by holding on to the ties.

When the bond is very strong, their survivors may keep a part of their home as a shrine, desperately trying in their sorrow to hold on to the memories by having an abundance of photographs of their departed loved one, their books on the shelves, clothes in the wardrobe, and musical instruments or other memorabilia about.

It's perfectly healthy to talk to departed loved ones, but not constantly—keep everything in moderation. People who hold very strong ties with a deceased person will often talk to them as though they are still alive, so it is difficult for the spirit to break the ties and move onward. The worst type of holdout is the selfishly possessive person, who still makes demands on the spirit long after death.

Excessive grieving holds back the deceased spirit's progress, so it is important to let go and realise the loved one must move on from the vibration of the Earth to the vibration of Light, where the next stage of the soul's development starts.

We all came from spirit, so when we die we go back to the spirit world—we are going home. It is a natural progression and simply a change of consciousness, as we only move on to the next dimension.

Some spirits become trapped, not by being held by love, but because they cannot bear to leave a loved one. Then there are those over-conscientious spirits who have died suddenly and unexpectedly, and are agitated because they have left unfinished work behind.

Concern Over Unfinished Business

A close friend of mine who passed quickly with a serious flu virus came through to me, asking that I send a message to his family. He wanted to apologise for the unfinished business he had left and the chaotic state of his office—he was so concerned it would inconvenience both family and clients.

A common reason for remaining earthbound is the very strong urge to send a last message. Perhaps the person died unexpectedly, so did not have an opportunity to say good bye, or say thank you to a loved one. Sometimes it can be a desire to explain the whereabouts of a will, or money hidden in an old weed killer tin in the garden shed. In this situation, the spirit will often open and close the shed door, or knock the tin off the shelf. They can be quite creative in their efforts to plant an idea in the person's head to visit the garden shed, or open the old file where the will is hidden. It is surprising how often they succeed, and then they move on happily.

Heaven Is Overcrowded—There's No Room

One ridiculous reason that some spirits remain trapped is they simply do not believe there could possibly be a Heaven or an afterlife, as there would not be space for all the people who have died since life began on Earth. I can understand their logic, as they haven't realised that we leave our body behind when we die, and only the mind and soul moves on. Nature recycles our body.

We are all made of energy, so space problems are resolved—without a body, spirits do not take up any space. Also, there are several separate energy levels in the spirit world, so there is plenty of room for everyone.

If you know anyone who is concerned about the space aspect and over-crowding, please reassure them. Having answers before you die enables you to find peace immediately.

Perhaps the group who most deserve our sympathy and compassion are the spirits of those folks who were victims of very powerful, inflexible religious beliefs. These people grew up believing everyone is a sinner and not good enough to get into Heaven—if you are told a fact often enough, you eventually believe it and don't question it.

I experienced an example of these beliefs when I first sat in as a beginner in a development circle. We were joined by the earthbound spirit of a vindictive preacher who was attracted to the light of the circle. This very angry spirit told us he had been cheated and hoodwinked, as he had believed everything he taught his little flock.

The poor man firmly believed he had done good work teaching about sin and Heaven, and as he spoke through the medium, he banged the table, again telling us he had been cheated, as Heaven was not the wonderful place he expected it to be. We bombarded him with White Light and healing energy to calm him down, while the circle leader explained to him that he had remained in "the passing through" area, and that she would guide him to the Light, where some of his little flock were waiting to greet him. This was our first experience of meeting an angry spirit—we were all a little awestruck.

Famous People Who Believed

It is sad that many people never know the peace of mind that comes with the knowledge that there is life after death, and that it is not the end of existence, as this knowing helps to reduce the number of earthbound spirits.

Many famous and powerful people have believed in this phenomena, and have used mediums to contact loved ones, or to receive helpful advice.

Princess Diana was reported to have regularly visited a psychic medium, and for many years, the much-loved Queen Mother was also a regular visitor to a medium, to communicate with her beloved husband, the late King George VI.

Formidable Queen Victoria also was a believer, as she regularly contacted her late husband through her medium, John Brown. This amazing monarch brought all her children up in the Spiritualist faith, which was rather surprising and a little ironic, since she was the head of the Church of England. It is reported that as well as royalty, world leaders have also used mediums to resolve problems. British wartime leader Sir Winston Churchill used the services of a medium for guidance during World War II. He was so satisfied with the invaluable advice and assistance he received that he recommended the medium's services to President de Gaulle of France. Last, but definitely not least, American president Abraham Lincoln was known to attend séances at the White House. Many of the world's greatest scientists have been involved in dealings with the spirit world and knew the importance of spreading awareness of this amazing subject.[5]

American Thomas Alva Edison, famous for inventing the phonograph and the first electric light bulb, was an active spiritualist. This brilliant man spent much of his time experimenting with mechanical means to communicate with the deceased (*Scientific American,* 30 October 1920).

The brilliant British scientist John Logie Baird, famous for his invention of television and the infrared camera, reported he had successfully contacted the deceased Edison through a medium.[6] Many clever scientists have conclusive proof that the spirit world does exist.

Have you noticed that although many sceptics deny the existence of an afterlife, none of these sceptics have been able to prove that there is no life after death, nor that the spirit world does not exist? It does seem ironic that there is so little knowledge of life after death when it is so important that we should all be aware of life's continuous cycle, and that the in-between world is not our permanent home.

That's a pretty impressive list of highly intelligent people who all tried to prove an afterlife by using the services of a medium. There is no way that world leaders or royalty could be fooled into regularly using this phenomena unless it was proved to be extremely authentic.

Mediums have a tough time dealing with criticism from the world's sceptics, who wage a constant war against them, since no amount of proof will convince them that messages are genuine. The poor medium, who is only using a skill that comes naturally, is called a cheat or a witch, or accused of preying on the vulnerable in their time of need. I have heard people say the medium makes it up as she goes along, and looks at the newspaper to see who has died! What a joke and what nonsense. Any good medium will give excellent proof of survival without receiving any clues.

My Proof There Is Life After Death

The first time I visited a medium, I did not know the difference between a medium and a clairvoyant. I had made the appointment for a sitting in the hope of receiving guidance on my life, which was in a state of upheaval. My marriage had unexpectedly broken down after twenty-eight years. I had known my husband since I was three years of age, so you can imagine my confusion.

I expected the medium to deal cards or look in a crystal ball, but I got a surprise. A whole new world was opened up to me, as I had never read about the spirit world and none of my family or friends were involved in spiritualism. I couldn't believe my ears at the confirmation I received that my parents were happy in spirit. It was a bit like a coffee morning, as the medium chatted with my mother and relayed the conversation to me. It included my getting a scolding from my mother for letting my standards slip, as I was not using my table napkin and tea knife, and even worse, I was eating my meals at the kitchen worktop, instead of sitting at the dining table, as I was always short of time. I was then told of relatives and family friends who were with my parents, and on checking up to confirm they had died, I realised I had been told the truth. The biggest shock came when the medium told me that I had two children in spirit. I immediately said "No," that my three children were very much alive, but she said the two who spoke had been miscarried. This was a shock as I had suffered two miscarriages, but had never thought that these souls lived on in the spirit world. The experience brought home to me how many people like myself had very little knowledge of what happens after death, and how easy it would be to become trapped by ignorance, through no fault of their own. This thought jolted me to become more involved in spiritual work, including spirit rescue and healing.

Every day in the Western world there are enormous numbers of people who die and leave their physical bodies behind, and move on smoothly to the next dimension without any apparent hiccup. Many of these deceased spirits have contacted relatives or friends on earth, through the channel of a medium, and tell of the wonderful release from pain or illness, money worries, and other limitations of life on earth.

They give reassuring messages of happiness, report a wonderful feeling of being surrounded by love and well being, and tell how they have been reunited with long-lost family and friends. When you hear these messages of love, it makes you feel sad to think that a small number of people who should be enjoying this wonderful experience are missing it, due to stubbornness, religious belief, or mental block

When you stop and think about life and death, your common sense tells you that it is a natural progression to move after death to the next dimension, so why is there a need for spirit rescue? The answer is often a closed mind. The spirit may, during their lifetime, have had negative thoughts that have sown the seeds that death is the end.

Clues of Spirit Presence

Deciding that you would like to become a spirit rescuer is fine, but how do you find the spirits to rescue? What are the warning signs that a spirit is present? Signs of spirit presence may simply be a whiff of sweet lavender or the strong smell of a man's pipe; at other times, it could be the sound of laughter or music, when nobody is present. There are many telltale signs, so ask anyone who is convinced there is a ghostly spirit in their home or office, and they'll tell you about the positive clues to confirm this unseen presence.

Unexplained Smells

Have you ever smelled an unexplained odor of freshly baked bread, reminding you of the wonderful bread your mother baked when you were a child, or it brings back other memories? Or perhaps you get the scent of freesia or lily of the valley, which reminds you of your mother or grandmother. This is not necessarily a clue that a trapped spirit is present, as it could well be a relative calling to say hello and to remind you of them. Often they will appear at the anniversary of their passing, or come to give support at a time when the family is experiencing problems.

A strong smell of cigarette or pipe tobacco is often a sign that the spirit of your father or grandfather is around. When the sign is present only occasionally, it is probably a deceased loved one dropping in to be near you. If the signs occur regularly, or the building has very negative energy and feels heavy, it is more likely that an earthbound spirit is present. I did some spiritual clearance work at a nearby shop where a spirit was making a nuisance of himself. This spirit created a really strong, almost overpowering, foul smell of stale pipe tobacco in the shop, which did not endear him to the staff, but he certainly let everyone know of his presence.

Are you ever aware of any unexplained smells in a certain room in your home, or does part of a room always feels cold? These are signs of an uninvited guest! Spirit presence can often be felt as a cold draft on one side of your body. The source is a mystery, as it appears to come without reason, when all the doors and windows are closed. You can't see anything, but you know they are there. The draught can be caused by a spirit visitor, but if it happens very regularly, or if a room has an uncomfortable, icy chill, then it may be time for a rescue.

Mysterious Sounds

It is normally a sure sign that an earthbound spirit is present when the family dog will give a low growl for no apparent reason. Alternatively, you may hear unexplained sounds—spirits often make sounds when trying to make you aware of their presence. Do you ever hear insistent tapping or eerie footsteps on the stairs when you know you are the only person in the house? It's amazing how many people report hearing music. It can be a tune that your mother liked, the wail of the bagpipes, a tin whistle, or a musical instrument a loved one used to play. Again, this can be a visit to acknowledge your birthday or offer comfort, but sometimes it can be an earthbound spirit who has switched on a tape. Should it be the date of the spirit's birthday, then silently wish them a happy birthday, or if it is your birthday, say thank you, as they will hear your thoughts.

I regularly hear the sound of my old dog Jock sneeze, or the sound of his tail thud. I know his spirit has come to visit me, so I say hello and acknowledge him. After all, they have made an effort to come to your home, so they appreciate a few words from you.

When you cannot explain the sounds, it usually means that a spirit is around you. These sounds are not always musical—as some people hear loud bumps in the night, or doors creaking.

Mischievous Spirits and Missing Objects

Trapped spirits try all sorts of tricks to make you aware of them and can be very infuriating when they turn on the television set or radio, or switch the kettle off when you are making a cup of tea. They can be very exasperating when they play tricks, as we are not always in the mood for it, particularly after a hard day at work.

Perhaps the most annoying thing is when they decide to hide your car keys or purse. It's a complete mystery why it goes missing. You remember placing it on the dresser or kitchen shelf, and you remember seeing it there, and yet when you go to get it, it's gone. All the family deny touching it, so how could it go missing? Isn't it frustrating when you find the missing keys turn up in another room, or somewhere you had already searched for them a few moments previously, and you know they were not there?

These tricks can often be played by spirit children who have been trapped in the building for some time. When an item is hidden by spirits, it is known as *asport*, so perhaps it's their idea of a sport. Asport can also occur when a deceased person is seeking revenge for some events in life that upset them. Alternatively, it can be the type of spirit who was often a selfish tyrant when alive and ruled with a rod of iron, and who now enjoys creating problems and chaos as it gives them the feeling of power. Try to remain calm and ignore their tricks and malicious behavior. Don't give them the satisfaction of causing an upset.

You'll often recognise this spirit as a cantankerous father or grandfather, so don't be too polite to him. This type of spirit is not easy to move as he enjoys the power, so it takes an experienced medium to talk him into moving along on his way home

Spirit Gifts and Tricks

Gifts given by spirit are known as *apport*. It's hard to believe but some people are fortunate enough to receive gifts from spirit. These appear when least expected, and can be anything from a nice plant suddenly appearing in the garden, to a semi-precious stone. This is a fascinating subject and is always confirmation that a spirit has been to visit you.

Many people who have visited Sai Baba in India will tell tales of having been given a beautiful ring or other jewelry he has materialised. I have not seen his work, but I have visited psychic surgeon Stephen Turoff when things have materialised. Ten years ago, I used to travel with a group of friends in a minibus to visit him, and as we were all healers, he allowed us to watch the operations on each other. At the end of the session, he would say in his deep, guttural Austrian / German trance accent "What is your favorite perfume?" We would each say our favorite scent, and sure enough, there it was on our hand! It was not psychological or auto suggestion, as we had not realised he was about to perform this feat and give us a quick squirt of perfume, so how did he do it? With the aid of his spirit helpers, I guess.

Asport is more frequent. Many folks will tell you of their experiences. This is a common story, as people often relate tales of their vanishing items, which mysteriously appear in another part of the house. The missing item is never of great financial value; it's just the inconvenience and the annoying wasted time.

The only advice I can give is to speak firmly to the spirit and ask them to please stop their little game. Pluck up your courage and talk to them. Yes, it feels a bit strange talking to an invisible spirit, but they do hear you as the mind lives on, and they will be happy to know you are aware of their presence.

Annoying Mischievous Spirits

Don't ever allow yourself or your family to be inconvenienced by an earthbound spirit, whether mischievous or malevolent. Realise it is time to call in the assistance of a local medium when you get to the "enough is enough" stage. The medium will guide the spirit home, and ensure you do not have any further frustrations. The spirits' tricks don't mean they are trying to annoy you, so don't be afraid. It's often their only way of trying to make you aware of their presence, and enlist your assistance to help them on their journey home, so don't think too hard of them.

Creaks on the Stairs

Have you ever heard strange footsteps on the stairs? This sound can be very off-putting—an unexplained footstep on the stairs is terrifying, particularly when you know you are the only person in the house. These ghostly sounds are guaranteed to make your tummy tighten as you listen for more. The footsteps are a cry for help, but unfortunately, it's you who feels like crying for help. Do your pictures or mirrors hang at an angle for no apparent reason? A slanted picture annoys most people, and there is an immediate urge to straighten it. Spirits seem to take great delight in adjusting them to tip slightly, just enough to keep you busy correcting their tricks.

They are also known to move an ornament or book from one shelf to another, making you think "How did that get there?" Sometimes an ornament or vase will be turned to face the wall. It's no good if scientific researchers are giving you a logical explanation that it was probably moved by traffic vibration, or the cat leaping nearby. When it happens at different times of the day or night, you know very well it's a mischievous spirit who is moving the picture, but there are times when they can also play helpful tricks.

My telephone is always very busy as people regularly call for healing, advice on ghosts, or geopathic stress. Recently I had one of those days when I seemed to get one call after another, and I mentally prayed that the phone would not ring during the evening, enabling me to relax and catch up with myself. Sure enough, the phone did not ring once, which was most unusual, and the following morning it was again quiet. In the afternoon I went into the seldom-used spare bedroom. I found the phone off the hook, and the receiver lying three feet away from the phone. Some kind spirit had heard my plea and taken the phone off the hook to allow me to rest. As I had not been in the room for several days, a kind spirit was the only explanation possible, so I mentally said thank you.

Have You Ever Been on a Ghost Walk?

It seems that the harder you try to see a ghost, the less likely you are to spot one—perhaps that's why "Ghost Walks" are so popular. There are a great many different reasons why a spirit remains earthbound, so whether it's an old tramp or a young child, all need help to move onward.

My first experience of an organized ghost walk was two years ago when I went along to the weekly ghost walk held in the next town. There you have a choice of a ghost tour around the old town or, alternatively, visit the ghost sites in old warehouses on the riverside area of the town. This ghost walk is part of the social calendar of the local chamber of commerce, a strange choice for their Christmas event you might think. It was a great event, even though I did not see any real ghosts.

The tour was led by a theatrical gentleman in a top hat and long black coat, who took us down lots of narrow lanes and alleyways and explained in a deep booming voice, with blood-curdling details, the story of how these ghosts met their death. None of these poor departed souls seemed to have had a normal death; they either died brokenhearted, were murdered, or worse, but then that made the story interesting and blood thirsty, and added excitement.

To add to the atmosphere, several ghostly figures ran past us in the shadows, or jumped out to frighten us from dark doorways. Yes, it was an evening of excitement and, sadly, it had a real ring of truth, as I was aware of spirits and so realised the evening was genuine, and there were actually spirits needing assistance in the old town. As the spirits do not show themselves to the tourists, I knew that releasing some of them from their bonds would not spoil the future ghost walks, so when I arrived home, I sat down and rescued a few of these poor, tormented souls.

The town where I was living has a lot of history and has an unbelievable number of ghosts—so much so that a local author had enough material to write five books about the ghosts in the area, and an abundance of incidents to fill several more books. Although it makes a story more interesting if the ghosts are found in an exciting place like a castle ruin, churchyard, battlefield, warehouse, or large old house, the vast majority of ghosts and earthbound spirits are to be found in very everyday places, like a shop, a flat, a bungalow, or a house.

Ghosts have been described over the centuries as all sorts of frightening apparitions, whether making loud, wailing noises, or eerie sounds of something being dragged along the ground. One most interesting ghost hunt took place recently under the South Bridge in Edinburgh. This old city has a large number of recorded ghost sightings, and is well known for its horrific tales of the past.

The highly organized hunt involved 250 members of the general public, who bravely volunteered to stand in the vaults deep under the bridge, an area famous for its ghosts. The results of this spooky exercise showed 44 percent of these brave volunteers had experienced some kind of unusual goings-on. These included temperature changes, a sure sign of a ghostly presence, and even more convincing, the sound of someone breathing close to them, while others felt someone touching them, or a pull on their clothes.

This research was organized by Dr. Richard Wiseman at Hereford University, so it was neither a fun event nor publicity stunt. I received details from a friend who had been present, but then was told confirmation of the facts had been published in *The Daily Mail.*[7]

Edinburgh is a magnificent historical city with areas of both great wealth and extreme poverty. It is a city that lends itself to ghost walks, with several areas where buildings steeped in history date as far back as the 1700s. A ghost walk is an entertaining way to spend a holiday evening, as there's always the possibility that you may be lucky enough to see a real ghost.

These tours usually have lots of atmosphere as they take place in old parts of cities and towns, where there are ancient courtyards and dark alleys. The first recorded ghost walk in England was held in the beautiful old city of York, which today offers several different walks. All are in the historic part of the city. For those who want a taste of the macabre, trips are available to York Dungeons' "Deadly Events."

Ghost walks are not exclusive to Scotland and England as these events occur regularly in many parts of the world. Many cities in the US have ghost tours. If you look at the website of the International Society for Paranormal Research (http://www.hauntings.com), you will find several hundred ghost walks listed, which confirms that there are a lot of people interested in seeing a trapped spirit.

The chances of seeing one of those poor souls is small, but if you do sense or see an unhappy ghost from the past, mentally ask them to go to the Light—then your trip will have been really worthwhile.

Basic Spirit Rescue Work

Most people agree the thought of rescuing earthbound spirits from old buildings does sound a bit scary, but I assure you it feels exactly the same as talking to a person who is still very much alive. As the mind never dies, the spirit can communicate, and that's when the fun starts!

Rescue work is like any other sort of work in that you learn as you go along and by your mistakes, so you gain confidence with experience, and just when you think you know all about it, a really unusual rescue comes along. That's when you must remind yourself you are not doing this work completely on your own, as helpers are always there in the background. As soon as you have doubts, you should call for their assistance, so don't ever be too proud to ask for help, as they are only too happy to oblige.

One of the difficulties of doing rescue work is that, until recently, there were absolutely no training classes available, and no set of guidelines to follow. Other mediums will often give a few words of advice, but I have found that very few mediums do regular rescue work, particularly dealing with entities, so it's trial and error.

There are several basic facts to establish before you start a rescue operation, but do you, like so many people, find it difficult to accept the idea of speaking to invisible spirits? Love is a very powerful energy, so send them lots of love, and mentally put your arm around their shoulder to lead them to the Light. Actions often speak stronger than words so they will be aware you are taking them home.

Ask spirit helpers for answers to your questions about the spirit's background, and if you are unable to hear answers to your questions, it is possible to dowse to find the history of the spirit. If you use a pendulum, be sure to cleanse it of negative energy before use.

Becoming a Spirit Rescuer

1. Ask what is the spirit's relationship with the area.

2. Are they a member of the family? If you do not see the spirit, then ask their sex!

3. Are they a previous resident? How long ago?

4. Were they in service in the house? Spirits of servants are often found trapped in manor houses, castles, or large properties.

5. Do they want to take an item or animal with them?

6. Have they a message they'd like passed to someone?

7. Are they lost? And are they afraid or lonely? If so, I usually visualise putting my arm around them to reassure them, and tell them everything is fine, and I will help them to get to their loved ones.

Mentally ask some of the above questions—the answers will give you a clear picture of why the spirit is there, and the best way to coax them to move on. Once you have established the reason they remained earthbound, you can guide them home. Most spirits will go happily to the

Light after receiving a few kind words and some healing energy. Those more determined spirits can be tempted with a promise that there's a new motorcycle awaiting them at the Light, or lots of alcohol, in the case of a drunkard! It's a case of matching the bait to the individual spirit's needs, so that they get the momentum to move on to the veil.

I agree we should not tell white lies, but if the spirit's presence is causing problems by keeping a person awake at night, or creating a strain on their nerves, then it is important to ensure they move onward. It is also in their best interest to move from this grey area, so never feel guilty when you use a bait to coax a spirit to move. I usually mentally ask their spirit guide for permission to move them to the Light. When a spirit does not want to leave without an animal or material things, tell them it's no problem, as they can bring the animal with them to the Light.

If the spirit has been earthbound for many years, you can say that their much loved family is waiting to welcome them at the Light. The rescue medium's job is to help souls realise they are still between worlds. This may entail penetrating a wall of darkness or negative energy that surrounds some spirits. We must always remember the spirit has free will, so we must never force them to move to the Light; all we can do is guide and encourage them onward.

Most spirits are relieved to see you, want reassurance, and are keen to move onward, so these rescues are done in a matter of minutes. Others create a challenge and those are the cases I really enjoy, as it becomes a battle of wits. As our helpers will feed us information to assist us, even the most difficult and obstinate can be helped home.

My business background is in sales and marketing, and never in my wildest dreams did I expect to use my skills to sell to earthbound spirits the idea of going to the Light, but sometimes it is necessary to make the spirit feel needed, so enticing them to the Light by telling them their assistance is urgently needed by their wife, child, etc., will work in some cases, while others require more persistence.

Rescue work is like taking stepping stones into the past, like a trip down memory lane, as often the earthbound spirit's problems remind you of places in your childhood. It can be demanding both emotionally and physically, so it is important never to let yourself become emotional over sad circumstances. It could be very easy to become upset by the unpleasant details of a spirit's death, or their hard and difficult life as a victim of violence and trauma. You will hear many sad tales but must remain detached, as your energy level drops when you become upset. Although you must never become emotionally involved, it is important to be kindly and sympathetic—compassion is the secret of success.

You are almost certainly the first human contact they have made since their death, which could have been a hundred years ago. Never fear a ghost or earthbound spirit. Many people instinctively fear the unknown, but remember, most of us face much more threat of harm in our daily lives from other people we meet than we ever will while doing rescue work on spirits or entities.

To work as a spirit rescuer requires complete faith in yourself and your Creator, a strong will, and a good working relationship with your spirit helpers—you will know instinctively when you meet a no-go situation that it's time to call in their outside help. All earthbound spirits still retain the gift of free will, part of the Universal Law, which should always be honoured. Thus, the spirits are entitled to stay in this no man's land if that is their choice. If a spirit refuses to move after several attempts, then you should respect their wishes to remain in limbo. You may have succeeded in planting the idea in their mind that there is a better place to settle, so they will change their mind at a later date.

You can use several options and variations when doing this work, so you must never feel you should use the same technique for each rescue, or as other mediums do. It's essential that you use a method that feels right and natural for you at the time. We all work on different levels of energy vibration, so a method described in a book, or at a class, may not be suitable for you. The basic rule is: "Listen to your gut feeling, and to your helpers"; then you won't go far wrong.

Using Healing Energy in Rescue Work

When doing rescue work, you need all the tools available, and one invaluable tool is the ability to channel healing energy to the spirit, as this makes the rescue easier. The love energy felt in the healing gives the spirit confidence and comfort and, most important of all, it has a calming and reassuring effect on them. Also send White Light, as this powerful energy will help to dispel any negative energy, and its importance should never be underrated.

Would you like to become a rescue worker? Then it will happen and probably when you least expect it. We acquire the necessary skills when the time is right, and when our energies are strong enough to cope with the many situations that crop up. There are basic courses on spirit release therapy available in many countries, varying in length from a weekend to five days. All that a short course can do is give you information about a rescue technique, the problems you may meet, and the options available, but like learning many other subjects, it's only when you start doing hands-on work that you begin to learn your subject and gain confidence.

Please don't be fooled into thinking you can learn spirit rescue in a few days. You can learn the basics as the course opens the door for you and gives you confidence and other rescue contacts, but you learn from each case, and that's when the fun starts!

Once you start on this path, you soon develop your own style and tools, and it does not matter whether you work alone, with a partner, or in a rescue circle, as the results are the same. Any time you lose confidence and think you may not be good enough to do this work, remember that, whatever our religion or beliefs, we can all follow Jesus' instructions. A large part of his healing work was casting out devils and moving spirits onward. We have all heard his famous words quoted many times, asking us to "do as he does and more." These words are confirmation that we are all able to do this work. I always work alone, as I do my rescue work at different times each day, depending on the situations I meet.

If you would like to learn more about this form of spirit rescue, classes are available in the UK and the US.

When you start to do your first rescue case, remember *you* are not doing the rescue entirely on your own, although it may feel like it! You are only the channel, so don't panic if your first few rescues are not casebook rescues. This is when you use your initiative and think fast! Rescue work is not an intellectual skill, it is a spiritual skill that we learn when the time is right.

Moving on a nice, friendly little lost child, while you sit in a development circle, is one thing, while dealing with obstinate earthbounds who are not keen to move to the next dimension is another, but always remember your helpers are a thought away, so mentally yell for assistance. The spirit world will hear you, as their help line is open twenty-four hours a day.

Distance Rescue Work

There are times when it is not convenient or desirable to do the rescue work from the site—in those cases, it is possible to work from a distance. The rescue is exactly the same, and you talk to the spirit as though it is in same room as you, instead of at a distance. As it is all about positive thought and intent, the thought will get to the earthbound spirit, so you can complete the rescue comfortably from anywhere in the world.

Scientific Study Group

In 1981 the Association for the Scientific Study of Anomalous Phenomena was founded to establish the truth about observed phenomena. Their investigative groups use infra-red cameras and other electronic equipment to locate ghosts. If you are more interested in finding out about earthbound spirits and proving their existence than rescuing them, there are many similar groups in both the UK and the US.

Helping the Dying to Cross Over Safely

As well as rescuing lost spirits, this work can involve helping those who are seriously ill and close to death to pass to the other side on their journey to the Light. Compassion is needed when a rescuer sits with the dying person, reassuring them and helping them to pass over peacefully, and guides them to the Light. This type of work can be done in a hospice, hospital, or in the person's home. It is important work as it eliminates the fear of death and makes the passing easier for the patient and their relatives to accept.

Rescue Work at the Scene of Major Accidents or Disasters

Is it possible to do rescue work at the scene of a natural disaster? The answer is yes, although most spirits will often move on together, because many people from all areas are sending healing energy and prayers to the site. It's usually a simple task to escort those souls remaining there to the Light as they are stunned, and they are grateful for friendly guidance. Since there is much confusion, it is helpful to appoint one of the deceased spirits to lead the group to the Light, so ask for a responsible spirit to take charge. In the case of an air crash or sea disaster, ask the captain to take charge, or appoint officers, and it usually works. Then check several days later to find if any spirits have remained at the site.

The human body is quite unique—our Creator designed this highly sensitive and extremely intricate piece of material to perfection, so remember, the mind is capable of hearing various frequencies after death, when it has moved from the physical to the spiritual plane.

Learning Rescue Work—The Rescue Circle

The ideal way to start learning rescue work is in a development circle, where you are protected by the group leader, and are gently taken step by step through the rescue.

Development circles often grow into rescue circles as the sitters become more experienced, and a leader is in charge of the circle. She or he will tell you when a spirit has been drawn to the spiritual light of the circle to be rescued, and will lead the group through the rescue, while talking to the spirit, reassuring them and guiding them to the Light. During this time, every member of the circle sends healing energy to the distressed spirit. Lost earthbound spirits will often be drawn to the light of a circle, and the selection of spirits who come along will vary from one extreme to another.

The rescue circle is formed when a few like-minded people commit themselves to meeting at the same time each week to give earthbound spirits the opportunity to receive comfort and direction home. Years ago, a circle was known as a séance and was shrouded in mystery. The format of the rescue circle is simple: the group starts with a prayer, then a meditation, which attracts the earthbounds to the bright Light of the group. Once the lost spirits have made themselves known, they are given healing and directed to the Light. The number of spirits rescued varies from week to week and from group to group. Sitting in a rescue circle is satisfying work, as these lost spirits are grateful for guidance.

Rescue Work and Opening Your Third Eye

What is the third eye? If you are not familiar with chakras, it may sound like something seen on an alien. In fact, the third eye is equivalent to the mind's eye, and is a very necessary part of spiritual and psychic work. Where is the third eye? This power point sits on the centre of the fore-head, slightly above the level of the eyebrows, and can only be seen psy-chically. You may have heard someone say, "Oh, the medium said my third eye is open."

The third eye looks like a normal eye—it is the same shape, but in-stead of being used to see everyday things in life, it is the tool used in meditation to see spiritual scenery and spirits. Once your third eye has opened for rescue work, it will not close again.

This unusual eye, which we all possess, is normally opened by doing regular meditation, or by developing your psychic abilities as a much-worked healing channel. The opening of the third eye is essential if you want to progress in spiritual work, as it enables you to sense when a spirit wants to contact you, to see and hear spirits, and also communi-cate with them when doing rescue work. It also enables you to have the all-important contact with your spirit guide and helpers.

The White Light

What is this mystical White Light and where is it? This bright White Light has been described by adults and children of all ages and nationali-ties who have experienced near death experiences. The description var-ies little, as all have described the unbelievable brightness of the Light, and said its magnificence is almost indescribable. It appears to shine very far beyond everything on our planet, and leads to Heaven.

Those who are Christians know this Light as Heaven, others may know it as Nirvana. This Light is the source of all being; it is the Godhead.

This all-powerful Light is eternal, it will always be there to guide us home. It is completely indestructible, and is the source of all creation in the universe, so never doubt its overwhelming love and power.

The Midway Stop—A Passing Through Area

So few people are aware of this grey midway stop area, which was created in yonder days at the beginning of time as a place to give a soul space to deliberate, and perhaps say good bye to a loved one, before making the final journey in this life. Through lack of knowledge, many souls have made this their prison, so we must all try to spread awareness and talk about this "passing through area" on every available opportunity. It is not always easy, as it can be a real conversation stopper, but it's time to start talking.

Much of my rescue work is done with spirits who do not make their presence known; they were crews on ships sunk by torpedoes, soldiers killed in battle, passengers in aircraft disasters, etc. There are all types of disasters and accidents that have happened a long time ago, and as we may be unaware of the history of a site, we should be tuned in at all times—there are trapped spirits waiting to be helped in every town. Get into the habit of mentally asking your guides and helpers if there are any spirits in the vicinity who need your help, and once the spirit world realises you are keen to do this work, you will be guided to those who need a helping hand to guide them home.

Different Sectors of Rescue Work

There are three very different sectors of spirit rescue work, so choose which feels right for you.

1. Rescuing earthbound spirits—this is easily done without any training—and is an act of kindness.

2. Treating fragmentation cases and doing soul retrieval work, which requires specialist training in the field, and is usually carried out by shamans or hypno/psychotherapists.

3. Removing all types of negative entities from people and buildings. Again, it is essential to become a trained spirit release worker before tackling this area of rescue work.

Summary

Earthbound spirits need your help. There will always be those folks who believe in earthbound spirits, and those who say it's all in the imagination, but my experiences convince me that a few spirits do remain earthbound for a variety of reasons. To many, these reasons may sound a bit mundane and not a good reason to become earthbound, but to the spirit, their reason for remaining in the in-between area is very real.

Should you become aware of an earthbound spirit in your home or another building, pluck up your courage and say hello. They will be pleased to hear a friendly voice and will most likely follow your advice to go to the Light. Earthbound spirits turn up in the most unlikely places and, as they have free will, you cannot force them to go on their journey until they are ready to make the move.

In this chapter, I explained some of the reasons why these spirits become stuck, and the warning signs of spirit presence. If you are aware of the cause of the spirit's delay in returning home, then please put his or her mind at rest by explaining that their worry will be resolved. Often, by establishing the identity of the spirit, it is easier to guide them to the Light. Perhaps they are concerned that nobody will feed their beloved cat, or they are worried about unfinished business. When you find the cause of their concern, you can reassure them that it will be sorted out. It is amazing how often a few kind words will reassure a concerned spirit and encourage them to move to the Light. Helping a lost spirit to complete their journey is one of the most important tasks a human can perform, so never underrate the importance of spirit rescue.

Notes

1. *Spiritualist National Union Hymn Book,* 20th edition. Headquarters Publishing Co. Ltd., London.

2. Raymond Smith. "Sir Oliver Lodge." *For Those Who Are Willing to Listen.* ConPsy Publications, UK.

3. *Psychic News.* "Insurers Offer Paranormal Policies."

4. Findlay 1955:350.

5. Victor Zammit. *A Lawyer Presents a Case for the After Life. Irrefutable Objective Evidence.* www.victorzammit.com Book 8. "Scientific Observations of Mediums."

6. Ibid.

7. Dr. Richard Wiseman. *Rod and Pendulum*, No. 16. June 2001. *The Daily Mail.*

chapter four

Spirit Rescues—
They're All Different

Strange Noises in the Night

Spirit rescues occur in a wide variety of places and circumstances some are very amusing, while others are infuriating or sad, and the case of the strange noises in the night was all of these situations. I received a telephone call from a lady who'd been given my name by the British Society of Dowsers, as she wanted her cottage cleared of geopathic stress (GS) to make her home more peaceful. Before agreeing to clear her home of GS, I was urged to ask why she felt this work was necessary. When she started telling me the sad tale, I soon realised that although the energies did need clearing, the root of all her problems was an obstinate spirit who was in residence in her home.

This distraught lady explained that over the past twenty years there had been strange noises in her home during the night, which kept her awake. These noises ranged from a strange whooshing sound to loud, unexplained bangs. This caused her considerable stress, to the extent that she was receiving medical treatment for very high blood pressure and nervous strain. In sheer desperation, she had invited almost every type of expert to her home in an effort to diagnose and clear the problem. The water supply and drains had been checked, the heating serviced, the chimney swept, but none of these services could account for the noises.

In a desperate effort, she turned to alternative therapists and arranged for the layout of her home to be checked by a feng shui consultant, and for a dowser to check the energies of the property. Again, no explanation, so as a last resort she decided to have the building checked for geopathic stress (GS) and that's when I joined the story.

As soon as she started telling me her sad story, I realised the cause of the noise was linked to a trapped spirit, so I cleared the building of geopathic stress from underground water and balanced the negative energy, which had built up in the little cottage over many decades.

It was now time to search for the culprit and, as you've probably guessed, there was an earthbound spirit—an elderly gentleman—who had made himself at home in the building, He told me he had died eighty years ago after having lived in this little cottage on a country estate in the south of England for a large part of his life. He had been employed as head gardener on the estate and this, he told me proudly, was the head gardener's cottage. The home went with the job, so he was not prepared under any circumstances to leave the cottage. This was his home and he had earned it.

I felt as though I was up against a brick wall as he was utterly inflexible. He firmly believed he had a right to be there, and was not lonely as his loyal brindle terrier dog had stayed with him. My instincts were telling me that it was not going to be a simple task to move this determined man and his loyal dog to the other side. He had positive ideas on that subject, and so dug his heels in firmly when I tried to talk him into going to the Light to meet his family. He was adamant he was staying put, so I faced failure in this rescue, unless I could use slightly devious tactics to coax him to leave his beloved cottage.

After several refusals, I considered various options and decided that as the man was obviously very attached to his little dog, it made sense to use the terrier as a lever. I told him that there was a really juicy dinner for his dog sitting up at the Light, and suggested that he should take his dog for a walk there, and that the lady in the cottage would look after it for the short time until he and the dog returned from their walk.

Success, at last, as he fell for my bait and went off happily to the Light, where he was met by his family.

When I do rescue work, I always ask spirit to give me proof that the person has safely gone over, as it's possible for spirits to change their minds at the last moment and return to their earth links. The proof shown to me is always different each time, and often is related to that particular case.

Sometimes I will be shown a flight of stairs, an escalator, or a ladder, other times it may be a flag or a horseshoe. This time when I asked for proof that the man and his little dog had actually gone to the Light, I was shown two blue birds, which I assumed was telling me that he was happy to have flown over. When I told the concerned lady he had gone safely over and that I had received confirmation by the sighting of the blue birds, she became very excited and explained that she believed every word I said, as she had two blue birds in her cottage. As this rescue had been done from a distance, I had not visited her cottage, so I was not aware of her love for budgerigars, or the fact that she had two of these birds in her home, so, as you can imagine, I was astounded by the accuracy of the proof.

I later received a letter of thanks telling me the cottage was completely peaceful, all noises in the night had ceased and there was an amazing improvement in her health, as her blood pressure had dropped to normal almost immediately. The budgies, who had suffered mites in their feathers from their cage being located over the geopathic stress energy line, were now healthy and the cat's fur was now shining. This was not due to the gardener's presence, but to the effects of exposure to GS.

She was absolutely delighted with the results of the energy clearance work and found it very hard to believe that the problem had been resolved from a distance, since I had not visited her home. This is just another example of the amazing work of the spirit world.

When I have to tell a white lie to move an obstinate spirit to the Light, I always ask permission from their spirit guide to use this tactic to help them continue on the next phase of their spiritual journey.

Trapped spirits and geopathic stress are often linked, as this energy is sometimes present where these spirits are found. When the negativity has been cleared, the spirit's journey is made easier. In buildings where there are several underground streams crossing so the GS is very strong. It can create a wall of negative energy, which acts as a barrier and can stop spirits from moving onward, so clearance of this energy is a priority.

The Holiday Camp Ghost

My son Mike was an entertainer at a large holiday camp and thoroughly enjoyed all the buzz and excitement, but one day he contacted me to enlist my help as he was aware there was something wrong with the energy in the chalet where he stayed.

When I linked into the chalet, the energy felt very heavy, full of anger and frustration, certainly not a nice restful place to sleep, so the first job was to clear the negativity and fill the chalet with positive light, then proceed to look for the cause.

I found a very unhappy young man who told me he had been stabbed to death. He had been employed as a cook and said he had been attacked by a drunken youth. When I asked him why he had stayed in the chalet area for years, he said he could not possibly go without his beloved motorcycle. I told him that his bike had been cleaned and serviced and was waiting for him at the Light, ready for him to enjoy a ride. My white lie did the trick, as he was soon off to the Light where I knew he would be in safe hands.

Mike reported that after I'd cleared the energy in the chalet, it felt like a different place and he and his friends were now sleeping well. It's quite amazing how an incident like this one can have a dreadful effect on a property, so that it is no pleasure to live there, and yet, when the energies are balanced and the ghost moved on, the place feels completely different.

A Perthshire Ghost

Many years ago I attended a week's course on Earth energies at a centre in Perthshire, Scotland. The owner of the hotel where I stayed asked what brought me to the area, and when I explained I'd come to learn more about earth energies, she asked me if I knew anything about ghosts.

She then told me a tale of an old cottage in the village that was haunted by a very old lady who'd been there for over a century. I had no difficulty making contact with this lady, who told me her name was Anne, that she had died in the 1880s, and that her job was looking after the herd of goats on the estate. I tried four times to get Anne to go to the Light but failed abysmally each time, as she refused to go without Mary.

I eventually discovered that Mary had been her faithful donkey, so once the cause of the delay was known, it was a simple task to rescue this lovely lady. I told Anne that Mary was waiting for her at the Light, and that she was in a nice, green field. Without hesitation, she was off to join her faithful friend.

Once I have carried out a rescue, I seldom remember the details and think no more about it, so it was a surprise a year later, to receive a telephone call from a friend who had a "sitting" with an international medium who was visiting the area. The medium asked her if she knew anyone named Wilma, and when she said "Yes," the medium said this little old lady called Anne wanted a message passed to me, to thank me for helping her to the Light. She explained that she had been very confused, so this was a nice message to receive. It is very seldom that earthbound spirits send a message back saying "Thank you."

A Spirit Child and the Family Dog

Perhaps the saddest and yet most rewarding part of rescue work is finding a child who has been earthbound for a very long time, and is desperately keen to find her parents, so here are a few details of some of the children I have taken to the Light.

I received an urgent request to check the energy of a nice family house nearby, as the owner "felt something," and grandchildren visiting over a period of years had reported waking up to see a grey lady standing at the side of the bed, leaning over them to check if they were asleep. After clearing the energies, I found the grey lady, who told me she had been a nanny half a century ago, and had stayed in the house to look after the children. The poor, confused soul, even in death, was still looking after the children and checking that all visiting children were safe in bed.

When I explained to the nanny that there were a great many little children at the Light who badly needed her love and protection, she immediately cheered up, and went off enthusiastically to find them.

A few months later I received another call from the owner, saying "There's still something unusual here," so I agreed to search for any other spirits who might be lingering in her home. To my surprise, there was the spirit of a dear little girl, nine years old, who told me she had died of a childhood illness a long time ago. I asked her if she would like to go to the Light to see her mummy and daddy again, but she firmly and politely declined my offer, as she said she wanted to stay here with Josephine, her doggy friend.

Josephine was one of the family dogs, a beautiful black Labrador, slim and elegant, with a shining coat, and her companion was Napoleon, a gentle giant golden Labrador. I'd always thought Josephine was a very psychic and spiritual dog, as the first time I visited the house, I was told that "Josephine does not like strangers, so always stays in the kitchen when guests are in the house." No sooner had I sat down than Josephine proved her owners wrong, as she walked into the room and stood firmly against me, mutely asking me to heal her injured shoulder.

Having seen this side of the lovely bitch, I was not surprised she had been looking after this little girl, and they had become firm friends. My problem was how to coax the child to go to the Light without the dog? This was another occasion when I had to use devious tactics, as I felt it was important to reunite the little girl with her parents.

As Josephine was a very obedient dog, I explained to this little girl that we could take Josephine for a walk to the Light, and as she is a very good dog, she would sit and wait at the Light, while she went off to visit her mummy and daddy. My story worked well, as the child was happy to come to the Light with Josephine and me. As we both watched, her parents welcomed her, and at last they were together again.

I did not feel too guilty about separating her from her doggy friend, as once she had settled down on the other side, she would be able to come back to visit the dog.

When they die, most children will go directly to the Light and be welcomed by parents, grandparents, aunts, etc., but a very small percentage will stay in the area close to their home or the site of their death, whether a hospital or disaster.

Occasionally someone will sight a child ghost, usually because the child is confused, sometimes a child who has lived in poverty, with no parents to look after them. On death, they do not know where to go for safety. This situation was common in the 1800s, when sad little souls lived in real poverty in old buildings, and rarely grew to adult life, due to malnutrition and lack of resistance to illness. Many children under the age of five years are able to see spirits and will have a spirit child as a playmate to share their games and fun. The parents often refer to the spirit as an imaginary playmate, but little do they realise the playmate is a very real friend. So real, in fact, that the child does not realise their little friend and playmate is a spirit, and will ask for a biscuit or drink for their friend.

Trapped Spirits of Children

Until the age of five, many children are very psychic, but seem to lose the gift when they start school. Were you ever really frustrated by your children being emphatic about the presence of their little invisible friend, when you could not see or sense their presence?

Some parents report hearing sounds of a child playing in the nursery when the room is empty, or hearing childish laughter in the house, when only one child is present. These are not always earthbound spirits of children, as often they can be spirit children who come down to play and help a lonely child. It is really amazing how many times, when the subject of spirit children comes up in conversation, that adults will recall having a child spirit as a friend when young.

They also recall on other occasions how their parents used to calmly reassure them there was nothing there, yet they felt the presence of a negative spirit, and were not happy being in a certain part of the house, or were afraid to go to sleep in their room.

Today more people accept that young children below school age are very sensitive and can see spirits of departed relatives and pets, so the days of being told "Don't be silly, there's nothing there," are less common. I can still remember my fear, as a child, each time I went upstairs, as I had to walk along a long, dark gas-lit landing to get to the bathroom. My tummy always felt tight, and my heart thudded as I rushed past the old dresser and the dark shadows on my way to the bathroom and bedroom.

I was always aware of a strange energy in that area of the house, which was not improved by the fact that it was wartime, so the windows had blackout curtains making the house unusually dark, plus there were no friendly street lights outside.

Some of the earthbound children have a sad tale to tell, so it is vitally important to avoid becoming emotional, as they would pick up this energy. To give them confidence, I must always remain calm.

One little girl told me she was four years of age, and had been killed when she stepped in front of a motorcycle and had died instantly. She was so happy to make contact and told me she wanted to take her dolly along—she skipped with me to the Light, and waved me good bye as she was met by her loving grandmother.

Another upsetting rescue was three young children who had been drowned when playing in a rowboat while on holiday at the seaside. Confirmation was given to me that they are safe now—when I took them to the Light, I was very clearly shown Jesus standing, waiting to welcome them home. The only time I am ever shown Jesus is when I am doing rescues that involve children.

On a recent trip to the city, I started talking to the lady sitting next to me on the tube train. I had spotted a book on healing in her bag, so asked if she was a healer. This meeting was definitely arranged by spirit, as we were both getting off the tube at the same station and were both early for our appointments, so we found a nice little café nearby where we could have coffee and continue our chat. She asked me if I knew about ghosts and when I said yes, she asked me to rescue a little girl ghost who had been seen many times in a building in the area.

It was a delight to link to the little girl who said she had been there since 1898. She was very excited when I told her she was going to see her family again, so came happily to the Light. After I had left her in safe hands, I made my usual request for proof that she was safely on the other side. I was shown a sign of a new moon tipped on its side, and a voice said "She's over the moon," so I knew she had gone home.

The Gipsy Boy and the House Mice

I was asked by an estate agent to clear geopathic stress from a house, and when doing so, I found the earthbound spirit of a little boy of about eight years of age. He was a very bedraggled looking little lad, as his clothes looked like "hand-me-downs." He told me he was a gipsy boy and had lived in the countryside. He had been living on the site where the house now stands, and he did not know where to go. He said he died after falling from a horse and being seriously injured.

When I asked why he had not gone to the Light, he said he liked staying here, as he'd become friends with the house mice and spent a lot of time playing with them, so was never lonely. I offered to put the mice in a little box, so that he could take them to show his family. The ruse worked, and he went happily to the other side of the veil.

As I watched him go off, I saw an old gipsy caravan and a large group of gipsies waiting there to welcome him, so I knew he was in good hands.

The great bonus of doing rescue work is you experience a wonderful feeling when the lost spirit goes to the Light, as your body feels an indescribable peace moving through it when the spirit crosses over. This is a form of confirmation that all is well.

The Children of the Glen Cinema Fire in Paisley

A strange coincidence happened recently when I was reading a copy of *Psychic News* and noticed a letter from a lady in Paisley, Scotland, asking for assistance dealing with the ghosts of mischievous child spirits, who were creating havoc at her place of work. This modern office building was built on the site of the old Glen Cinema, which was the scene of a dreadful disaster over eighty years ago.

The cinema had been packed with children for the Saturday afternoon matinee when someone shouted "Fire," which caused great panic. Many of the children stampeded down the stairs to the fire exit, but the exit door was firmly locked from the outside. The children fell on top of one another, and bodies piled up behind the door, so those first down the stairs had no chance of survival.

This tragic event happened before I was born, but I knew the details of it as I was born in Paisley. My grandfather was in charge of the welfare in the town, so was responsible for sending assistance to the bereaved families, most of whom were very poor.

Many years later, at school, my class was asked to write an essay on the disaster, which is part of the town's history, so when I read the article in the *Psychic News*, it brought back many memories, and I knew I was meant to do some work on the site, to find the trapped children. I lit a candle and sat down quietly to link into the site and see what I could find there. Sure enough, there was still a group of nine children lingering there who had been victims of the disaster. These little souls were waiting for guidance and needed help to reunite with their families, as they had been there for over eighty years. Most of their parents had already passed to spirit, so they would be there waiting to welcome these little children.

My job was to organise the children, to get them to come with me to the Light, which turned out to be an easy task as I remembered these children had been poor. I was able to bribe them to come to the Light, with a promise of lots of fresh fruit and sweets, and a great welcome from their parents.

When I had safely handed them over to the other side, I asked for my proof, and was shown a zebra standing on the middle of the road. He was a beautiful, healthy animal, who stood smiling at me. At first I could not understand the significance of the zebra, and then I realised my spirit helpers were having a little joke and trying to lighten the energy with humour, so the zebra was telling me the children had crossed over safely at the "zebra crossing."

I was feeling somewhat emotional due to the sight of these little children meeting their parents, and the fact that it happened in my hometown, which I had left over forty years ago as a bride. It was the first time I had rescued so many children, so my spirit helpers were working hard to lift my energy. They succeeded as the thought of the zebra crossing sent me into peals of laughter and released my tension.

Ask any spirit rescuer about the spirit world's sense of fun, and they will immediately confirm that the helpers who work with spirit rescuers, as well as having great compassion, have a wicked sense of humour. They can create humour out of sadness, thereby making the job easier.

The Little French Girl of Newport

Last year, I was contacted by BBC Television to appear on a programme about the use of dowsing, to find ley lines at the ruins of the ancient church on the waterside near my home. The ley line ran across the site of the ruins and was an area of beautiful energy, in a perfect setting overlooking the natural harbour.

This part of the filming went very smoothly, apart from an upsetting incident when an explosion occurred on a small boat in the harbour.

When filming was completed, we moved to Newport, the main town on the Isle of Wight, where I was instructed to dowse to find the trapped spirit of a little French girl called Francesca, who had been sighted many times over the past two hundred and fifty years by people in the old part of the town.

Francesca was an orphan who'd been brought to England in the 1700s to work, and the story is told that she'd been sold to the landlord of a coaching inn and had a very hard life. She fell in love with Ralph, a stable lad, but unfortunately, a lecherous local printer raped her and she became pregnant. To stop her naming the father, she was murdered and her body thrown down a well. The stable lad was blamed for the pregnancy, and he also was murdered, and his body suffered the same fate.

This story has been passed down for generations and recently, in the room where she had lived her short life, a cupboard that had been boarded up for several centuries was opened, and Francesca's little shoes and blood-stained nightdress were found. Francesca's story was an interesting tale and one to appeal to viewers, so the TV crew took me to the old court-yard, where the coaching house had been sited all those years ago. This was the area where her spirit had been seen regularly and many people believed she had stayed to try to prove the innocence of Ralph, her beloved stable boy. When I started to walk around the courtyard, I was unable to find any trace of her spirit, so I asked my guides and helpers for confirmation that she was still in the vicinity of the courtyard. You can imagine my discomfort when they told me positively that she had already moved to the Light, and was now reunited with her Ralph. What a dilemma now faced me. Should I tell the viewers that I had rescued Francesca and that I had taken her to the Light, or should I risk spoiling the programme and tell the truth by saying she was no longer there, and was now safely home?

As the bulk of the programme was about this little waif, I had to make a quick decision. I decided I must tell the truth and risk disappointing the producer. It's so easy to be found out if you fake a rescue, as another medium could be watching the programme. I told the viewers I was very pleased to say that Francesca had already safely gone to the Light some time ago, and was happily reunited with Ralph.

The following day I had good reason to be glad I had been honest, as I received a telephone call from a local medium, who told me she had done a lot of work with little Francesca and had taken her to the Light several months ago. This call proved to me that you should always tell the truth when doing this work. If you'd like to read more about little Francesca, you'll find details in Gay Baldwin's book *More Ghosts of the Isle of Wight*.

Loyalty to Their Ship

Once each month I used to meet a friend for lunch and as she was interested in rescue work, but not confident enough to do it alone, we would sit eating our lunch in the local pub at a table in a large bay window area that always seemed to be empty and waiting our arrival.

While we were eating our food, we would be doing rescues at the same time, as my helpers would be giving me continuous details of ships that had sunk in the bay over the centuries and the number of spirits still aboard the wrecks. We also rescued both British and Luftwaffe pilots who were still trapped with their plane on the seabed.

One day, for a change of scene, we were sitting enjoying our lunch at another seaside pub and busy rescuing between courses. I was sitting with my eyes closed, linking into a sunken ship, and when I opened my eyes, I was in time to see the waitress taking my tea plate away with my tasty, uneaten bread roll on it. I quickly asked her to please return it to me—she laughed and said she thought my meal was finished, and I was saying a prayer of thanks, as my eyes were closed.

Following our lunchtime successes, I borrowed a book from the library that listed all the ships and aeroplanes lost in the waters around the island over a 400-year period. I sat several times with another friend to whom I was teaching this skill, and we worked our way steadily through the list of casualties, checking every vessel for earthbound sailors. Our efforts were well rewarded, as there were many poor souls from the Mary Rose and other vessels who had been there for a very long time.

This was a time-consuming exercise, but many souls were taken to the Light so it was time well spent. Should you know of any ship that sunk, or plane that crashed, please mentally ask if anyone is there, as you may be able to direct them homeward.

The Titanic

Many mediums have checked the Titanic for earthbound spirits over the years. I had searched there several years ago, but felt guided to try again last year with the friend who is learning this work. To our surprise, we located a few stray spirits who had not been noticed by other mediums or had hidden from them.

These earthbound spirits point blank refused to leave the ship. They were not loyal crew, but wealthy passengers, and I was told by a spirit helper that they were not prepared to leave their jewelry behind. The problem was that the jewels were locked in the ship's safe—how was I going to get around this little problem? I told them the ship's captain had taken their jewelry to the Light for safekeeping, and it was there waiting for them, so they went off in search of their jewels.

We were then left with three spirits who had no intention of leaving the ship. Eventually I discovered their reason for staying was that their limousine was in the ship's hold, and the owners and their chauffeur would not move without their beautiful car. It was a surprise to learn the ship carried vehicles in the hold, but as they were so adamant and I had not seen the film *Titanic* and knew very little about the ship, I believed them. By explaining that their limousine was waiting for them at the Light, where it had been cleaned and serviced, they went off at full speed to find their beloved car.

Naval Rescues

The Royal Oak battleship was torpedoed by the German navy at Scarpa Flow in 1939, with the loss of 800 lives. Spirit asked me to help those sailors still aboard this magnificent vessel.

As expected, I found a group of loyal crew who had remained with their ship. I explained to the men that the war had ended, and thanked them for protecting their country and looking after their ship.

When I said there was a big celebration party at the Light, with all their families waiting to welcome them home, they were happy to leave the ship and join the reunion. This rescue operation was a stirring experience, as when I asked the spirit world for a sign that they had gone safely to the Light, I was shown the Royal Navy ensign and heard the haunting, eerie sound of the boson's whistle, and watched as the men were piped by spirit to the Light, and I thought of the words of a spiritual hymn:

> *We do not die, we cannot die,*
> *We only change our stage of life,*
> *When earth temples fall and lie,*
> *Unmoving mid the world's wild strife.*
> *There is no death in God's wide world,*
> *But one eternal sea of change,*
> *The flag of life is never furled,*
> *It only takes a wider range. J.S.A.*[1]

My rescue work involves all nationalities, so I must include a German rescue as spirit directed me to visit the magnificent German cruiser, *The Scharnhorst*, considered almost unsinkable by the German Navy. She was sunk in World War II with the loss of almost two thousand lives. My spirit rescue team told me that my help was needed there, so I linked into the ship and found a group of loyal young men who stayed with this enormous vessel at the bottom of the ocean. They refused my invitation to come to the Light, to meet their families, so I had to think of a subtle approach.

After discarding a few ideas, I decided to tell them that they were requested to attend an urgent briefing of all crew at the Light. The request was accepted, and these loyal, well-disciplined men went off to the other side. It's really not surprising there are so many spirits earthbound, as trying to outwit them to get them to move onward is often like being on an obstacle course. I have a marketing background so my skills are put to good use, and with spirit's help, we win over most who are stuck in the grey no man's land.

Rescue at Pearl Harbour

The bombing of Pearl Harbour happened so quickly that naval and air force personnel did not have time to protect themselves from the hail of bombs. The *USS Arizona* was a serious casualty as she sank with 1,177 men aboard. I was asked to rescue those who had stayed with this grand ship and when I linked in, I found forty-seven men who had remained with the vessel, while the others had gone safely home. Once I had reassured the men that the war was over and help was coming to raise their ship, they were happy to go to the Light.

Over-Sexed Spirits

It's time to change the subject and tell you about some over-sexed spirits.

An Over-Sexed Spirit Near Reading University

A concerned mother recently contacted me to enlist my assistance as she was very worried about the energy of the flat near Reading University that her student son was renting for a year. This caring lady's fears were very justified, as she had visited the flat to help her son redecorate and clean the rooms, and had stayed overnight there. During the night, she sensed an uncomfortable feeling of negative energy, but eventually drifted off to sleep, only to be awakened by the frightening experience of the full weight of a man lying on top of her body, trying to rape her while she slept. She managed to scream, which made the spirit move out of sight, but it was a terrifying ordeal she would not like to repeat.

This mum's main concern was that three pretty young girl students were going to share the flat with her son, and she felt they would be very vulnerable to this nasty, lecherous, debauched spirit, who saw all women as a target for his needs.

The flat was full of very heavy negative energy from this dark spirit, also from the previous occupant, and when I started clearing the energies of the flat, I saw the spirit of a heavily built, uncouth beer-belly of a man, a really objectionable spirit, who had nothing nice to say. It was essential to be as crafty with this man if I was going to move him from the flat, so I told him that if he hurried up to the Light, he'd find lots of beautiful, sexy girls who would love to entertain him.

The bait was sufficiently tempting to get rid of him for good, as he shot off to find his next victim. This was an example of people who do not change their character after death, as they hang on to their nasty habits. It was a great relief to see him depart, as this type of low level spirit can create many problems.

Having passed him to the other side, I knew he would be helped to see the error of his ways, and I hoped would change his attitude toward women. Perhaps, in his next incarnation, he'll come back as a woman.

That will teach him! One good thing about rescue work is there is such a wide variation, it is never dull or boring. By contrast, the next sexy nuisance spirit was female.

A Sexy Lady Spirit in the US—Three in a Bed!

A friend called me, saying "I need your assistance." She then explained that her recently married daughter and son-in-law, who live in the United States, were having a very serious ghost problem that was disrupting their life.

Before the wedding, the second bedroom had been converted to an office and that's when the trouble began! The bridegroom started waking up at 4:00 each morning, for no apparent reason, always feeling a bit strange, and sometimes feeling a heavy pressure holding him down on the bed. Sometimes he saw this lady with long blonde hair lying next to him on the bed. After the wedding, this lady made her presence felt, appearing in the bed, grinning in a seductive manner. When the groom swung his arm out to move her away, she instantly vanished. This sexy lady spirit was an unwelcome visitor in the young couple's home and was crowding their marriage. The mischievous spirit caused many sleepless nights, and during the day would show herself to the wife as a dull lady, with her hair tied back and wearing plain clothes and no makeup. The first time it happened, the husband described how his bride's eyes opened wide and became very large. She was so terrified that she let out an enormous scream, which frightened the spirit off. She described the woman as battered and angry, and not the glamorous lady seen by her husband. Although it was the same spirit, the story changed when she was in the presence of the husband, as her image became glamorous, with her hair hanging loose over her shoulders.

She was well made up and to complicate matters, she regularly appeared in the bed, close to the husband, so you can imagine the problem this situation caused, and why my friend pleaded with me to sort out this sexy spirit.

I linked in to this female spirit and had absolutely no idea how to coax her away from the young couple, as she seemed to know exactly what she was doing and had no intentions of leaving this home. It was a matter of urgency that she was moved onward, so I told her that if she hurried off to the Light, she would find there a very sexy black lace negligee, which the man wanted her to wear. That did the trick—she was off to the Light, and has not been seen since, much to the relief of the couple. Once I'd said good bye to the sexy lady, I checked the energies in the rest of the building and as often happens after you rescue one spirit and they have gone safely on their journey, another one who is quieter will appear. My search revealed a gentle black slave, who told me their home had been on an orange plantation and the entire family of slaves had been burned alive in their home. The attack was carried out by a group of people wearing white masks. These poor souls had been the innocent victims of a hate battle, although they were not personally involved. It was an easy matter to take this slave to join his family at the Light. He explained they had become separated in the confusion of the fire. The family had gone in different directions and he had been left on his own, so was very grateful for my support.

This home was built on the site of the old orange grove, and when I told the groom I had found the old gentleman, who had lived on a plantation, he said he believed me, as the next road to his home was called Orange Grove. He also said that the people rushing from the fire explained the flashes he had often seen when lying in bed during the night, but could not find any logical reason, so the jigsaw now all fitted together.

One of the problems rescuers face when doing this work is trying to get positive confirmation that a ghost was present, and that the rescue occurred. How can you produce evidence that you had a chat with a spirit and have taken it to the Light? Many serious-minded people will think you are mad, and the sceptics demand proof, which is almost impossible to present, so it was a pleasure to have confirmation that the area of the "sexy lady house" where I found the distressed man had, in fact, been an orange grower. I was working from England and the spirits and their home are in the United States, so I had no way of knowing the history, but for me, the orange grove was a confirmation.

This is perhaps the most frustrating aspect of rescue work, as spirits are seen by some people and not others, so there is a lack of proof to back up ghostly claims. There are no fingerprints or marks. How much easier it would be to prove you'd seen a live ten-foot gorilla, as a trail of footprints would be there for all to see. So often spirits are seen at a fleeting glance. They are gone so quickly that you can easily believe you have imagined it and your eyes are playing tricks on you, as you ask yourself, "Where is the evidence?"

You meet all sorts of people when doing rescues, and when I come across a spirit like this gentle man, who has had such a hard life, it really makes me count my blessings.

What Is a Portal?

A *portal* is an entrance to the spirit world—an opening in the energy field made by our Creator for spirits to pass through on their way to the other side. These ever-open, heavenly doors have an impressive history and could tell a few tales, as they have been there since the beginning of time. You'll find them mentioned in the Holy Bible, as there are references to portals in both Genesis and Revelations. Portals are often found by mediums in buildings or gardens where residents have regularly reported sighting lots of different spirits.

Portals come in a range of sizes and these beautiful, heavenly doors are found in many properties. I have worked with them in a range of places, including a kitchen in a large family house, a bedroom in a flat, a well in a garden, and others. These spiritual dimension gateways, which are areas of divine love and protection, are found in all sorts of places, including hospitals, churches, and homes.

If you suspect there is a portal in your home, garden, or workplace, then get out your pendulum and dowse, as you will be able to locate it.

The Happy Ghosts of Lake

Can you imagine the nightmare of living in a little retirement cottage and sharing it with nearly fifty ghosts and all their animals? Well that is what was happening to a lovely elderly couple when they moved into their dream retirement home just over a year ago. They thought life was going to be perfect bliss, but what a shock they got when it became a living nightmare. The man suffered from Parkinson's Disease, so local priests and others suspected that the ghosts were a figment of his imagination and a side effect of his medication, but they were so wrong!

The priest was called to bless the energies of the house. This made no difference, so he came on two more occasions and again blessed the little house, still with no success, so a full requiem mass was done, but again to no avail, and finally a local medium who specialises in spirit rescue was asked to assist.

The medium was able to reassure the couple that there were many spirits present and that she believed their story. She spoke to the spirits but was unable to move all of them on, as they told her they liked living here and did not intend to move. They explained that they were a group of adults, children, and animals who had lived in the area a very long time ago. They did not have any religious beliefs so did not worship any god. This allowed them to have no conscience problems about their wife swapping, animal sacrifices, etc.

When the problem persisted, I was called to help and found a large number of spirits who were full of negative energy and quite content with this situation. They told me they did not belong to a witches' coven, but did enjoy their lifestyle in the fields.

Again they emphasised life here was great, so here they were staying and apologies to the old folks! Why were so many spirits remaining on the site? Yes, their friends and relatives were there, but you would think they would want to move onward. These spirits told me they stayed there because they could not move as there was a solid wall of energy blocking them from going to the Light. This was correct, as the site had very powerful geopathic stress from underground water, and also powerful negative energy had built up on the site, due to the sacrifices and other negative activities that had occurred over the many years they had been on this site.

It is not difficult to tell the difference between sites with good energy and sites with very bad energy, as land that has very positive energy always amplifies peace, harmony, and a feeling of complete and utter wholeness, whereas land that has very powerful negative energy seems to emphasise a heavy disharmony.

The range of spirits seen was amazing. Young girls would dance on the bed when the couple were trying to sleep. They would sometimes awaken to find a face peering into theirs, or someone sitting on their head. Spirits were seen jumping into the wardrobe, up into the loft, where they disrupted the insulation, or swinging on the light flex. It all sounds a bit far-fetched, and I found it hard to believe when told, but relatives and near neighbours have also seen these activities. When a daughter stayed on an overnight visit, she complained of someone trying to push her out of the bed. Some nights there would be the couple and three spirits all in the one bed and a dog pressing on their feet. To my relief, when I cleared the site of negative energy and geopathic stress, many of the spirits moved to the Light. Shadows were seen every evening on the wall, when the couple were relaxing or watching television. Sometime they could hear strange music—it was unrecognisable, and had an evil sound. Often singing would also be heard and always draughts of cold air were felt in the house.

The bathroom was so cold that for the entire year they had lived in the place, the bathroom cistern and windows had run with condensation, even in summer. The room temperature was kept over 70 degrees, and the windows were double-glazed, so should not have run with water, certainly not all year round. This was by far the most complicated rescue I had ever been asked to assist—there was so much happening that it was difficult to know where to start.

Cleansing negative energy from the area was the first priority, as positive light energy weakens negative spirits, and these "grey guys" take their energy from negativity, so by cleansing the place, and filling it with positive White Light, strength is on my side.

When doing rescue work in an area where demonic forces and witchcraft have been taking place, it's terribly important to ensure that I am well protected, so the evil energies cannot affect me, as this is a battle, and they are as determined to win as me.

Having put on my cross and said a prayer of protection, I sat down to move the merry gang on to new pastures—alas, that was what I thought! They had other ideas, but after several attempts I succeeded in moving a large number to the Light by tempting them with all sorts of promises of girls, sex, good food, and grass fields.

About 70 percent of the gang moved on, but the rest stayed and I struggled but seemed to be getting nowhere fast. As soon as I moved some onward, another lot of different spirits seemed to appear, although these were from a different generation, and were often seen floating through the bedroom wall, wardrobe, or ceiling. Eventually I realised there was a very regular stream of spirits coming through the house, who were not associated with the previous group, so I looked for a portal, which is a spirit entrance to the next vibration.

Getting rid of the condensation raised morale, but we still had a long way to go, as each night the couple were wakened by dust falling on their face, dogs and cats around, and strange unpleasant sights, like a man spreading human waste on the bed, which created a dreadful foul smell; fortunately, it dematerialised. Other times they would be shivering with cold when the room temperature was 75 degrees, so how do you find a rational explanation?

Many people live in houses with a spirit portal, but as they are not sensitive to spiritual energies, they are unaware that lots of spirits share their home. This couple were both very sensitive to these energies, so could see spirits, while some of their neighbours were oblivious to the unseen company.

Once I had cleared neighbouring houses of geopathic stress and negative energy, the only real proof of the spirit presence in the home was the unexplained extreme condensation problem, which stopped when I cleared the energies of the house, and the complete disruption to the loft insulation. As the loft did not have any squirrels or mice living there, and these elderly people were unable to climb into their loft, although it sounds ridiculous, the party-type noises they heard in their loft surely must have been these spirits.

This was a truly marathon ghost hunt and I can't help wondering how many other sites have a similar problem. John Masefield wrote the lines: "He felt the hillside thronged with souls unseen," and that's my description of this retirement site.

A Scottish Battlefield

My next rescue took me to my home country of Scotland. Following a guest appearance on a BBC programme talking about geopathic stress, I received a telephone call asking me to go to Scotland to clear energies on the grounds of an estate. I was taken to the site where a vicious battle was fought between the Scots and English armies several centuries ago.

It was an area of countryside covered with gorse bushes and nettles, and although at first glance it seemed a peaceful spot, it was heavy with sadness remaining from the battle There were still many confused souls wandering around in the area, so I had some work to do. I was shown a scene of several piles of corpses and noticed they had been separated, so the Scots were in a different area from the English—even in death, they could not be friends!

As there were a number of spirits from both sides requiring my help, I wasn't too sure of the best way to get them home—I felt pretty certain they would not all go together. My experience of mass rescue at that time was limited, so I decided the best move was to rescue the Scots first, then deal with the English.

It was time to ask for outside assistance, so I mentally called for help, support, and guidance, and as usual, my helpers excelled themselves by giving me a simple solution, for lo and behold, a lone piper appeared, playing a haunting tune, and as I watched with tears running down my face, I saw my Scottish soldiers march off into the distance behind the piper, on their way home. Even now, while typing the details, I can feel emotion, as it was a truly stirring sight.

Don't worry. I didn't forget the English, as when I got over my sense of awe and goose pimples, I was able to arrange a bugle call and ask for their king to lead his men to the Light. This battlefield has now been cleared of negative energy and all the souls have gone home, but how many souls still remain on other sites? If your journey ever takes you to the scene of a battle or accident, please mentally ask any spirits still present to move to the Light. I know I am repeating myself, but this is important work.

While clearing the energies on this estate, as well as the battle site, this area so steeped in history had lots of spirits in need of my assistance. My next task was to take five magnificent knights to the Light, as they had stayed on the site to protect it from invaders. It did not take long to reassure them their work was done, and their rewards were waiting for them at the Light. I told them there was a huge banquet awaiting them. With the knights was a large dog called Toby, who looked like a deerhound. He had befriended the knights, so he too was taken to the banquet.

The next task on this large estate was not so pleasant, as there were a number of servant girls and their foetuses who had been killed, and their bodies thrown down the well. A previous land owner had been an arrogant man who had brought the young girls from a nearby village to work as maids on the estate. He had his nasty way with them, and when they became pregnant, they were killed. Life was hard for poor peasant families in those days. These girls and their foetuses were happy to be guided to the Light as all were relieved to leave this dark, dank area.

The Ghosts on a Scottish Estate

When I was invited to work on this site, I asked a spiritual friend to come along for moral support. The night before we traveled north, we were sitting chatting about the estate, when we were asked by spirit to draw a large picture of a flag. We were told this flag should be taken with us on our journey to Scotland, and hung on the flagpole of the great house. This all sounded a bit strange, but we obeyed and drew the flag and, as instructed, we drew it in four sections, with a different animal or crest in each section, and coloured it as directed. As neither of us had any knowledge of the subject, we sat and waited for guidance and were shown a picture of the subject in each section. Drawing has never been one of my talents, but fortunately, my friend is more artistic, so he drew the flag and the end result looked professional.

We flew from London to the estate the next morning, with the flag safely in our baggage, and trusted that spirit would guide us where and when to hang the flag. Our instructions were to hang the flag on the flagpole, and then to burn it. A strange request and a bit sad to see our artwork burn, but the reason for this action was to remove some of the black power from a previous owner. Light was thrown on this mysterious subject by the head gardener, who was knowledgeable on flags, and had looked it up in a reference book. He informed us that the flag we had drawn was the coat of arms of a landowner who had owned the estate several centuries ago. We were rather pleased with ourselves that we had succeeded in drawing a genuine flag, simply on directions from upstairs!

Were the happenings on this estate an isolated case? I don't think so—although we don't hear about those sort of incidents, I suspect they were frequent occurrences, so there are many advantages to living in the twenty-first century.

A Spirit of the Blitz in Cowes

While on the subject of battles, this week I cleared a home in Cowes, Isle of Wight, of geopathic stress, as the owner suffered from myalgic encephalomyelitis (ME). She mentioned that both she and her husband regularly heard noises on the stairs in the evening, and thought there must be a ghost in their home, since neither of them could locate the source of the sound.

When checking the house, I found the spirit of a thirteen-year-old girl who was very upset. She told me, "I was blown to smithereens by a German bomb during a raid." This was the first time I had rescued a child whose body had been blown to pieces, so it was an upsetting rescue. This sad little girl had been there for over half a century and was in a very confused state. She had been a victim of a blitz on Cowes during the last war, when the family had been wiped out by the force of the bomb explosion and the burning that followed the blast in 1942. Her mother and baby sister had been killed, also the family pet, an Alsatian dog called Judy. Cowes suffered severe bombing during this time— eighty people were killed and eighty-four injured during the raids. She was happy to go to the Light when I told her that her family and the dog were all waiting with a big welcome party. I watched as she went off, carrying a small Union Jack in her hand. The sight of the flag took me back to my childhood during these frightening times.

As I had no knowledge of the area affected by the drastic blitzing by the German aircraft, I decided to check at the council offices for details of the attacks, and my search unearthed details of the heavy bombing, which had caused dreadful casualties in the Cowes area. Looking at Cowes when the America Cup was being held, it was impossible to visualise this happy town's smouldering ruins half a century ago.

He Would Not Leave His Savings

When rescuing earthbound spirits, it's so very helpful to find what secret or reason holds them to the area, and this was the situation with one rescue case. I had to pit my wits against the determination of a local businessman who had died in the 1920s and refused to move on. He had money hidden in his building and did not want to leave, as he wanted to ensure the money went to his family.

This family man had refused to move when offered assistance by another medium so it would be a struggle, although I felt sympathetic that he wanted to leave his money to his family, but how was I going to resolve his problem? A few attempts failed, then a spirit helper told me that it was white-lie time! I told the man very confidentially that if he got to the Light quickly, there was a lot of money hidden, which he could claim for his family. The ruse worked and he went off happily, but the money is still missing—the building has since been demolished and rebuilt, so it's probably good bye forever to his savings, unless some lucky person with a metal detector finds it.

A Healing Ghost

Today I was asked to help rescue an earthbound spirit from a New Age shop—the staff were aware of the presence of the spirit of a gentle man who had practised healing in the upstairs area of the shop. When I was told the earthbound spirit had been a healer, I was convinced there was a mistake, as healers are very spiritually aware, and upon death would automatically travel to the Light. So why was this healer still in the building?

After the energies had been checked, and spirit confirmed that he was in fact still there, the first job to do was to establish what was holding him there, as it was very likely that he was not there from choice. It did not take long to discover that the building had very strong negative energy from geopathic stress, and this band of negativity was acting as a barrier, stopping this man from moving on. When the energies of the building had been cleared, I spoke to him, and told him there was a great queue of people standing at the Light waiting for healing, so he was off at speed to offer healing.

My Uninvited Guest

Another spirit in need of rescue resided in my new home. When I moved to live in this lovely area, I was aware of a pleasant-looking man who regularly sat in my armchair. My neighbours gave me a description of the previous owner, confirming he was the mystery visitor. This lovely man did not want to leave his home, as he had a little factory in his garden, a workshop where he made golf clubs. I don't know what he thought about the fact that I promptly redecorated it, threw out all the old bits of wood, then proceeded to convert it into a nice healing sanctuary.

I asked my helpers for some inspiration to coax him to leave his beloved golf clubs—as a keen golfer myself, I sympathised with him.

My bush telegraph told me he had owned a nice boxer dog, so when he heard the dog was at the Light, waiting for him to take him for a long walk, he promptly forgot about his factory, went off in search of his dog, and is now reunited with his faithful dog in spirit.

I'm often asked what language I use to communicate with foreigners. The answer is English, with a Scottish accent. Mediums receive messages in their native language, so a French medium would hear words in French, or a Spanish rescuer would hear the words in the Spanish language. I always mentally speak English, and if the spirit doesn't understand the language, they understand the energy of love and the positive energy that is sent to them. Also, intent and positive thought ensures the spirit receives my thoughts. Often that is enough to move the spirit onward, as some earthbound spirits are only held by negative energy. When they receive a boost of positive energy, it's enough to give them the momentum to be off—not all earthbound spirits have a complicated reason for staying in an area.

A Desperate Husband

People don't change temperament when they die. Even when they move to the other side, people who were aggressive, pompous, or inflexible when alive will be exactly the same as an earthbound spirit. These are the spirits I enjoy rescuing—I look upon it as a sport and a challenge, as they are often as determined as me to win. Our guides and helpers, as I've said earlier, only give us the cases we can handle, so I get the difficult, balshy ones! I never have any feeling of guilt when I've got them to the Light by false pretences, as I've had permission from their helpers to get them home.

Spirit directed me to an interesting rescue in Surrey, and warned I was dealing with a devious individual. As forewarned is forearmed I was ready for battle with this spirit who was causing an upset. Spirits don't realise that mediums like myself have inside information about them, so I had the advantage over this man who was upsetting the life of a lovely, gentle lady.

The distraught lady contacted me to enlist my help to clear this nuisance from her home. This angry man was making her life a nightmare by regularly tripping her up as she walked across the room, and on several occasions, she was violently thrown across the room. Many annoying incidents like the kettle being unplugged or lights switched off were a regular occurrence—in desperation she would move to sleep at her family's home.

This long-suffering lady was convinced that someone did not like her and was sending her witchcraft, or had put a spell on her home. It is easy to convince yourself this is the case when you've tried repeatedly to get rid of a problem, to no avail.

After several years of living in a tense state, a relative suggested she contact me. When I checked the energy of her home, it was full of negativity, which was not really surprising, as the struggle had been ongoing.

There he was, a cantankerous old man. I had already been warned by my helpers that he was cunning, so I used a gentle approach. He told me he was very angry and frustrated as his wife had consistently ignored him, so in desperation, he pushed and tripped her up in an effort to get her attention and accept his presence. As he did not seem to realise he was dead, it was essential not to upset him. After several attempts had failed to coax him to the Light, my helpers told me he had held a rank in the army. I used this fact as bait and told him he was missing all the fun, as his regiment was holding a reunion at the Light. All his friends were having a great time and waiting for him to join them.

The thought of missing a reunion with his army pals was too much for him, so he was off to join the fun, which put an end to the violence and this gentle lady no longer lived in fear. The spirit of her ex-husband meant no harm as his ungentlemanly behaviour was the only way he knew to attract her attention.

If you know of anyone who is suffering from this type of problem, please assure them it's not witchcraft, but simply a miserable or frustrated spirit trying to make contact, as they have become lost along the way. As a spirit rescuer, you meet all types and situations, but help is always at hand, as a spirit rescuer walks between both worlds and is comfortable with this co-existence with the world on the other side of the veil.

The Scene of a Major Disaster

I'm often told by my helpers that there is work for me to do at the scene of disasters and, like many other healers, I send out lots of healing energy to the injured and search for trapped spirits. There are usually very few earthbound spirits, as the power of healing being sent to the scene aids them on their journey, and many have reported through mediums of being helped by angelic beings.

There will always be a few confused spirits who stay around the scene for a few days to see what's going on, but spirit rescuers and mediums will check the site for any spirits who have lingered.

When a disaster on this scale occurs, healers and mediums automatically go into rescue mode, beaming out energy to where it is needed.

The power of prayer is also a very effective tool, as it fights negativity. A fine example was September 11, 2001, when we all worked hard sending healing light, love, and prayers to the scenes of disaster, so most of those killed made a very quick transition to the other side.

The length of time a spirit can wander the between worlds ranges from a few days to several hundred years. During the past few years, I've helped many thousands of trapped spirits from battlefields and disasters to move on to the Light, but an interesting fact I have noticed is that there are a higher number of earthbound spirits in the West, compared to the East. I've puzzled over this fact and the only explanation I can find is that more people in the East are aware of death, and that life carries on afterward. What do you think is the answer? The experience of meeting an earthbound spirit is exactly the same—whether it is in an English churchyard or an American plantation, nationality makes no difference.

Suicide Victims

I can't close this chapter without saying a few words about suicide victims, as I am often asked what happens to them after death. Some people worry that they live forever in a dark place, but this is not the case. A few of the people who commit suicide need help to move on, as they are trapped in a negative vibration. Some suicide victims have for a time slept or worked over a geopathic stress line—in fact, experts say that 75 percent of all suicides are people in that situation.

Research in Europe has shown a large number of people who suffer severe depression have slept over these geopathic rays, which has the effect of lowering energy and weakening the immune system, also making the person tired, lacking in energy and momentum, and suffering unexplainable depression or feeling suicidal.

I was asked to clear the energies of a home in Staffordshire, where a couple were experiencing upsetting events. The wife reported that on several occasions she felt she had been hit hard by an invisible object, and the husband found tools missing and other annoying little incidents.

The energy in the house was very heavy and on checking, I found GS in the bedrooms. It didn't take long to find the spirit who was responsible for the upsets. I tracked down a distraught young man who told me he had committed suicide by hanging himself with a rope because he had been in serious debt and saw no way out of it. The poor lad had been trapped in the house for almost fifty years, so was very relieved when I assured him he was now safe, and I would take him to find his family.

It is always sad when you find a spirit who has taken his own life, as he or she is usually desperately unhappy, very often regrets his or her action, and is in urgent need of help.

Another suicide victim who needed my help was a young man who had committed suicide by poisoning himself with gas fumes in his car. He told me he had blocked the exhaust, then sat in his car in turmoil, waiting to die. It's difficult to imagine the depth of his despair as he sat there slowly dying. Taking him to the Light was a simple task as he was keen to pour out his troubles to me, and happy to go and see his family.

This was not the end of the rescue, as a few months later I visited a medium near my home, who told me this young man was here to thank me for rescuing him from his despair after his suicide. I was surprised and absolutely delighted, as it is so seldom that people make the effort to say thanks. He told me he was very grateful to me for helping him to find peace and he said that he hoped that I, too, would find peace. This was a touching moment and events like this make the work rewarding—spirits have to make a great effort to contact a medium, so I appreciate it greatly.

Within a split second of death we have again become a spirit, and as every spirit consists of a fluid energy, it allows us to float around in space. When we pass to spirit, we leave absolutely everything behind except our mind, as the mind lives on after death. It is eternal; everywhere we go, our mind goes as well, taking all our life's experiences to the next phase of development.

The Human Mind After Death

When mankind can accept that death is not a permanent end of life, we will be able to release fears of death. It's time to accept that the human brain and the human mind are totally separate, that each has a function, and the brain is a tool of the human mind.

The mind is a truly individual phenomenon that works completely separate from the brain. It is linked to the memory that lives on after death. It is a gift from our Creator, it is eternal and everlasting, the centre of our soul, and is our permanent invisible link with the universal mind. This is the reason we are able to ask a departed loved one about a missing ingredient in a recipe for a favourite scone, or data about scientific research in a previous century from Sir Oliver Lodge. Long after the body has decomposed and been recycled by nature, the mind is still in 100 percent working order, so it's vitally important to get earthbound spirits moved on to the next phase of their development, where their minds can again add to their experiences.

Perhaps the most amusing tale I have read was about a gentleman member of the British Society of Dowsers, who wrote to the magazine saying he had been bereaved seven years ago and had discovered, by accident, how to contact his deceased wife by using his dowsing skills. His first question was: "What programme did you use on the washing machine?" He went through the alphabet until he got to the letter J, then received the "Yes" sign, so he has been happily using this cycle ever since, and regularly communicating with his late wife.[2] I will talk about the use of dowsing as a tool to find lost spirits and energy lines in a later chapter.

Can a spirit materialise as a butterfly? That's the question a lot of people were asking last year at the large funeral of a popular hairdresser, for as the coffin was entering the church, a beautiful butterfly landed on it and stayed there for the entire duration of the service, and did not leave until the coffin was removed for cremation.

It then calmly flew down the aisle and out of the church. Was this the spirit of this well-known man, come to see who had attended his funeral and that it was all to his satisfaction? We will never know the answer, but many mourners were convinced this artistic man was there sharing the service with them. Spirit can move in mysterious ways.

Are you concerned about an earthbound spirit in your home? Many people offer ghost rescue work, but one American firm, whose claims amused me greatly, had an advertisement on the Internet for a ghost busting firm boldly claiming: "ONCE WE KILL IT, IT STAYS DEAD." No other company can make this offer! Have you ever heard of a ghost or earthbound spirit who was not already dead?

Should you consider having a go at "do it yourself" ghost busting, or have any other dealings with negative energies, please remember to put on some protection.

Summary

Spirit rescue is rewarding and important work, so please don't feel nervous about attempting to rescue a lost spirit from your home or workplace, as he or she will be so grateful to you for your kindness. Being a trapped spirit can be a nightmare experience as it is possible to be trapped in this between-worlds area for many years, feeling isolated and confused.

When attempting to guide earthbound spirits on their journey to the Light, always remember that they can hear every word you say to them, so choose your words carefully, and keep instructions simple.

If you are aware of the identity of the spirit, the job is often easier, as you can coax them to move by telling them their husband or wife is waiting for them at the Light, or any other member of their family whom you know has already passed to spirit. The difficult cases are those where the spirit does not want to move on for a personal reason, and this is where you have to mentally ask their guide for permission to tell a white lie to encourage them to leave the area. When a spirit is causing alarm to a person, or disrupting sleep, it is important to move them onward, so don't feel guilty if the only way to inspire them to move is by bending the truth. It is the right thing to do as you are helping them on their journey, as well as removing the disruption.

Earthbound spirits appear in the most unexpected places and all need assistance to move to the Light, which means that when you are aware of their plight, you should offer assistance.

Once you have rescued one or two lost spirits, you will become confident and it becomes a perfectly natural thing to do. It's hard to believe, but it can become automatic, so that when you become aware of the plight of one of these spirits, you do the rescue work in a flash without being apprehensive or having to think about it! When you become aware of the presence of an earthbound spirit, try reminding yourself that this spirit was somebody's son or daughter, or grandfather, and needs your help!

Good luck!

Notes

1. *Spiritualist National Union's Hymn Book.*
2. Michael, Jack. "Dowsing Today." British Society of Dowsers, Kent, England.

chapter five

Are Animals Psychic?

————————————●————————————

What happens to our pet dogs and cats when they die? "Do they go to Heaven?" ask worried owners. I believe the answer is yes. There is plenty of proof that animals that were loved by their owners have developed a strong spiritual bond, and they will be together when the owner dies. When there is a strong link of love, it is a very powerful energy, an eternal link that cannot ever be broken.

On many occasions, I've heard a medium give a message to a person in a spiritualist church, describing the colour, size, and breed of a loyal dog or cat that has shown itself to the medium, to be remembered to that person. This has often brought a tear to their eye. Animals, like humans, do survive death, as every living spirit returns home when their life on earth has ended, so please don't worry about your pets, as they will be happy, being loved and looked after by your relatives.

There are many stories of animal spirits—usually these have been much-loved pets and part of the family. The strong affinity encourages them to visit their much beloved owners, and make their presence known. This does not mean they are an earthbound spirit, as usually the animal has gone safely to the Light, but comes back on regular visits, or even to warn of danger. Simply sending out a loving thought to them will bring them closer to you. Do you ever wonder if your pets will be there to greet you when your time comes to move to the other side? The answer is yes, they will be waiting there patiently to greet you and return your love.

Dogs and cats are the most frequently recorded animals that come back to visit their owners, although tales of horses appearing in their favourite field or nuzzling the owner's neck are common, and bird lovers tell tales of their deceased parrot or budgerigar calling to say hello. They feel a draught from his wings, or hear his happy chirp.

Animals, like people, are not all on the same spiritual level. Some animals are more evolved than others, often noticeable by their behaviour and understanding of what's expected of them, and how well they are tuned into their owner. You'll often hear a loving owner say of their pet, "He's so knowing, he's almost human!"

Several years ago, a medium told me that my dog Jock was on the highest canine spiritual level. At the time I thought "What a lot of nonsense," but she has been proved correct by the many unexplainable incidents that have occurred since then.

Jock was a border collie/terrier cross of unknown origin. I found him, or perhaps he found me, in the midst of winter when snow lay nearly two feet deep on the ground, and I was walking my two dogs, both black and white crossbreds, at a local field. As the wind was cold and snow was falling, I walked around the field with my head down, and my old woolly hat pulled well down over my eyebrows to protect my face as much as possible from the cold wind.

This was a regular safe route, so I did not need to keep an eye on the dogs as they knew the routine. You can imagine my surprise when I got back to my car to find that instead of two black and white dogs, I had three of them. I had no option but to take the stray dog home. Jock was cold and very hungry, so I fed him and prayed that his owner would claim him. Alas, nobody wanted to own him, so I coaxed my husband to allow him to stay with us. Within a few years, my other two dogs passed away, and so Jock and I became a team.

Each time a person visited my sanctuary for healing, Jock would sit at their feet and beam out powerful healing to them—so much so, that people regularly commented that they could feel great heat coming from him, although he was often a few feet from their chair.

I discovered to my astonishment that Jock did astral travel to heal the sick in the small hours of the morning. My first knowledge of his night-time activity was when I received a phone call from a patient, asking if Jock had died? She assured me she had wakened at 3:00 AM and seen Jock sitting on her bed, giving her healing.

The first time it happened, I thought it was the person's imagination and she must have dreamed it, as I knew Jock slept at the side of my bed each night. When it occurred again, I realised he was doing this wonderful work in the night and it was not purely a visit to a loved one, as he had only met these people once during a short visit to my centre.

This made me realise how little we know about the spiritual side of our animals, and that other cats and dogs almost certainly do this astral travel work. It all sounds very farfetched, but when sensible, well-balanced people who don't know one another tell the same story, then it's got to have some truth in it.

Jock, who departed a few months ago at the grand old age of seventeen, is often here to visit and I'm regularly told by visitors that they see him sitting by my chair. Last month I received amusing confirmation when an Australian medium called to visit me. We had not met before, but she knew my treatment had cured her friend's knee problem, so wanted to meet me.

We went into my healing sanctuary for her to receive some healing for various aches. As I was giving her healing, she was giving me messages from spirit about my work and good wishes from relatives and friends. Suddenly she burst out laughing and exclaimed in her lovely Australian accent, "Who is this cocky-looking black and white dog that's walked in, looking as though he owns the joint?" I said "Oh, that's Jock. He comes to join us. He used to heal with me, and still comes to give a hand."

Can Animals See Spirits?

Dogs and cats are very psychic and have a natural ability to see spirits. Cat owners often describe how their cat stares at a blank wall, concentrating hard when there's nothing to be seen, not even a fly. Dog owners are often mystified and intrigued, as they describe how their dog's hackles stand upright on its back bone for no apparent reason. There is nothing unusual to be seen in the room and no unexplained noises, so why does the dog give a low growl, or the cat stare at the wall when nobody is there? The only thing the owner feels is a slight draught. The psychic ability of animals goes much further than seeing ghosts. Very few pet owners realise the full extent of their pet's psychic abilities, and before I started working with Jock, I would have found it very difficult to believe the full extent of their psychic powers.

Animals Can Recognise Negative Entities

Animals are very tuned into energy, so they are well aware of the presence of any negative beings and will often react strongly. Some cats register their disapproval by moving from their home permanently or live most of their life outside, only coming indoors for meals. I recently cleared the energies of a house nearby, as the owners had very nasty entities attached. They told me that their much-loved cat spent very little time in their home and they wondered if the reason for the cat's unsociable behaviour was dislike of the family dog. I knew better!

Jock was very tuned into energy and gave a low growl when anyone who had an attachment was present; all very embarrassing when the person was keen to make friends and he chose to ignore their overtures, particularly when he charmed everyone else present. Many dogs respond in this manner, but this does not mean that everyone whom your dog chooses to ignore has an entity attached. It can simply be that he does not like the person.

Animals are able to link their thoughts to their owner and know when they are worried or in trouble, and they also have the uncanny ability to link with mediums, as I found to my astonishment last year when Jock excelled himself. The previous year I had been contacted by an animal medium who helped to find lost animals and resolve behaviour problems. She asked me to clear energies in a farmhouse where two little Jack Russell terriers were sleeping over geopathic stress lines, which was blamed for their lack of bladder and bowel control. This gifted medium linked to these little dogs who told her they were messing in the house to try and draw attention to their plight. They were very unhappy because their bed was located over negative energy lines.

I was enlisted to clear the geopathic stress from the farmhouse and, in return for my assistance, I asked the medium to link into Jock and ask about his life before he joined my household. I received a delightful reading in the mail from this medium, whom I have not yet met. She wrote about her conversation with Jock, and the information she gave tied in with the few details I had collected, so it all made sense. He told her he had been dumped out of a car in the snow and how his owners had driven off and left him alone, but he was not worried, as he knew I would be coming along to find him, and we would work as a team. Jock said he had been a mischievous puppy who was very curious, so the family had been fed up with his antics. He was certainly overactive when I found him, but luckily, my other dogs tired him out.

Some time ago I experienced terrible problems in the form of psychic attack from an unstable woman who spent time every day bombarding bad energy to Jock, myself, and a group of friends, which had a serious effect on our health.

Jock thought enough was enough and, without my knowledge, decided the situation needed outside help, so he astral traveled to this medium's home, over 100 miles from my home, arriving there around 11 PM. According to the medium's letter, he point-blank refused to leave until she had promised to help by sending us an herbal remedy to counteract the evil effects. Sounds like a story from a spooky film, but it is very true!

I was mystified and overwhelmed with emotion when I opened this surprise parcel, which arrived in the post, as inside were two little bottles of herbal tincture, one marked Jock and the other marked Wilma. Also enclosed was a letter explaining the tincture was being sent at Jock's request.

Friends have asked "Why didn't your guide or helpers protect you?" I think the answer is simply that had I received their protection, I would not have learned that dogs are able to astral travel to get assistance for their owners. When someone is working on the dark side and is very dedicated and knowledgeable, it can be difficult to combat these vibes, but this witch had underestimated Jock's spiritual abilities.

Many pet owners describe how their departed pet is never far away and still joins them on their daily walk. I often hear Jock sneeze, or his ear flap, so I know he is with me, and it's a nice feeling to know your pets are protecting you. Animals are quick to sense those they can trust, guided by their intuition. This is very evident when you take a dog to a psychic surgeon for a spirit operation, which is done without anaesthetic. The dog will sit perfectly still and show none of the usual signs of nerves most dogs do when they visit a vet. Animals can see the spirit doctor, who works through the medium, so they are in tune with the exercise—all quite amazing!

A friend's old Labrador dog was treated on several occasions by a well-known psychic surgeon, and showed no sign of nerves, as he was able to see the spirit doctors who were working on his aches and pains.

Never underestimate the psychic ability of domestic animals, as they know a great deal more about the spirit world than we'll ever know. Because of their natural ability to see spirit and to sense invisible energy, there are times when we should be guided by their reactions.

Rupert Sheldrake wrote an interesting book titled *Dogs that Know When Their Owners Are Coming Home, and Other Unexplained Powers of Animals* (Hutchinson). He researched 1,000 randomly selected pet owners to collect information on this unexplained behaviour—more confirmation that animals have a direct line to the spirit world.[1]

Dogs enjoy the spiritual energy found in a spiritual church. I have seen many dogs attend services each week and all behave impeccably, with never a growl or bark. They appear to be very content in the presence of this energy.

In an interesting and controversial book on animal souls published two years ago, Professor Andrew Linzey of Mansfield College, Oxford, claims animals have souls and so can go to Heaven. His book, *Animals Have Souls,* includes church services for animal baptisms and funerals.[2]

Newspapers occasionally report a story of an animal who has traveled from one end of the country to another to find their owner, and cats who keep returning to their previous home, apparently preferring it to the new home. This is further confirmation that they are more in tune with spirits and energies than we humans will ever be.

It's not only dogs who can heal, as many cat owners will swear their feline friend sits on their lap and pours out strong healing energy, and bird lovers won't be outdone, as they too claim their affectionate little budgerigar or canary gives healing when they feel low. Owners who have an emotional bond with their pet will all benefit from their healing energy, although not all animal lovers realise their improved health is due to the healing energy being sent by their pet.

Animals Can Heal

There is a lot of evidence of pet healing, and the medical profession accepts that having a pet has a healing effect on its owner. Pets As Therapy (PAT), a service for sick and depressed lonely patients, does a great job of arranging home visits of pets to the sick and to hospital wards, as well as to hospices and nursing homes. The animals give out warmth and help to stimulate interest in life, and remind folks of the love of their departed pet, so they are always welcomed, and usually people look forward to the next pet visit.

When visiting my aunt in a home for the elderly, I was delighted to see that a friendly, well-balanced mongrel bitch belonging to the matron was always in the lounge, giving love to these frail ladies.

It's easy to talk about dogs as there are so many of them giving healing, but what about dolphins? These friendly creatures are wonderful healers and are very generous with their healing energy. We regularly hear of very sick children who have been taken to swim with the dolphins. These highly intelligent creatures seem to understand the plight of the children, and pour out love to them.

Never underestimate the power of an animal, as they have a natural ability to interact with our life. An amazing rapport builds up between pet and owner, to the extent they seem to be able to read our minds and they can plant ideas in our thoughts without making a physical movement.

How often have you felt guilty because you haven't taken your dog for its daily walk when your back aches, or the weather is wintry with driving rain, and you hope he will forget he has not had his walk? No such luck, as you find yourself being urged to leave the warm fireside, don Wellington boots and waterproofs to take the dog for a walk. Don't be fooled into thinking it was your idea, as it was your clever dog who sent you a positive thought. Many times I have donned my woolly hat and winter coat to go out on a walk against my wishes, knowing my crafty four-legged friend has used his wiles to plant my guilt.

Research has been done on animals that know when their owner is due back from work or holiday, even when they come home at a different time each day. My wise mongrel always sat upright from a snooze when I was a few road's distance away, as I would send him a telepathic message, telling him I would be back with him very soon. The friends who were looking after him in my absence would tell me that they knew when I was due to arrive, as Jock would get up and have a big stretch, then go to sit at the front door to welcome me.

Animals do not become trapped spirits, as they do not have the problems of religious beliefs to block their progress, so if an animal has stayed in this between-world area, they have chosen to stay in loyalty to their owner. It's very seldom that anyone will report regular sighting of a ghostly animal. Some folks have reported hearing the sound of phantom animals, usually the clear clatter of horses hooves, but this is usually a memory imprint from the past.

Summary

To recap, animals can see spirits and are at one with the spirit world. They do not suffer the same mental blocks as humans since, to them, it is a normal part of their existence to see spirits and sense atmospheres and energy.

Next time you are feeling low, have a backache, or would like to receive some healing energy, mentally send out a thought to your pet, asking them to channel some healing energy to you, and you will be pleasantly surprised as you feel the energy being beamed to you. Not only are animals able to channel healing energy to people and other animals, they can also give their owner an early warning when the onset of an epileptic fit is imminent. Rupert Sheldrake relates how a rescue dog could warn his owner fifty minutes before she had an epileptic fit so that she could take preventative measures.

If you want to communicate with your animal, sit down and consciously send a message to him and he will respond. I regularly send a message to my cat telling him I will be home soon to give him a cuddle! It's all about positive thought and intent, so if you send out the message intending it to reach the animal, it will get to him.

All animals can give healing, whether to each other or to their owner, and they can communicate telepathically, so who says animals are dumb? They can teach us a lot of sense.

Notes

1. *Life and Soul* No. 16. Roy Stemman, Karma Publishing Ltd. No. 18. "Are Animals Psychic?" Dr. Rupert Sheldrake (Hutchinson).
2. Ibid. *"Animals Have Souls Too, says Christian Professor,"* by Professor Andrew Linzey. Mansfield College, Oxford. Professor Linzey is holder of the first Academic post in "Theology and Animal Welfare" at this university.

chapter six

Your Spiritual Development Circle

●

"What is a circle?" No, we don't all sit cross-legged in a circle on the floor, and it is not a gathering of weird people! A development circle, as the name suggests, is a group that meets regularly to learn more about the spirit world, and how to develop their spiritual and psychic gifts. Most people who are trance mediums do automatic writing, rescue work, or other psychic work started learning their skills in the shelter of a circle.

The Closed Circle

The main difference between a closed circle and an open circle is that whereas anyone can attend an open circle, the sitters in a closed circle have usually been invited to join the group.

If you are serious about your spiritual development, then the closed circle is the place for you. The great advantage of this type of circle is that an energy balance is created. As the same sitters gather together each week, the rapport, trust, and energy builds up to become a power- ful energy vibration. In this type of circle, you are well protected from negative energy, so have no worry when going into trance or meditation. Numbers can vary in this type of circle—it is usually between five and ten people—but numbers often depend on the size of the meeting room.

There is an accepted, strict code of conduct that all sitters follow. The energy of the circle should not be broken by anyone leaving the room, so leaving the circle while in session is forbidden. In other words, everyone is advised to take care of personal needs beforehand.

The format includes opening the circle with a short prayer, thanking spirit helpers who are present, and asking for protection for the circle. In a beginners circle, you are taught how to open and close your main chakras (these are the body's power points). You also learn how to protect your aura from negative energy and how to cleanse your aura.

A meditation follows. This may be led by the circle leader, who takes you on a journey to a beautiful beach or woodland, or to meet your guide. Meditation in circle is usually a wonderfully peaceful, experience, as the spiritual energy has built up in the room and many guides and helpers are present. Some people are fortunate to see or hear all sorts of things at this time, while others don't see a single thing. You may find that the more you relax and don't try to see anything, the more you become aware of sights and sounds or smells.

There is an unwritten rule in mediumship and in all circles, that "you give what you get," no matter how ridiculous it may sound—unless it is very personal. There are times when your common sense tells you that you can't possible say what you've seen or heard, as it sounds nonsense. An example of the importance of giving what you get occurred many years ago in a development circle. When linking into the lady sitting opposite me in the little group, to my surprise, I saw the Lone Ranger and Tonto! As this lady was roughly fifty years of age, I felt the message was wrong, or someone was playing a joke on me, but having been told firmly that it is essential I report anything seen or heard, I somewhat hesitantly gave her the message, while expecting her to burst out laughing. She did laugh but only with delight, as she then told us that she was making a Lone Ranger and Tonto birthday cake for the little boy who lived next door!

This confirmation gave me confidence to "give what I get" the following week when linking into the same lady, as a picture of the "black and white minstrels" appeared. Here again was a dilemma, as it sounded so theatrical to say "Oh, I have 'black and white minstrels' here for you!" Remembering my lesson of the previous week, I took courage in both hands and said "I've been shown a group of black and white minstrels," whereupon she said "Thank you, that's lovely. My grandfather was a minstrel." More confirmation for all the group that we should always pass on anything we have seen, never doubt our abilities, and remember that we cannot choose which messages are right for another person, or which are wrong, as it is often the most unlikely one that can mean a lot to the person.

Warning Tingles

When you start to receive messages from spirit, you become aware of little signs that confirm it is genuine. Some tell of a tingling feeling on one side of their head, others say the message always comes in the same ear, while others say their confirmation that a message being given is correct will often cause a cold shiver to run down their body.

Almost every time I dowse, a needles-and-pins sensation runs up the side of my right hand from my small finger to my wrist, before the pendulum moves. This sign confirms the message is genuine, and lets me know the answer is correct. Often, when giving a spiritual message to someone, they will say "I know that's correct as I've gone all goose pimples," which is their sign that a fact is correct.

On entering a building that has negative energy, meeting a person who has negative energy, or looking at a picture of a person in this group, I feel my upper arms tingle, warning me to beware of the problem. Sometimes when a person gives me information that is completely wrong, the warning sign from my helpers is a strong thud on my solar plexus area. So look out for your body's little warning signs. It'll make life a lot easier and you'll be glad you listened to the alarm signals. Perhaps you already feel them, but have not recognised the full significance of these very helpful and valuable tools, which are free and are there to be used! How often do you hear someone say "I had a bad feeling about it, but ignored it. I should have listened." Many mediums who do rescue work started by learning about it in a closed circle, as the bright White Light given off by the spiritual gathering shines like a beacon in the grey area and attracts lost souls to the Light and to the circle. I have sat in several different circles where lost spirits have popped in to ask for help. There have been many unhappy adults who needed guidance, as well as young children who are lost. These little souls were searching for their mother and were always very easy to guide to safety. Normally the circle leader would talk to the spirit and gently coax them to the Light, while the rest of the group sent healing energy to help the spirit on its journey home. In a teaching circle, the leader will often allow a member of the group to do the talking, so they become confident about doing this work, and most people report a wonderful feeling of upliftment as the spirit goes over to the Light.

The closed circle falls into three separate types: the development circle, the healing circle, and the rescue circle. Each does special work.

The Rescue Circle

The rescue circle is formed when like-minded people decide to commit themselves to meeting at the same time each week to do this work.

The Healing Circle

The healing circle, as the name implies, is a group of people who meet weekly to send healing to those on their healing list, and also to various parts of the world where there is war or starvation and healing is urgently needed. The entire group sends out healing energy at the same time, so the strength of the energy builds up and the collective energy is very powerful. This type of circle starts with a short prayer, then the absent healing begins.

The Open Circle

The open circle is often held in a Spiritualist church and is a spiritual development circle open to everyone, so anyone can come along to explore, to find out whether it is right for them. This type of circle is a starting point in spiritual development for many folks, as it gives a basic understanding of circle work, and the opportunity to meet other like-minded people, who also want to learn more about the spirit world. .

The format at an open circle is very relaxing and informal. It starts with a prayer, then a meditation led by the circle leader. This is followed by discussions on spirits seen or messages received, or questions arising from the meditation. Some people will not see or hear anything, but feel tremendous benefit from the peaceful meditation and the positive energy of the group.

When attending an open circle, it is very important to put a protection around yourself before arriving at the circle, and cleanse your aura afterward, as anyone can join this circle. This, of course, applies to everywhere you go and not just to an open circle, but it's a wise precaution always to cleanse after an open circle. Your gut feeling will guide you when it is time to leave the open group and join a closed circle, where you can develop your gifts and start to open your third eye.

The Circle and Your Third Eye

When you start to take an interest in the subject of spirit or join a development group, you will hear the third eye mentioned. It sounds a bit mysterious and from a different planet, so what is the third eye? No, it is not something from *Star Wars*, or from the TV series *Star Trek*! It really is our third eye and is located in the centre of the forehead, just above the eyebrows. It starts to open slowly as you develop your psychic and spiritual knowledge and progress is speeded up by regular meditation.

Have you ever been told by a medium or circle leader that your third eye is almost open? Or that it is now fully open? What exactly does this mean? I remember my feeling of excitement many years ago, when I was told my third eye was opening. At that time, I was a beginner and knew very little about spiritual development so felt a sense of wonder—to me the third eye was veiled in mystery. Can the third eye see things? Yes, when this amazing eye is fully open, you do see with it, but not everyday things—it's only used for seeing spiritual things, such as spirits and events. Once open, it stays open and is your special window to the world of spirit, and to your guardian angel, your guide, and your soul.

In other words, when your third eye is open, your spiritual development will move quickly and open up new knowledge.

What does this mind's eye look like? It is the same shape as a human eye, but without the eyelashes, and the colour is always the same, so it does not match the colour of your eyes! This amazing eye is the tool used in clairvoyance, clairaudience, and clairsentience, and is often described by mediums as a television screen, which shows them a very clear picture of spirits and places.

Learning Trance Work in the Circle

Once the third eye is fully open and the link with the spirit world is strong, many people develop the ability to go into trance to work with their spirit guide. What is trance? It's more than just daydreaming—it is the wonderful experience of someone in the spirit world talking through your voice, usually a spirit guide or a helper, and the messages are words of wisdom.

There are different types of trance. Light is the most common and is learned in the protection of a closed circle. As you begin going into trance, you become aware of a feeling of being overshadowed by someone. It's not an unpleasant feeling, so don't worry. It's as though someone is tickling you, as you become aware of a light feeling close to your face, but there is nothing to be seen. When in trance, you are in a state of being that allows a spirit helper to link into your mind and relate words of wisdom to you. What you feel is the energy of the spirit who is going to speak through you. Not all mediums describe the same symptoms, but all know when they feel a spirit close to them and when they are about to start speaking through them.

Trance is not a special gift that only chosen people possess, it's a tool that we can use to communicate with spirits who many years ago lived on the earth plane and those more advanced mediums can speak to archangels who have never been on the earth plane. When the time feels right, the circle will allow you to develop this skill. You don't have to be highly intelligent or very spiritual to channel communications. All that's required is the intent to link into the spirit world and be a channel to pass helpful information to those who are meant to receive it.

The big problem that must be avoided when channelling messages is that old enemy "Ego." Many people who channel messages see themselves as special, so they take the liberty of controlling the message. In other words, they say what they think should be said, rather than what they hear. Some frauds are known to hear very little but make it up as they go along, as this gives them a feeling of importance.

Channelling—Watch Out for the Ego!

Genuine channelled messages to a group should always be uplifting and have words of encouragement, so any messages of gloom and despondency are usually fake, given by a low-energy entity who is attached to the medium. Messages channelled never instruct you to *do* anything, as all humans have the gift of free will, so spirit never tells us what to do. If you hear a channelled message instructing you to do something, do not take it on board unless your gut feeling tells you its right. This type of message is quite likely to be the medium's personal opinion, or she has picked it up psychically. Do not ever be influenced by a channelled message, unless you feel it is right, as fake messages can be very convincing.

The first time you see a demonstration by a trance medium or hear channelled messages in a circle, you can be tremendously impressed, but as you see more of this work, you begin to differentiate between the quality of the various trance works. Sometimes mediums give amazing proof of survival and also information about the world's problems, while others allow their egos to enter, so the quality of their message is garbled, as some of the message is from the spirit world and some has been made up as she goes along!

My first experience of an exhibition of a medium's ego happened many years ago when I sat in a circle where the medium went into trance and was overshadowed by a North American Indian guide. The guide spoke through the person in a very deep voice. We were all very impressed, until we realised that the messages we received all related to our social life and subjects we had discussed before the meeting started.

Again, please don't take everything channelled literally, as 100 percent correct. If it feels comfortable and right, then it is right, but if it sounds theatrical, or too farfetched, then forget it, so that you are not influenced by it. Channelled messages are usually uplifting. It is an awe-inspiring experience to sit in a room when the medium is in a light trance and channelling a conversation from the higher realms. These messages are often about what's happening to Planet Earth, how we can help our world to survive, etc. Most messages pass on great love to all present and even the most insensitive people can feel the soothing energy of love in the room.

Channelling can be done on many different levels, depending on how developed the medium is, so some will give messages from archangels, etc. Others will give messages from their helpers, who may not be particularly old souls, so although they may give roughly the same message, the language may be more modern. Mediums cannot always choose when the spirit communicates with them, as the spirit guides and helpers decide when the energy in the room, church, or hall is suitable. It is difficult for the spirit to channel if a lot of negative energy is present, so prayer and singing are used to raise the energy level in churches.

You can learn spiritual development in a circle, but you cannot start channelling from spirit until you have established a good strong link with spirit, and feel the presence of a guide or helper's energy around your head. The first step is to invite them to use you as a channel. They should never use you as a channel until they have your permission, so never worry about starting to channel against your wishes, or before you feel ready for the work.

You can give your guides a list of names of the spirit helpers you may wish to channel who are allowed in, and arrange for all others to be shut out. Again, please ask your guides to take action if any negative or dark entities attempt to enter your aura.

The most common type of trance done in a circle is the inspirational trance, which is a link with their spirit contact, where the messages are channelled while the person is fully conscious and in control of what's being said.

Many people sitting in a circle express surprise when they channel, as they feel their body become larger or taller, depending on the shape of the spirit. Perhaps they become aware of facial features changing, a feeling of having a beard, or being stooped. A medium friend in London told me she had channelled words from the Buddha energy while at the College of Psychic Studies, and had felt her tummy become enormous, which was a strange feeling, as this lady was tall and very slim!

Powerful spirits like Buddha, Jesus, and Archangel Michael will often give a message at a circle, and people will say "It couldn't have been Buddha or Jesus, because he was giving a message at our circle, at the same time you say he was at your circle!"

The explanation is simply that highly evolved souls give off very powerful rays, which allows them to carry out the feat of being in several places at the same time. Spirit channelling is part of our Creator's great plan, so you should not be sceptical of the existence of these greatly evolved souls in your midst, as they are constantly around all of us.

I cannot say often enough that when channelling, it is vitally important to ensure your aura is completely protected from all negativity, as you are vulnerable since your crown chakra is wide open. Once you advance to channel in deep trance, you have more experience of this work so will automatically wear protection, and instruct your guide to oversee protection.

Deep Trance

You must never forget that spirits of many deceased liars, manipulators, thieves, negative entities, and parasites are out there, many of them still in the between-world area, awaiting their opportunity to join an unsuspecting person, so get into the all-important habit of thinking *protection.*

What is deep trance? This is the state used when communicating with very highly evolved spirits, and it's quite normal for the person to become completely still and lifeless, looking as though they are in a complete trance. To become a deep-trance medium you must be very healthy, physically strong, well earthed, mentally stable, and unflappable. Whereas you can develop most spiritual or psychic abilities, you cannot learn deep trance unless spirit has already selected you to do this work. Only a certain type of medium has the temperament, health, and energy level that allows them to be suitable for this sensitive work.

Sometimes the medium will have the ability to speak in a foreign language, or in the case of psychic surgery, be able to do spirit operations on a patient, with no prior knowledge of medicine.

Full deep trance is not as common as light trance, and it's important that a knowledgeable person is present when deep trance occurs. You must ensure no noise or upsets disturb the trance medium—a mobile phone ringing, or a door banging can jolt the medium, and the abrupt interruption of the link, can make the medium feel ill.

Look closely at a person in deep trance— sometimes called control trance—and you will probably see the medium's features change subtly. They may look younger or older and their features may become slightly Asian or Indian. This work is known as transfiguration mediumship and I recommend going to a demonstration, when one is offered.

Direct Voice Mediumship

Direct voice mediumship is a very rare gift that enables the medium to allow the spirit world to speak through the medium, but at the same time using the spirit's own voice. In other words, the medium's voice alters to sound like the relative who is sending the message from the spirit world. The person sitting with the medium can actually hear their father or mother's voice, or that of a friend or loved one. As the spirit is giving the message in their own voice, it is a truly overwhelming, emotional experience for the recipient, and is wonderfully positive proof of life after death.

Most direct voice mediums have developed and strengthened their spirit link while sitting in a circle. Of these, perhaps the best-known direct voice medium in the UK is Lesley Flint.[1] Over the years this man has been thoroughly tested, and an impressive list of over 1,000 different voices of departed spirits have been recorded, speaking through him in many different languages and dialects. Perhaps the most impressive and convincing were those who spoke through the medium in languages unknown to him, and, even more impressive, in languages no longer spoken on Earth. How can sceptics explain this phenomena, particularly as Lesley Flint's mouth was taped up while the work was recorded? How did he manage to speak while his mouth was sealed closed? Impossible though it may seem, this medium did not use his own voice box when channelling the messages, as a new and separate voice box was constructed of ectoplasm by the spirit doctors. More about this fascinating and difficult-to-comprehend subject is found in Arthur Findlay's book *On the Edge of the Etheric* (1931) and also in Lesley Flint's book *Voices in the Dark* (1971).

Electronic Voice Phenomena (EVP)

We don't hear much in the media about this amazing phenomena, but rest assured the popularity of EVP is growing rapidly on both sides of the ocean. High technology is everywhere these days and it has now reached the world of spirit, where it is being used to help simplify communications with the spirit world.

Tape recordings of spirit voices have been made regularly over the past half century, but many of them are personal messages. If you are very interested in this subject, have a look on the Internet. By using a search engine, you will find more than 50,000 listings for this fascinating subject. Simply type "electronic voice phenomena," sit back, and enjoy some fascinating viewing, as there are many thousands of researchers in different countries all working on EVP. Experienced researcher Colin Smythe published an excellent book, *Voices from the Tapes*, which is full of exciting examples of EVP. In one session lasting twenty-seven minutes, a total of 200 different voices were received. This controlled exercise did not involve any gimmicks or trickery.[2] An organisation specialising in EVP is the American Association of Electronic Voice Phenomena which was founded in 1982 and has 30,000 members in eighty-seven countries. They record paranormal voices, pictures, and information from departed friends and loved ones through the use of tape recorders, telephones, fax machines, television, computers, or video recorders. This association is not about religion, nor is it an association full of dreamy people—its members are practical people who want to discover information about EVP techniques.

Does it surprise you that the Roman Catholic Church in Rome has been actively involved in this phenomena? Two of the earliest investigators of this phenomena were Catholic priests. They came across EVP by chance while recording the beautiful and much-loved Gregorian Chants in 1952, reports an expert on this subject.

The International Society of Catholic Parapsychologists, at their conference in Austria in 1970, devoted a large part of the event to discussion, using papers on the subject of EVP. The Vatican has continued to sponsor extensive research into the many areas of parapsychology, including EVP and ITC (Instrumental Transcommunication).[3]

British television, on December 9, 2001, showed an interesting documentary film called "Voices of the Dead," on the wonders of electric voice phenomena, which gave viewers a behind-the-scenes look at this fascinating and little-known subject.

Instrumental Transcommunication (ITC)

Since the early 1900s, scientists have experimented with electronic devices that have opened up a whole new world of communication with the spirit world. These scientists were completely flabbergasted by the mind-boggling results of their experiments, as they found they were able to make voice contact with departed spirits. By the 1940s, they had developed the technology to audiotape conversations and music, which when played back made it possible to hear faint voices communicating from the other side of the veil.

Now over the many start-up teething problems, ITC has been used effectively since 1980 by many psychic researchers to communicate with people who have passed to spirit. The equipment used by the researchers is similar to that used in EVP. It's very hard to believe, but it's true that, in European research laboratories, technicians are able to receive information and video images showing actual places in spirit.

What is the difference between ITC and EVP? They are very similar methods, but whereas EVP captures the faint spirit voices on tape in short messages, and many people around the world use EVP, the ITC form of communication can only be used when the researcher and the spirit person are in unison. The researcher must be on a direct spiritual link to those in spirit, as it will not work if the technician is using it as a technical exercise. All these new forms of communication are great for the technically minded, but like many people, I prefer simply to link mentally into the spirit world and to my guides and helpers.

Your Spirit Guides and Helpers

We hear people saying "My guide says this or that," and it always sounds very impressive, but what is a guide and what do they do? Spirit guides and helpers are evolved spirits who dedicate their time to guarding each one of us and acting as one of life's teachers. They have progressed by learning wisdom and have the knowledge to guide you on your spiritual pathway. Each person has a guardian angel, a main spirit guide, who is your principal teacher, doorkeeper, and helper.

Your Guardian Angel

Your guardian angel has been with you from the moment you were conceived in your first life on Earth, and is with you until the end of your final journey. This wonderful angel holds a complete blueprint of all the events you have experienced in each life on Earth, or other planets, and also holds details of your behaviour.

No matter how badly you have behaved, this angel loves you and is always close to you, so it is possible to ask your angel for protection from physical attack. Start getting to know your personal angel now, build up a strong relationship, and once you have a strong link, you will have confidence in their ability to protect you. Your guardian angel is there to look after you, so is happy to assist when necessary,

You should never ask them to do anything that you can do yourself—in other words, they should only be asked to assist in tasks you cannot control. You can ask your guardian angel to help you find the money to purchase a car to replace one that is worn out, but not to find money to replace a two-year-old car with a new model. It's no good asking them to help you win the lottery as they will probably turn a deaf ear to that request!

Your guardian angel is a very useful ally in any family, neighbourhood, or business dispute or conflict, as you can ask her or him to contact the guardian angel of the person concerned, and try to guide the person to resolve the dispute. It's certainly worth a trial, as this is a simple and painless way to resolve many disputes and is usually successful.

Although my cloak of protection is wrapped around me, I always ask my guardian angel to look after me when I am traveling on the motorway and ask if she can guide me to start my journey at a time when there is a gap in the traffic. I also ask for protection for all the birds and animals on the roads I will be traveling, so that I do not injure any animal who is on the road. The law of nature dictates some birds and animals must die, as they are food for other animals, but I don't want to be the cause of their death.

The Angels of Protection

Many people report hair-raising events in their lives when they were convinced their guardian angel intervened and saved them. My guardian angel and helpers were certainly looking after me last week as I was getting into my friend's car after a visit to the car boot sale on the local village green. I had bought a small pram for my granddaughter and was in the process of getting myself and the little pram into the car when a car driven by an elderly lady, who was driving on the wrong side of the road, drove her car into my car door as I was entering. The violent bump caused the door to crash against me, knocking my entire body out of alignment, but miraculously not doing any severe damage.

At the second her car hit my passenger door, I was halfway getting into the car. The upper part of my body was leaning into the car, but my legs and feet were still on the road. As I was about to get my legs into the car, the force of the bump caused the car door to slap against my body, so should have cut both my legs off, but I was aware of an angel grabbing the door. It was a very strange feeling as I felt the angel grab hold of the car door and take the full force of it, so that I was not seriously hurt. The car received £2,500 in damage, so it was a major bump. Needless to say, my first words were "Thank you," when I got my breath back. This was proof for me that my guardian angel was very close.

Tussle with a Taxi

I have had several hair-raising experiences when angels have intervened and saved my life. When eight years old, I crossed the road at a T junction on my way home from school and a taxi came around the corner and hit me. The force sent me up in the air and an angel caught me and placed me gently on the ground, so no bruises.

The taxi driver asked for my name and address, and then I ran off home and was too afraid to tell my mother what had happened, as I knew I would receive a row for not looking where I was going! Alas, my guilty secret was disclosed when a policeman arrived at the door that evening to ask if I was hurt, so I had to own up.

Miraculous Driving Skill

Another time I had breathtaking proof that the angels saved my life. It occurred when driving down the motorway. It was a lovely summer evening and there were very few cars on the motorway. I was relaxed and happy as I was on my way to sit in a weekly circle. My car was traveling at 70 mph, in the outside lane, when I was aware of a car joining the motorway from a slip road. I assumed the driver had looked in his mirror and seen the road behind was clear. Alas, he had not looked over his shoulder, or he would have known that my car was level with him; he proceeded to join the road at high speed and drove across my bows onto the outside lane. The only way to avoid hitting his car was to swerve onto the central reservation, which fortunately was grass. As my arms swung the wheel round to take evasive action, my car ploughed through the grass, cutting a track in the mud. At that second, an angel grabbed the steering wheel and turned the car around on this narrow space so that my car ended up beautifully parked, but facing the wrong direction on this narrow central reservation.

It would have been impossible for any driver, even the most experienced, police-trained driver, to turn the car round in this narrow space at such a high speed, so the only explanation was that I had help from the spirit world. The car did not have power steering and I was not strong enough to control the car as it hit the central reservation; also, it was impossible to turn the car around in a space its own length, while traveling at high speed, so again I said "Thank you" and meant it!

When you talk to people about the London Blitz or other horrific experiences, they will often relate a humorous thing that occurred, and the funny side of this hair-raising motorway experience was that I had a good laugh when I looked at myself in my driving mirror. Instead of seeing an ashen face, I saw my face covered with splashes of mud. Angels work in many different ways and so when you ask for their help, it can come in a form that you least expect. If you ask their assistance in finding a new job or a nice flat, you may find that their help comes in the most unexpected ways. Perhaps you are invited to an event but don't want to go, but something makes you go, and you meet someone who knows a job vacancy is about to occur at their firm, or knows someone about to move from a flat that is in the right area and at the right price.

The Dog Fox on Sentry Duty

Help came from the angels while I was living on the Isle of Wight, but I did not find out about it until some time later. Before each trip to the mainland, I would ask the angels to protect my home until my return and always found the house safe on my return home. One day recently, when talking to a neighbour, she mentioned that she was very puzzled why each time I was away from home, there was a large dog fox standing sentry in my driveway in the middle of the night.

She explained that each time she returned home in the small hours of the morning from the late shift, she saw this beautiful animal standing rock still, appearing to be guarding my home. You can imagine my surprise and delight on hearing this news—although I instinctively knew my home was protected, here was positive proof. I explained to this mystified lady that I always asked the angels for protection for my home and this was symbolic of the powerful protection given to me.

When something like this happens, it makes us realise how little we know about the world of spirit, and helps us to become more aware that help is there, if we remember to ask for it, and that always saying "please" and "thank you" is a must.

Angels Can Make Miracles Happen

Angels are able to make miracles happen and there are certain angels who specialise in helping to resolve specific problems. There is so much unrest in the world, it's time to ask the assistance of the Angel of Air to help create world peace.

Sit down and relax, then quietly link into the Angel of Air, as she is in charge of the atmosphere, and we need to request that the clouds of negative energy floating above countries at war are balanced with positive energy. Every country where there is war or corruption has an excess of negative energy, which gives power to the evil ones, and influences behaviour and the health of its people.

History has shown that most wars are caused by religion and so we can enlist the help of the Angel of Fire, as her job is to cleanse and purify, which creates a new beginning. Since long before the birth of Christ, there have been battles caused by racial or religious hatred. The energy of that hate, fear, anger, or hurt lingers on Earth, so needs to be cleansed.

Please sit down quietly and link in to the Angel of Fire, as her help is needed to cleanse the Planet Earth. Ask this powerful angel to please cleanse our planet of negative energy and to balance the energy. Also please ask her to help resolve wars and unnecessary bloodshed, and help to create peace in countries where there is unrest.

The World Water Shortage

War is not the only problem facing planet Earth, as a very serious water shortage is looming and many experts forecast the next war will be about water, so it's time to enlist the help of angels before this world crisis arises.

When you look at an atlas of the world, you will see that more than half of the planet is water—mainly oceans and rivers—and a very small percentage is drinking water. An added complication is that a large proportion of the drinking water, particularly underground supplies, is contaminated with chemicals, or polluted with other harmful ingredients. Please sit down and relax and ask the Angel of Water to enlist her helpers to cleanse contaminated oceans and drinking water—if enough people ask for help, the power of the collective energy can make miracles happen.

We had proof that the power of prayer is a mighty tool when Britons prayed for help to end the war with Germany, so never underestimate the power of prayer or the power of angels, as the spirit world can summon great power when necessary. When you add positive thought and intent to angel power and prayer, then miracles do happen.

As well as our guardian angels, there is an enormous army of angels on the other side, all wanting to protect us and waiting to help when asked.

Have you ever seen an angel? Since we moved into the new century, more and more people report seeing angels, and their acceptance and popularity is growing rapidly. There are many lovely books available on angels, and workshops where you can learn about angels and how to work with the angelic kingdom. Angels are big business in America where hundreds of different angel books and several angel magazines are on sale. There are also lots of angel shops that sell nothing but angel-themed merchandise.

Astronauts and Angels

Angels are no longer simply beautiful, kindly beings in a story; they are real and have been seen by many sensible, highly intelligent people, including crew members of the NASA space shuttles, Russian cosmonauts, and regiments of soldiers.

American astronauts have seen a great many angels floating about in space. In fact, they have reported seeing several hundred of these celestial beings, while flying in orbit. Imagine the astronauts' reaction when one of the team looks out of the window and says "Gee guys, there's an angel!" One astronaut had the amazing experience of seeing an angel hovering over his body, protecting him while he walked in space.

These sightings cannot be doubted, as they were seen by astronauts from both Houston, Texas, and Cape Canaveral in Florida. They have reported seeing these heavenly beings on almost every single space mission, and one crew member reported that an angel had escorted their craft back to Earth.

Don't think this is all a bit of American publicity or drama, as very similar experiences have been reported by Russian cosmonauts, who have described seeing huge-winged angels floating in space in the belt between Mars and Jupiter. The cosmonauts reported one of their craft was escorted by six angels for three days, while they circled the planet.

What an amazing and reassuring sight that must have been, quite unforgettable, particularly as these beings were flying very fast. A Russian crew member succeeded in measuring their speed at 50,000 miles an hour.[4]

The Angels of Mons

My grandfather, who fought in France in World War I, used to tell me the story of the Battle of Mons and how during that war, when British soldiers were outnumbered, many angels appeared to the soldiers and gave them momentum to carry on and win the battle. This was a case of angels giving support to the army of men fighting for human freedom and against aggression. The last thing British soldiers expected to see when in the midst of a bloody battle against the German army at Mons in the warm summer of 1914 was the figure of an enormous male angel, clad in white, appearing in the sky. This amazing sight was reported by many soldiers and it is said that the German army, not surprisingly, turned and fled. The vision was good news for the British troops, who were truly outnumbered. Sightings of both male and female ghostly beings were also reported over a period of days by hundreds of soldiers.

My father was in the Air Force during World War II, and used to tell me the story of the Battle of Britain, and how many British planes continued to fly and fight after their crews had been killed. At the time, I thought it was one of my father's fairy stories, but this was no fairy story, as many pilots reported seeing this occur, and Air Chief Marshal

Lord Dowding. Many articles have been written about the sightings of angels in both these war events, confirmed by Diana Cooper in her book, *A Little Light on Angels.*[5]

Our world needs a visit from the angels of Mons today, as many countries are weighed down by negative energy created by violent fighting and hatred. The miraculous appearance of a few Mons angels would bring much-needed love and positive energy to our planet to help resolve battles and hatred. Angels bring the energy of light, and this would help to create much-needed balance.

Throughout history, there have been reports of the existence of angels, dating as far back as the Essenes pre-Christian writing, and the numerous references in the Bible. Famous scientists over the centuries have written about angels and Austrian philosopher Rudolf Steiner writes of the presence of angels. In his book *Angels,* Paul Roland lists details of angels in history,[6] and perhaps the best known and most beloved person to report seeing angels was the late Princess Diana, who stated on a television interview that she had once seen three large angels.

The Angel of the North

What does an angel look like? Certainly not like the famous Angel of the North. This sixty-five-foot tall angel sculpture by Anthony Gormley was built with lottery cash, and stands higher than four double-decker buses.

She is certainly doing a good public relations job, as she has succeeded in getting people talking about angels. With her wings the width of a jumbo jet plane, this is one pretty impressive angel. She is made of weather-resistant steel and is the largest angel sculpture in the entire world. Home is a former colliery pithead site, which is now landscaped, reclaimed land on the boundary of the Great North Forest near Gateshead in the North of England.[7]

About Angels

My mental picture of angels had been little, childlike beings with wings, so it was a shock the first time I saw angels, to discover that they were larger than adult-size humans, and had enormous wings. Many times I have seen these wonderful pure spirits, who are on a much higher and purer vibration than humans. They have always appeared very large. These beautiful, gentle beings have shown themselves to me many times, but mostly they have appeared unexpectedly when I was doing rescue work.

Angels are very natural beings. They are God's special messengers and helpers, and are always present in times of trouble, although they remain invisible most of the time, and only choose to show themselves when their help is required. They tend to stay in the background, supervising what is going on until their help is needed. Angelic beings are viewed in many people's minds as creatures in nice stories, but these pure spirit beings are very real and practical, and do wonderful work. Just because we can't see them doesn't mean they don't exist—it's like saying "Healing doesn't work, because you can't see it!"

Angels do all sorts of very special work. You'll often hear a child who has been very seriously ill, say "A beautiful angel was beside my bed smiling at me, and I was not afraid." These celestial beings are nothing new, as they have been around since the beginning of time and there are many references to angels in the Holy Bible. They were created by God as intermediaries. These supernatural beings are go-betweens, acting as a direct link to the Creator.

Channelled facts about angels tell us they are eternal, they live forever on a glorious dimension, and they do not, like us, have a family, as they each have a job of work.

These beings reflect a divine peace and are immortal, ageless, indestructible, and gifted with the uncanny ability to move faster than the speed of light. All angels have a direct link with our Creator, so are guided to where help is needed. It's great that so many books have recently been written about angels, as it helps us to become aware of the love and help available from angels and encourages all of us to invite them into our lives, to be around us. The more you talk to angels, the more you establish a relationship with them, encouraging more of these wonderful beings to be near you.

When Diana Cooper (*A Little Light on Angels*) was interviewed on British TV, there were many enthusiastic viewers, and 114,000 of them telephoned the studio following the programme for more information about Diana and her work with angels. This was the highest number of telephone calls ever received on this show, and prompted the producer to invite her back the following day—definitely one up for angels.[8]

Angels are not the same as your guardian angel, guide, or helpers. They are simply loving beings who offer love and protection, but do not interfere in our pathway. They can see the past and the future, so are there to give support, but *only when asked.*

Asking the Angels for Help

Before you have any problems, try calling angels to be near you and remember to give them permission to assist you, as they will not help unless you have already given them authority to intercede when trouble approaches.

As well as assisting you when problems arise, they will help you with basic chores, like threading a needle! You can, like me, always ask the angels to assist in threading a needle for you, as it saves a lot of time and frustration, and the job is done quickly. Try asking the angels for guidance next time you want to purchase a book on a specific subject and are undecided which one will have the most useful information. They will encourage you to choose the most suitable book

As mentioned earlier, I always ask the angels to create a gap in the traffic, also for protection when entering a busy motorway where there is a lot of fast-moving traffic. I also ask their help when I am waiting to drive out of a side road, when the traffic on the main road will not slow down to let my car out to join the traffic.

Help Finding Missing Objects

We have all experienced the frustration of lost objects, usually when we are in a hurry to keep an appointment or catch a train. You are running around lifting things, pulling out drawers, searching pockets, and looking frantically in the most unlikely places. You can become almost irrational, even start looking in places where you know the missing object should not be found, but to no avail. This is the time to enlist help. Take a deep breath, relax, and stop for a few seconds to ask the angels to help you to find the missing keys, book, etc. Usually, when you ask their help, you will find that you suddenly remember laying the keys on a chair, where they are now covered by a newspaper, or they are in the pocket of a jacket in your car. It's amazing how the answer comes when you ask for assistance from the angels. After asking their assistance, if you are still unable to find the missing object, try asking St. Anthony for assistance, as finding missing objects is one of his specialities. Another option is to dowse for the missing item.

Each morning when you put on your protection, this is the time to ask the angelic kingdom for guidance and protection. Remember part of the Universal Law is that if you want help from the angels, or want to channel in trance, you must always invite these beings to work with you. Our gift of free will is always honoured by the spirit world, whatever the circumstances.

When you raise the subject of angels in a conversation, it's quite amazing how many people will say "I've seen an angel," or "I believe in angels," so it's not very surprising that many reported they had seen the angel at a time of great emotional upset, such as sadness from a bereavement, when an angel came to give love and comfort. Others tell of an angel coming to pass on an important messages, but perhaps the most intriguing tales are from those who have experienced the angel rescue service.

Many people believe they have been snatched from death by an angel, within a split second of drowning, or being killed by a car or coach. Interestingly, a high number of people who believe they were rescued by an angel had no knowledge or preconceived idea of what an angel looked like, but they described the appearance of the angels as having large wings, wearing a white gown, and having a glowing halo above their head.

One of the most interesting reports about sighting angels happened during a baptism service. An angel was seen by half of the congregation, and by the vicar, curate, and organist. "They can't all be wrong," and "Yes, they were all cold sober."[9]

Planetary Connection magazine in 1995 reported that a Gallup Poll in the US found 72 percent of those interviewed believed in angels, and of this group, 40 percent had felt an angel presence at least once in their lifetime.[10]

Angel Research

The UK's *Daily Mail* in 1998 commissioned ICM to do a survey on angels and results showed positively that over 25 percent of the population believed angels do exist, and that number has risen considerably in the past couple of years, as more and more books are published on the subject and regular workshops are being held on "Getting to Know Angels."[11] We can't forget the lovely little angel cards that are so popular today; they also confirm the popularity of angels. From angels we move on to our other spirit helpers.

Do You Know You Have a Doorkeeper?

As well as guardian angels, guides, and helpers, we all have a doorkeeper whose job is to protect us during meditation, or at any time when we are vulnerable to negative entities. They guard our psychic doorway and allow only helpful energies to enter, so get to know your doorkeeper. A medium will be able to tell you their name and nationality, as once you know the name of your guide or doorkeepers, it's much easier to build up a relationship with them.

When new to my spiritual pathway, a medium told me about my doorkeeper. It gave me a feeling of wonder and importance to learn that I had my own special doorkeeper. It was a lovely surprise to hear that this spiritual helper would always be there to protect me from harm. I had never heard of them, so was pleasantly surprised to find that every human being has a personal guard. I was fortunate to meet a psychic artist at a psychic fair who drew a picture of my spirit doorkeeper. The painting exactly fitted the description of the man described to me by a medium some time beforehand, more proof for me that the spirit world exists. When doing any rescue work or other spiritual work, always remember that your doorkeeper is close, so thank him for protecting you from all risks. Although your doorkeeper's job is to protect you from evil, it is still your responsibility to protect your aura from all negative energy.

Your Spirit Helpers

We all have many spirit helpers who are constantly around us, ready to assist and guide us when necessary. Some helpers may be relatives or friends, while others are people who in their life on Earth were experts on subjects that include our work or hobbies, so they are able to guide us and give help when necessary. You often hear people say "I was hesitating and felt as though someone gave me a positive push in the right direction."

Most people who channel healing or do other spiritual work are very aware of their guides and helpers—some are fortunate to be able to see them. As well as having spirit experts helping us, we also have family members on the other side who send love, and try to help when possible.

How do spirit members of your family manage to come to visit you to give comfort at a time of need? All spirits are pure energy—by positive thought they are able to travel through space. Solid objects are no obstacle as they can also travel right through walls of buildings, windows, and doors, and through the four natural elements of the world, Earth, Air, Fire, and Water. Perhaps the words of this verse from a spiritualist hymn sum it up:

Friends never leave us. Those we call
The dear departed never do,
They are around us, though the pall of earth,
Conceals them from our view.[12]

Psychic Art from Spirit Artists

Other spiritual gifts that never cease to amaze people are the ability to sit down and write automatically, or draw or paint beautiful pictures, when you do not have a natural talent. People who are able to produce psychic pictures of our departed relatives never cease to astonish us, as the likeness is usually remarkable. When you stop and realise that the artist has never known the person in the drawing, it is truly proof that they can see your loved ones clearly. Psychic artists have the gift of being able to draw an accurate picture of a person, in spirit, who wants to make themselves known to their loved ones on the Earth plane.

Most of us feel admiration and a touch of envy for psychic artists, but a great many of us who feel envious can do good psychic art, if we take the time to develop this spiritual gift. Some psychic artists can produce such an astonishing likeness to a person's departed partner or parent that a normal artist could do no better. Some psychic drawings of family members are so good that anyone would think they were portraits.

It is possible to have two pictures of the same person drawn by two different psychic artists. Although the styles and colour will be different, the pictures are recognisable as the same person. A team of doctors works through me as a channel for psychic surgery and I am fortunate to have two different psychic drawings of the doctor who is in charge of the team. These pictures were drawn several years apart and the style is different, but it's easy to recognise the same gentleman. The first picture was drawn at a psychic fair held near my home, while the second was drawn 100 miles away, so the artists had no contact with one another. All these little happenings are confirmation of the world of spirit.

How is psychic art done? That's a question many people ponder. The person who is doing the psychic sketch or drawing does not have to be a brilliant artist as the spirit helper takes control of the pencil or brush and draws the picture. All that is needed by the psychic artist is a strong link with the artist helper and to be relaxed enough for them to control the pencil. If you are too tense and holding the pen or brush tightly, they will not be able to work successfully through you.

Psychic Drawing

Automatic drawing is a bit like doodling while you are chatting on the phone. You are relaxed and your mind is blank to what you are doing with your pen, but some reasonable drawings of animals, flowers, or interesting shapes will appear on your phone pad. These were not linked to what you were thinking or what was being talked about; the same thing happens with psychic drawing.

The channelled drawing can appear in any style, often a style unfamiliar to the artist. Sometimes the medium will produce a painting or drawing that is well beyond their normal artistic ability. The process is exactly the same as psychic painting, in that the hand of the person is taken over by the spirit who is controlling the pen or pencil while doing the drawing or sketching, or when doing automatic writing.

The Magic of Automatic Writing

Automatic writing is a fascinating subject that has to be seen to be believed. My first ever experience of this form of spirit communication was when an elderly lady in our circle started writing messages from spirit. The sight was hilarious, as the lady had a job to control the pen—it was writing at such a high speed and the writing was large, so that you could sense the enthusiasm of the spirit writer.

This form of spirit message can be difficult to read, as words run into each other and spaces are not always left between words. It takes a bit of time and experience to perfect the system and build a good rapport with your spirit helper, so you can act as a team.

Many experienced mediums set aside time each day to do psychic writing, and some of them have written long articles on philosophy and many spiritual subjects. An interesting fact about spirit writing is that the handwriting is often written in a very old style, with a noticeable absence of punctuation. It is so completely different from the medium's everyday handwriting that it is obviously a genuine communication, so much so that some mediums find it very hard to believe they have written this work. They often exclaim it is not possible to recognise the style of writing and they need the confirmation of the circle to convince them that it is their work.

When you are doing automatic writing you are in a light trance, which accounts for the fact that the writing is done much faster than it would normally be possible to write legibly. Because the writer is in a trance state, they are usually completely unaware of the contents of the writing, so don't have any influence on the subject matter.

The style of handwriting is usually bold—it's easier to write fast in a bold style, whereas it is impossible to write very fast in small letters. It would be difficult for spirit to control the pen, since the pen is held in a tighter grip when writing in small scale, whereas the hand and wrist is relaxed when writing is flowing.

There are many variations in automatic writing, as some mediums write in a foreign language, others will write backward across the page, or up and down. Is this the preference of the spirit, or are they perhaps playing games with us?

In my circle there is an efficient medium who writes pages of beautifully channelled messages during the Circle, all in legible shorthand, which she then reads to us. The spirit world realises they must move with the age of technology, so many mediums do automatic writing on their computer or word processor.

As you would expect, there are two very separate schools of thoughts regarding the source of this form of writing. Sceptical people argue it's the writer's subconscious mind that is writing the message or article, but how do they explain messages in foreign languages, or subjects of which the writer has no knowledge? Those of us who are aware of the power of spirit know that the information comes directly from the spirit hot line.

Another form of automatic writing is inspirational writing, which happens when a medium asks for assistance when writing a thesis, article, manuscript, or book. Some mediums have succeeded in writing a complete book in record time with the aid of spirit helpers, and they say the plot of the story was given to them by spirit. This applies also to musicians, as famous ones in the past have claimed they received great works in this manner, and many people believe Mozart was aided by spirit musicians when he wrote an entire symphony in a miraculously short time.

Although I do not write in trance, I am very aware of the fact that my scribe helper is always on call and works with me. When a word eludes me, although it's on the tip of my tongue, I ask, "Please, what is the word I need?" and sure enough, it's there in a flash. When you are researching facts for a book or thesis, simply ask for assistance from the spirit world and you will invariably find you are guided to the information, often by opening a book to the correct chapter and page.

I have a fairly good working knowledge of the subjects I write about, but spirit assistance makes writing a lot easier. They occasionally remind me of certain facts I may have forgotten to mention and when to introduce them, so I am always grateful to them for drawing my attention to an error. This form of spirit assistance is priceless and certainly speeds up the boring process of research by eliminating a lot of time wasting and frustration. If you decide to write a book, poem, or magazine article, remember to ask your spirit helper for guidance. Automatic writing, like all other spiritual matters, must be treated with respect and caution, so it is essential that if you decide to experiment with this form of mediumship, you have someone present. It is also important to say a prayer of protection before you start and ensure your solar plexus chakra is tightly closed, so that any lurking entity cannot enter.

Telepathic Research and Remote Viewing

Remote viewing is a method of psychically linking to a person and location, to discover someone's secrets. It is another form of mental communication, a person-to-person telepathy, and has been explored by secret service and the military in several countries. Russia has done extensive research with animals in the field of telepathy over the past twenty-five years.

It is also being researched by the Consciousness and Transpersonal Psychology Research Unit at the John Moore University in Liverpool, England, where a research unit to study the mystery of telepathy was recently opened.

The team will investigate several different ways of making telepathy a reliable form of communication and their results will certainly be of great interest to the government. The people involved in this research are students from a Liverpool School of Performing Arts, so do not already have extensive knowledge of this subject. This group was chosen for the research because the scientists want to try and establish if creative people have much greater extrasensory perceptions.[13]

Remote viewing is used extensively in many countries with amazing results. Remote viewing is the ability to link into other countries, cities, buildings, safes, or files, and scan information. In other words, nothing is safe from a gifted remote viewer. How can you become a remote viewer? Simply by using all of the senses given to you when you were born. Normally most of us use only our five senses in daily life, but by developing our other senses, which most us don't know we possess, it is possible to develop the ability to view from a distance.

US and Russian military have used remote viewing to obtain information about secret locations. It's a thriving exercise that has been proven to work effectively, having received very thorough testing over the past twenty years. Major David A. Morehouse removed the lid of secrecy from remote viewing when his book *Psychic Warrior—the True Story of the CIA's Paranormal Espionage Program* was published. This book offered a fascinating look at behind the scenes of the secret service, and created great interest in remote viewing.[14]

This differs from out of body experiences, as the viewer is able to register detailed information clairvoyantly about military sites and targets. In his book *Remote Viewing Secrets* (2000),[15] Joseph McMoneagle describes how viewers can link into a desired location or target.

It is a well-known fact that the US military considers remote viewing a very valuable and vital part of research and over the past twenty years have used their annual seventy-million-dollar budget on psychic research and this form of viewing. Remote viewing is big business as several ex-military viewers now run companies specialising in this service. Use a search engine on the Internet to look at remote viewing sites. You'll find more than 800,000 entries, proof that there is widespread interest in this fascinating subject.

The Chinese government is known to finance psychic phenomena research. In China, gifted mediums are well respected—how different from the West, where we are often considered strange. *China's Super Psychics* by Paul Dong and Thomas E.Raffill[16] gives lots of information on China's attitude toward this subject.

Would you like to learn more about remote viewing? The Farsight Institute's website has a list of free materials available for scientific remote viewing. One stipulation is that you must be over eighteen years of age to use equipment.

The Western Institute of Remote Viewing also has an interesting and informative website with information on remote viewing and training. In the future we may be able to remotely view a holiday resort to see if we'd enjoy a holiday there, view a company to learn if we'd like to work there, or even check up on our husband's business trip. In other words, the possibilities are endless.

Psychic Photography—How Do You Explain It?

Examples of inexplicable psychic photography crop up regularly, and invariably no one can offer any explanation for the presence of a ghostly figure in the photograph.

I was shown a photograph taken in the gardens at Stanstead Hall, headquarters of the Spiritualist National Union. The photograph showed very clearly a ghostly figure standing beside a tree in the beautiful garden in front of a charming old building, but no explanation was offered for the presence of this visitor.

Some people refer to psychic photography as spirit photography— don't be confused, as it's exactly the same thing! These photographs are proof of the spirit world, accepted for many years, but psychic photographs are often disappointing as they may show only part of the figure; at other times the spirit will appear as a bright white blob of light, which seems to be almost transparent. Not all photographs with a white blob are a camera fault, but it's worth taking another look at it, as it could well be a spirit light, sometimes called an orb, in the photograph. If the temperature dropped when you were taking the picture, or if you felt a chill, then a spirit was almost certainly present when the photographs were taken.

One of the quickest ways to develop your gifts of clairvoyance, automatic writing, and other psychic abilities, including making contact with your guide and helpers, is to meditate on a regular basis. Yes, finding time is difficult, but when you start meditating, you'll find you look forward to the next session.

The Amazing Benefits of Meditation

Meditation has been practised for thousands of years in the East, although today its popularity is growing in the West, where it is now well respected, and meditation classes are held in adult centres, also as part of yoga classes.

Perhaps the most surprising place to find meditation is in schools, where it has proved successful and beneficial, particularly in London's poorer areas. Children attending a meditation class become calmer, develop a feeling of well being, and are less aggressive—there is also a noticeable improvement in self-discipline. The Meditation in Education Network (MiEN) was formed by a group of educators to create awareness of the benefits of meditation in all schools, and is having success.[16]

The popularity of meditation is growing in St. Petersburg and other cities in Russia, also in Australia, where a global meditation group called Earth Mother Marine Meditation beams love and healing during meditation to the oceans.

Meditation has always been a part of India's culture and is now practised in most prisons where both prisoners and wardens meditate. Since the meditation practise was introduced, behaviour problems among prisoners have decreased, and many have found it changed their outlook on life—they've became reformed characters. In one of the most notorious prisons in Delhi, over 1,000 prisoners and staff regularly attend training in meditation, with quite outstanding results. Many prisoners seem to emerge from this training with a completely transformed attitude, as the meditation mellows their terrible need for revenge.[17]

In the UK, Buddhist shrines introduced in a few prisons have proved so successful that the spiritual director of the Buddhist chaplaincy is planning to introduce the shrines in all 130 British prisons.[18]

Big business has become aware of the advantages of meditation. There is a strong incentive to meditate if you live in The Netherlands, as a Dutch insurance company has taken the unusual, very forward-thinking step of offering 30 to 50 percent discounts on automobile insurance to all policy holders who practise transcendental meditation.[19] The biggest bonus for drivers is that once they establish a pattern of meditation, they become more relaxed and stress-free, which reflects on their driving ability—another example of how meditation clears negative energy.

Your Brain's Different Vibrations

Anyone who meditates regularly will be quick to tell you how much better they feel after meditation and how they really miss it on days when they do not meditate. What happens to the body when you meditate? Your brain enters an altered state of consciousness. There are four separate groups of electrical activity linking to your brain, the alta, beta, delta, and theta, so during meditation it's all change.

Your Brain's Two Sides Control Different Actions

There are four vibrations operating in the brain: Delta, Theta, Alpha, and Beta, and the brain contains two parts or hemispheres.

a) The left brain hemisphere is the logical/numerical section.

b) The right brain hemisphere is the creative/artistic section.

When you hear someone saying a person is in alpha, you know they are in a meditative state or healing mode, as alpha is the frequency used in meditation and is also the healing vibration. This is the vibration of the energy around the Earth—roughly ten beats every second.

It is good for all of us to spend a little time relaxing in alpha as it gives the brain a rest and the body an opportunity to relax and heal itself. You may wonder "What is the point of meditation?" Perhaps the biggest benefit is the feeling of complete quietness you experience, almost impossible to find in modern-day living. Although most of us don't realise it, we all have a need to meditate, to give the mind and the body the chance to shut off and heal itself. When you meditate, you completely divorce yourself from your everyday problems and even a short meditation will leave you feeling refreshed.

Are you a person who finds it impossible to visualise scenes during a guided meditation?

The secret is in being able to relax. When your mind is clear of everyday thoughts and your body is also relaxed, the mind is able to create the picture. Meditation slows the busy mind and the body's metabolic rate, creating a real bonus, as the body then requires less intake of oxygen. When your metabolic rate slows down, your body's major organs can rest, which is great for anyone suffering from stress, blood pressure, or heart problems. If someone in your family suffers from any of these health complaints, try coaxing them to experiment with meditation—even if they are sceptical, they will soon thank you.

Meditation helps all of us to reach our full potential, freeing the mind of all unbalanced attitudes, and enabling us to escape from daily suffering, drudgery, and emotional problems. During this time your mind is pure and peaceful, free from all worldly thoughts and pressure.

So how do you meditate? To find this refuge, sit in an upright chair, don't slouch—by sitting upright, you allow the subtle body energies to flow freely and to keep alert so you do not go to sleep during the meditation. Start by placing your hands on your lap, then relax and calm your mind by emptying it of the day's activities and events. Take a few deep breaths to help you unwind, then when you feel comfortable, with each deep breath, imagine that the *out* breath is taking all the negative energy out of the body, then the *in* breath is filling your body with bright White Light.

You can either meditate on a particular problem to find an answer, or you can find yourself going off on a beautiful journey. Some people meditate concentrating on the flame of a candle, but it's what feels right for you. Whatever type of meditation you experience, you will benefit greatly as it will strengthen your aura and help to ensure you do not have problems with negative entities. Meditation when sitting in a circle can be an extremely overwhelming experience. A build-up of positive energy in the room makes it easy to have a very deep meditation and to go off to wonderful, far-off places.

There's always a magical touch of wonder when sometimes a sitter will say they have been to the "Halls of Learning" and seen these wonderful buildings with their enormous libraries, where they learned something useful. Others will say they were taken to see the Akashic records. These are the universe's super-efficient filing system, sometimes called the collective unconsciousness or the universal mind, while other mediums will refer to is as the cosmic mind, but whatever name is used, this is an energy source almost beyond comprehension.

The Akashic records capture our every single thought and deed from the past, from the day we first came to Earth or another planet, thousands of years ago, keeping our data up to date and also holding a record of our future. In other words, we have no secrets!

Meditation is one way to link in to the spirit world, see the Akashic records, and visit the Halls of Learning. It is also a stepping stone to developing other natural tools, like healing and psychic surgery.

Summary

When the door opens on the spiritual pathway, your life takes a new, exciting turn as you discover the joy of sitting in a circle and the feeling of excitement when you start to see or hear things. It is an indescribable feeling when you first discover your psychic abilities and a whole new world to be explored.

Once you become aware of the spirit world, you will find that you somehow seem to be led from one subject to another, as the spirit world has many facets and all are interlinked.

Joining a development circle is an ideal introduction to the other world as it gives you the opportunity to learn how to tune into the energy field of others, also to recognise the presence of a spirit and become familiar with the feeling of energy. As you advance, you may be drawn to develop your healing abilities, or find that you would like to become a medium.

The most important lesson you can learn when starting to develop your psychic abilities is the importance of psychic protection, and once you become used to putting a cloak of protection around yourself, you can start to explore the subject of spirit rescue or become more adventurous and learn about astral travel. The secret of speeding up your psychic abilities is meditation. This allows your brain to rest and the spirit world to connect with you, so that when you start to meditate regularly, you will find that it opens up new possibilities and enables you to make contact with your guides and helpers.

With this door open, you can explore your channelling abilities and may find you have a gift for psychic art or automatic writing. Go with it and enjoy it, as the more you learn, the more you will realise that it is a never-ending subject and there will always be more to learn.

Notes

1. Book 12. "The Direct Voice Mediumship of Lesley Flint." Lesley Flint, "Voices from the Dead," 1971. Arthur Findlay "Voices on the Edge of the Etheric" 1931. *A Lawyer Presents a Case for the After Life: Irrefutable Objective Evidence.* www.victorzammit.com

2. Ibid. Book 3. "Electronic Voice Phenomena" (EVP). Colin Smythe.

3. Ibid. Book 17.

4. *Planetary Connection.* No. 15. "Angels in Space." NASA.

5. Diana Cooper. *A Little Light on Angels.* Findhorn Press, 1996.

6. Paul Roland. *Angels.* Piatkus Books, 2000.

7. *Planetary Connection.* "Angel of the North Wins Lottery Prize" Positive Living. No. 10.

8. Cooper (1996).

9. *Life and Soul.* Roy Stemman. Karma Publishing Ltd. *Testing Telepathy.* Dr. Matthew Smith, Consciousness & Transpersonal Research Unit, John Moores University.

10. *Planetary Connection.* Gallup Poll in USA on Angels, 1995.

11. Ibid. "Getting to Know Your Angel." No. 15.

12. *The Spiritualist National Union Hymn Book.*

13. *Life and Soul.* Roy Stemman. Karma Publishing Ltd. *Testing Telepathy.* Dr. Matthew Smith, Consciousness & Transpersonal Research Unit, John Moores University.

14. Zammit. Major David A. Morehouse. "Psychic Warrior: The True Story of the CIA's Paranormal Espionage Program," 1996.

15. Ibid. "Remote Viewing."

16. *Planetary Connection.* "Meditation in Education MiEN. Calmer Classrooms Clearer Minds." Positive News. No. 18.

17. Ibid. "Prisoners in Delhi."

18. Ibid. "Buddhist Chaplain in Prison. Prisoners Go in for Meditation." No. 5.

19. Ibid. "Transcendental Meditation." Autumn 1993. "Meditating Dutch Save on Insurance." (Source: Catalyst November/Dec. 1992.)

chapter seven

Becoming a Spiritual Healer

───────────────●───────────────

Are you worried about having healing? It is natural and can only be used for good, as this pure energy is channelled directly from the Creator, so it can never be used for black magic or satanic power.

Spiritual Healing—A Gift from the Creator

Spiritual healing is a gift that comes directly from our Creator; it comes from the highest spiritual level and can do everything that Reiki can do. This healing energy is simply a thought away, as those in spirit are always ready to channel healing rays to anyone asking to be healed. It's a direct link, like a telephone line that is open twenty-four hours a day.

The power of thought has a communication point, which allows us to make immediate contact with healers and doctors in the spirit world. Spiritual healing, as well as healing the body, is equally beneficial to heal the disturbed mind, as the healing rays create harmony and balance in the body, so banishing disharmony.

Healing is done in many countries. In Britain alone there are roughly 14,000 qualified spiritual healers who are fully trained and insured members of a healing organisation. There are also probably the same number again who still practise in a quiet way, but do not renew their memberships.

Although you don't hear many people say they have been to a healer, it's all going on quietly behind the scenes.

Centuries ago, healing was the only form of treatment available for injuries and illness, and was complemented by the use of herbs and plants with great success. It has stood the test of time, being used since man was created.

Healing energy is channelled by the healer. It comes in through the crown of the head and out through the hands. Healers do not use their own energy, we are simply the channel used to pass the energy to the patient. Healing does not have to be serious—it should be relaxed and can be fun—a truly fascinating exercise. It is an unknown quantity and has an air of mystery and of being very special. It can make you giggle when you see or feel something jump for no apparent reason.

Often, when a spirit doctor is working on an injury, you can actually see things move, and the wonder of it can give you goose pimples! People often ask me if I don't get very tired doing a lot of healing. The answer is no. It seems to work the opposite way, as the healer absorbs some of the healing energy while she or he is channelling it to the person being healed.

Many people think healing doesn't work unless you believe in it, but they are wrong. There's lots of proof that it works in spite of us—it is a very effective treatment for young children and animals, and is particularly good for animals who are very fearful when visiting the veterinarian. So how do sceptics explain the fact that it works very well on babies and toddlers who are too young to believe in healing, so not influencing the results, not aware they are being given healing treatment? There will always be sceptics who will say they would probably have gotten better anyway. Many people report that healing treatment cured their health problems when traditional medicine had failed.

Where Does the Healing Energy Come From?

Healing energy comes from the source of all energy, the Creator, or what others prefer to call the universal energy. It's natural and works because of its simplicity—the energy travels around the patient's body and can effectively jump-start any sluggish area. There are very few illnesses that do not respond to healing.

How Do You Become a Healer?

Sit down quietly and relax, hold your hands out, and then mentally ask your Creator or the universal energy (depending on religious beliefs) to be used as a healing channel. As you relax, you will feel the energy start to come through your fingers. It may be a very subtle feeling at first: a mild tingling, needles and pins, heat or cold. The more you use this energy, the stronger the channel becomes. When you first start healing, it's a good idea to practise on your dog or cat, as you won't feel self-conscious and they love receiving healing. Once your pets discover you have the ability to give them healing, they won't be shy about coming to ask for more.

Where Can You Learn to Heal?

Now that you have decided you would like to become a qualified healer, you can join one of the many healing organisations that offer excellent training, and where membership includes insurance coverage. Training usually takes roughly two years and involves attending several weekend courses and working as a probationer with a healer. I have been a member of one of those well-respected organisations for many years and know they offer excellent training and advice.

We have been told so many times by spirit that what we give out, we get back tenfold. This refers to life generally, but is particularly applicable to healing, where it has a strong boomerang effect. When you send someone healing, you'll notice afterward that you feel better. This is proof that the love you give out returns to you.

Why Do Some Healers Channel More Powerful Energy than Others?

Some healers have amazing results and can cure an illness in one session, while others can take a year to show results. It's not that one healer is physically stronger or more healthy than another; it's a case of healers working on different levels of energy vibration. We are all on different energy vibrations—the more spiritually evolved healers work on a more rapid vibration, so channel from a higher source, and work with spirit doctors and healers. All healers, whether doing Reiki or spiritual healing, are only providing a safe and loving, supportive environment, which facilitates the powerful interaction between the higher energies and the patient's energies. Today the media is beginning to accept the power of healing and it is often introduced into a weekly soap opera, a television programme, women's magazines, and daily tabloids, which regularly favour the subject.

More and more people today are turning to healing as an alternative to taking medical drugs, which can create uncomfortable side effects.

Can Healing Be Given Anywhere?

I have channelled healing to a buffet car attendant on a train traveling at seventy miles per hour so I know healing can be given anywhere. My funniest experience occurred ten years ago, when I was about to open a healing centre in a local community centre. I went to a nearby fish and chip shop, which was fifty yards from the centre, to ask the owner to put a poster on his window advertising the centre.

When I entered the shop, there was a queue of people waiting for their fish suppers, so the big dilemma was: should I go in front of the queue, or should I wait my turn with the customers? I decided to join the queue and when it came my turn to be served, I asked in as quiet a voice as I could manage, if I could please put a poster on the window. The owner asked what the poster was for, so I had to explain about the opening of the new healing centre, whereupon the gentleman standing next to me in the queue promptly asked me if he could have some healing. To my surprise, he meant *now*, and asked me to please put my hand on his sore ankle to heal it.

As no chairs were available, there was no option but to sit down on the dirty shop floor, while wearing my good white trousers, and channel healing to his ankle. Great entertainment for all the people in the queue, as they watched the performance with interest and amusement. My patient told me he had received healing before, as he used to go to a centre in London every week, so I asked if he had been seriously ill. He replied that he was not ill, but he liked going there as it made him feel relaxed.

Healing the Dying

Healing is not just helping people to live, it is also used to help people pass peacefully to the other side. Many healers work at preparing seriously ill patients for death. If you are interested in learning more about this side of healing work, I recommend Allegra Taylor's book, *Acquainted with the Night: A Year on the Frontiers of Death*.[1]

Magnetic Healing—It's Your Own Energy

Magnetic healing occurs when people are not aware of the basics of healing and so, in error, use their own energy. It can happen when someone is really keen to help relieve another person's pain. By trying very hard to make the patient feel better, they are unwittingly giving their own energy.

A typical example is when you meet someone who is feeling a bit sorry for themselves and you try to cheer them up and make them laugh. It is simply a straightforward transfer of energy, but it's your energy that you are giving away and it will leave you feeling depleted.

Have you ever visited anyone in a hospital who is lying in the bed, looking very sad when you arrive, but by the time you leave they are sitting up very cheerfully, and say they feel so much better since you arrived? That's magnetic healing. You have given them your energy, and now you feel exhausted. The next time you go to visit someone who is ill, make sure you close your chakras and put yourself in a protective bubble before you arrive there! Also ask any healer friends to send the person absent healing.

Absent Healing—Distance Is No Problem

Absent healing or distance healing is an extremely effective form of healing and can create all sorts of miracles. It is particularly useful if anyone is trapped under rubble or in a car accident, where they are inaccessible to medical assistance. The healing will reach the person who needs it if the healer simply thinks about it. It's amazing and hard to believe, but you don't need to know the person's full name, or where they live, as long as you know they are Jack's father, Anne's daughter, or Mary's neighbour. Our spirit doctors know where the healing is being sent, so simply by sitting down and channelling the energy to the person, they will receive the healing.

People will often describe how they felt the energy arrive and can even tell you the hour that it was sent. I don't usually tell the person what time the healing energy will be channelled as it is so easy for the treatment to be delayed due to a telephone call or unexpected visitor, then they may be sitting patiently waiting to receive healing.

Wonderful results can sometimes be achieved from one session of absent healing, which are truly difficult to comprehend. After I'd been a guest on a BBC programme a woman wrote to me, asking me to send healing to her friend who was losing her eyesight. As requested, the healing was sent, then forgotten about, until the following week when a letter arrived saying thank you for the miracle, as the lady's eyesight had returned to normal.

Another woman in London contacted me as she had a cyst on her jaw and was due to have an operation the following week to remove it. The cyst vanished after the healing had been sent, so the operation was not necessary. This type of healing is carried out with the aid of spirit doctors and is a form of psychic surgery done from a distance. Last month I channelled healing to an eighty-year-old woman in India who had gangrene in her foot, and had been told the foot would need to be amputated. After received an urgent phone call saying "Please do something," with the aid of my doctor friends upstairs, the channelled energy succeeded in drying up the gangrene and the woman is now home from the hospital, feeling greatly relieved. With the skill of my team of doctors, distance healing repaired a problem that was stopping a young woman from conceiving a much-wanted baby. She had been told by the hospital she could not have children, but she is now four months pregnant and overjoyed.

Perhaps the most satisfying results of absent healing occurred recently after I received a phone call from a friend in Scotland, telling me that her grandson, who was only a few months old, had been diagnosed as having a large lump close to his liver.

Healing energy was sent for twenty minutes—my fingers were jumping so I knew the spirit doctors were working on this lovely baby. Yesterday evening my friend called to tell me the good news—that a further hospital scan showed the lump had disappeared, whereupon I silently thanked my spirit doctors, who work so quietly to help the sick.

Absent healing is just as effective as hands-on healing, and is often much more convenient, as no time is wasted in travel. Many churches have an absent healing list, so if you would like to receive absent healing, they will be happy to add your name to their list.

How Does Absent Healing Work?

The healer is not acting on the patient's physical body, they are acting on the patient's super energy body. Some healers, by using positive thought, can link their patient to the quantum energy waves in the universal energy. It has been proved many times that the separation of thousands of miles can be overcome simply by intent. The healer mentally connects to the patient by positive thought, which is a form of physical interaction with the universal energy and our Creator.

No Name or Address Is Needed

Perhaps the most mind-boggling fact about absent healing is that it works successfully without you knowing the name or address of the person receiving your healing. As long as you know who you are thinking about, that person will receive the healing. This also applies to people involved in a natural disaster or victims of war. By sending the healing energy to those who need support, whether emotional or physical, the healing will get to its correct destination. When you see pictures of victims of powerful tornadoes, flash floods, war, or famine, please sit down for a few minutes and send healing energy. They may not know that you have personally sent it, but they will be aware of feeling better.

Absent healing is also a very useful treatment for a sick animal who shakes in fear when visiting the vet!

Animal Healing—They Love It

All animals are very receptive to healing and are quick to ask for it when they have a problem. I have several doggy friends who come and ask me when they want healing. They stop directly in front of me and stand very still. I now recognise the signs, and the strange thing is that animals who do not know me seem to know that I can give them healing. Dogs that I had never met before have come and asked me to give them healing—more proof that animals are very psychic.

Healing is very effective, whether it is treating animals, rodents, insects, birds, trees, or plants. All respond very well as there are no barriers. Next time you notice your pet is looking a bit sad, give him some healing as he'll love it! The same applies to wild animals. If you notice an insect that has been injured or a pigeon with a sore leg, send them a blast of healing and ask for healing to be sent to them. I am not asking you to spend a lot of time sending healing to every bird, stranger, or beastie you see each day, but by sending them a blast of energy as you walk or drive along a road, and by passing the responsibility to the spirit world, the unknown animals will receive healing.

Is Your Dog Hyperactive?

I visited my sister in Scotland who owns two beautiful bearded collies. Bracken, the male, was very laid back and well behaved, while the bitch, Penny, was as mad as a hatter and never still for more than a minute.

We wondered how to remove fur balls from a dog that refuses to sit still. Penny seemed to have a never-ending supply of energy and romped around the lounge, so as a joke I offered to send her some healing in the hope of encouraging her to settle down and relax. The result was beyond our wildest expectations as, after a few minutes, the dog lay down on the carpet and completely relaxed.

She was like a rag doll—when we lifted a leg, it flopped down—so we were quick to take advantage of this opportunity. Gail and I had the satisfying job of removing every fur ball. She sat at one end of the dog and I at the other. Luckily I was at the nose end. We each soon filled bowls with fur and met no opposition.

I had a similar experience a few years ago, when a lady brought a ferret to me for healing. This little beastie was intent on running around my body and seemed to have no intention of settling down, so the healing was channelled while he explored my body. After a couple of minutes, he suddenly curled up into a ball on my lap and went to sleep. Again, more confirmation that animals do respond to healing energy.

Amazing Psychic Surgery

Psychic Surgery is a natural form of surgery, done without the use of any anaesthetic or pain killers. There are different methods that I will talk about later. Some surgeons will sometimes use a small knife or use their fingers to open an area of the body. They then put their hand inside the person's stomach or chest and remove the offending part. The length of time taken depends on the technique used by the surgeon.

How Long Does an Operation Last?

Often an operation lasts only a couple of minutes and when the surgery is completed, the hole is then closed by the surgeon, who zaps the area with high-frequency energy. He simply presses the sides of the wound together and it seals completely, so the only proof that the event happened is something resembling a small scratch by a cat. When major surgery has been carried out, there is sometimes some bruising to be seen in the following days, which helps to convince you it was not all a dream!

Some psychic surgeons use water for a disinfectant, but it is really only to reassure the patient, as no disinfectant is needed since these specialists can channel disinfectant and anaesthetic when needed. You will know if you see a small bowl of water, that it is the only disinfectant used and it can instantly be changed to ether, when doing a major operation. This is sprinkled over the patient's body before major surgery. The first time I smelled it, I couldn't place the smell, so asked him and he grunted, "Ether," in a deep gutteral accent, so that gave me something to think about!

Different Methods of Psychic Surgery

Several completely different types of psychic surgery are done in various parts of the world. Because the surgeons work on different energy vibrations, some are more comfortable working one way and some another.

Perhaps the most famous of all psychic surgeons is João Teixeira da Faria, known as João de Deus, "The Miracle Man," who is known to treat and cure up to a thousand patients in a day at his healing centre in central Brazil. Carloads of patients travel from many countries, including England, to visit this amazing surgeon, who has been studied by many scientists and doctors and been subjected to all sorts of tests. I recommend Robert Pellegrino-Estrich's book *The Miracle Man,* for those wanting to learn more about this fascinating man.[2]

Filipino surgeon Alex Orbito, whose many psychic operations have made news, opens his patient's body with his fingers and pulls out the offending part. This surgeon does not go into full trance, so is able to talk to patients and answer questions, which makes the operation a much less frightening experience. If you'd like to learn more about this surgeon's work, have a look on the Internet, as there are over 1,500 websites to choose from.

Compared to these wonderful surgeons, my work is very limited, although I have been used by spirit as a channel for a form of psychic surgery for five years. I never touch the patient, as the spirit world uses me for mental psychic surgery, which allows my hands to remain about four or five inches away from their body, while the work is done in their energy field. When this form of healing is being done, it feels as though strong currents are traveling down different fingers and my fingers feel as though they are jumping in peculiar positions, yet my hands appear to be perfectly still. The amazing thing is that the person being healed will describe all sorts of sensations of being pulled or pressed, or feeling a needle injecting their body.

Like all healers who do this work, I have a team of doctors and a "ray master" who work through my channel. Spirit medical specialists are available in every field, including heart surgeons, gynaecologists, eye doctors, acupuncturists, and chiropractors, so all types of illnesses can be treated. The huge advantages of mental psychic surgery are that neither the healer nor the patient feel discomfort or pain, whichever area of the body is receiving the treatment, although while this healing work is being carried out by my spirit doctors, the patient may be aware of unusual activity in their body.

Yes, it all sounds a bit far-fetched, but hospitals have confirmed to patients that they no longer require an operation—the problem has vanished and they cannot explain it! A young woman came to me for help because she was unable to conceive a child. After one treatment her fertility problems vanished—she became pregnant and gave birth to a healthy baby. The local hospital told this mother that they could not understand how she had conceived, as it was not physically possible due to her gynaecological problems. There is no point in trying to explain to a surgeon that you had a spirit operation.

Where's the Large Cyst Gone?

Some folks scoff at the idea of psychic surgery, but those who have benefited from this natural and drug-free surgery have the last laugh. One such person is my friend Celia, who suffered uncomfortable pain that the gastroenterologist surgeon at the nearby hospital confirmed was caused by abnormal enlargement of her right ovary, due to a 6.3 cm x 4.6 cm cyst. The remaining ovary contained further small abnormalities.

The hospital scan also confirmed that Celia's uterus contained a 2.4 cm fundal fibroid. In a desperate effort to avoid major surgery, my friend visited psychic surgeon Stephen Turoff, who removed the ovarian cyst. You can imagine the hospital staff's surprise when a further scan showed clearly that both ovaries were normal and there was no evidence of the large cyst on the right ovary. Where had the big cyst gone? Some folks doubt that psychic surgery can possibly remove cysts or tumors, but my friend had the last laugh as she no longer needs to have surgery. There is no other logical explanation for the case of the vanishing cyst!

I have often puzzled why the spirit doctors work through me in a different manner from many other surgeons, so was very relieved when I learned that surgeons in other countries are also used for this form of mental psychic surgery. One of those is a very famous Filipino surgeon the Reverend Joseph Martinez, who also does not touch his patients, but like me, works in the auric field. The great advantages of this type of surgery are first, that because the patient is never touched by the healer's hand, there is never the threat of prosecution, which is a hazard linked to this work, and second, that it can be done at any distance from the patient, so can be carried out without the patient being present.

There are thousands of people in America and other countries who will describe how they were cured of a serious illness by psychic surgery, so it is no fluke. For more details on the work of the Reverend Joseph Martinez and other psychic surgeons, I recommend the website www.uri.geller.com/ps6.htm.

When psychic surgery is being done, there is no need for the surgeon to cut open a body, as they are all able to work in the auric field. I was told by the surgeon I visited that cuts are made and blood appears as proof for the patient that an operation is taking place.

As we are all made of energy, it is possible for these surgeons to remove damaged tissue without physically operating, but who would believe a psychic operation had taken place?

Some time ago I had a patient in Scotland who had too much mercury in his body, which was creating a health problem. While channelling healing to him, my doctors removed all excess mercury from his body. It sounds wonderful, except that they removed all the mercury/amalgam fillings from his teeth, as well.

Psychic Surgeons Do Not Need Details of Your Illness

You do not need to give any healer or psychic surgeon details of your health problem, as the surgeon will only do the work that the spirit doctors think is most urgent. This means that if you go along for treatment to a sore knee, you may find that an operation is carried out on your stomach where you could have a problem that has not yet shown itself to you. It's a sort of preventive surgery.

Psychic Surgery—The Big Plus

1. No long hospital waiting list. You can choose when to have your treatment.

2. No time off work.

3. These operations cost very little money (around £20 in the UK and donations in Brazil.)

4. There are no unpleasant side effects of drugs or medicine.

5. You avoid the use of anaesthetics.

6. Very little risk of infection.

Apart from being emotionally tired the next day, most patients have no other aftereffects. You are always advised to take it reasonably easy for a few days as your body has experienced an operation, although there's nothing to be seen. With this form of surgery, like any other type of healing, you learn as you go along so it becomes second nature.

People who have had a successful psychic operation will usually make this their first port of call when they develop any future illnesses.

What Illnesses Can Be Cured by Psychic Surgery?

This form of healing has been used very successfully to: remove gallstones and malignant and non-malignant tumours; relieve ear, nose, and throat blockages; balance the uterus and ovaries; realign the spine; heart surgery; remove bone splinters; and treat liver and kidney disease. These surgeons will tell you that every illness can be cured if the time is right. Sometimes more than one operation is needed, as it could be too big a shock to the body to do more than one major operation at one time.

Many of tomorrow's healers and psychic surgeons are the youngsters of today whom we often refer to as "old souls," or the "indigo children." You may often hear someone spoken of as "an old soul." This is a spirit who is highly evolved, has lived many lives, and learned many lessons. These children seem to be so wise for their age, kind, placid, and almost too good to be true. You'll often be astonished at their inner knowing, as they seem to know without being taught—they are tomorrow's leaders.

Definitions

Clairaudience

Clairaudience is the ability to hear voices from beyond the normal human range of hearing. In other words, the voices are from another dimension and are usually helpful and friendly messages from the spirit world. You don't have to be a medium to receive clairaudient messages—any non-psychic person can hear a voice—so don't doubt it and think it is your imagination. Like many mediums, I tend to hear spirit voices when I am talking on the telephone and will sometimes have the caller talking in the ear nearest the phone, and a spirit voice talking in the other ear, so joining the conversation. They will interrupt to diagnose a patient's health problem or tell me if their body is short of minerals and the information is accurate, so always trust the voices you hear if your gut feeling tells you it is correct. When talking to someone about a geopathic stress problem, the voice will tell me if there are two or three streams under the home and how many hundred feet down to look for the water. Usually when I dowse to check the information, I receive confirmation it is correct.

Clairvoyance

Clairvoyance is a tool used by mediums and psychics to communicate with the spirit world and receive messages. It is an ability to use the third eye as a screen to view people and places, often described by mediums as looking at a television screen that is located in the centre of the forehead, just above the eyebrows—a fascinating and useful gift that can be developed when sitting in a development circle. This second sight gift allows clairvoyants to see into the future, which is an invaluable tool when reading tarot cards, the crystal ball, or palms.

Clairsentience

Clairsentience is the ability to understand and decode accurately shapes and images shown by the spirits on another dimension. These symbols and pictures appear in the medium's mind, so many people new to a development circle will think they have imagined it. You will often hear a person say "I saw a tall, dark-haired lady, but it was probably my imagination." It is difficult to get rid of self-doubts when you first start to develop your psychic abilities, but you must trust the spirit world and accept what you are shown. They may not mean anything to you, but they could make sense to someone else in the group.

Psychometry

Psychometry is an exciting gift as it allows you to read the energy of any object you touch. Simply by holding a ring or watch, you can find out a lot of information about the owner and many clairvoyants include psychometry as part of their sittings. This gift enables you to lift a second-hand ring or necklace in a shop and get a detailed picture of the previous owner. In other words, there are few secrets from people with the gift of psychometry

Photopsychokinesis

Photopsychokinesis is simply mind over matter, enabling you to move an object using the power of your mind. A fine example is the world-famous Uri Geller, who can start broken watches from a distance. Never underestimate the power of positive thought, as it is a very powerful and effective tool.

Precognition

A few people have the ability to see into the future, and are able to foresee events. Some people who can see a scene of disasters or accidents have this gift and can often tell when an earthquake is about to occur, or a plane crash will soon happen. It is surprising how often this is accurate, but the frustrating thing is that they are unable to prevent it happening.

Telepathy

Telepathy is the ability to read a person's thoughts, not only when they are in the same room, but also when they are a distance away. It is sometimes a good thing and sometimes not so good, but it's certainly cheaper than a phone call. We regularly get examples of telepathy when we think of a friend we have not seen for some time and that day unexpectedly receive a phone call or visit from them, or a card will arrive in the mail. We tend to think it is only a coincidence, but this is telepathy at work.

Summary

Becoming a healer today is an easy matter, as there are many Reiki and spiritual healing classes available locally, and churches and major healing organisations that offer training. Before you invest any money in courses to becoming a Reiki healer, or learn other methods of healing, sit down and mentally ask to be used as a healing channel. You will feel the energy start to travel down through your hands and the more regularly you practise, the stronger the energy channel will become.

Everyone is able to channel healing energy, so don't doubt you can pass this energy to others. When you are confident that you can channel the healing energy, you can start to experiment by sending absent healing to sick friends and animals.

I advise everyone who would like to become a healer to read as many books as possible on this fascinating subject, also to attend as many workshops and talks as are available, but do not be impressed by everything you hear, as you must only take on board the facts that feel right to you. Once you feel you know a few facts about basic healing, perhaps you might like to learn about psychic surgery or animal healing, as there are many avenues to explore. Each one leads you on your spiritual journey and gives you the opportunity to learn and to meet like-minded people. Giving healing to someone who is sick is one of the most satisfying things you can ever do, so start healing—there are so many sick people in the world who need you.

Notes

1. Allegra Taylor. "Acquainted with the Night, A Year on the Frontier of Death."
2. Robert Pellegrino-Estrich. *The Miracle Man.*

chapter eight

Psychic Protection — Is It Really Necessary?

A frequently asked question is: "What is psychic protection and why do we need it?" It sounds as though it's a strong defence system against any form of psychic attack, but don't be alarmed, as it's only a simple and wise precaution done by positive thought. This protects the aura from invasion by any incoming negative energy, hangers-on, or anyone you may meet who drains your energy. The more love you give out in your life, the less chance there is of a hanger-on-type lodger joining your energy field. By keeping the score in your love bank account on the high side, you are much less likely to attract negativity, as love is by far the strongest power in our universe. It is the most powerful energy in existence.

Spiritual protection in its simplest form is maintaining a clean and healthy aura, the most effective way to keep the door firmly closed to unwanted intruders.

Earthbound spirits, negative entities, and spirit possession all sound very far-fetched and difficult to accept. It is not until you, or someone you know, has been directly affected that you realise protection is a *must*. It's often only after experiencing an unusual phenomena that your attitude toward this subject changes, when you realise it was a lesson to help you on your pathway. Suddenly you begin to accept that the dark side really does exist around us twenty-four hours each day and they are never off duty—they really are not just horror stories! There are so many conflicting facts told about the dark side, so take on board whatever feels right for you and ignore other facts. There are several different ways of using psychic protection, so it's very much a case of trying some of the variations and exploring this subject until you find a system that feels comfortable and right for you.

Calling on the help of Jesus when you experience energy problems is okay, but you have a responsibility to protect yourself, as we are each responsible for running our own life. It is not God, Buddha, or Allah's responsibility, so you must put on your own protection, although you can ask your guardian angel or the universal energy for protection. If you do not have any religious faith or are concerned that your body may have a hanger-on, in addition to wearing your protection you can try using positive thought to instruct it to leave your body, but say it as though you mean it.

Think Protection

Whatever method you use, please do not listen to anyone who says that you don't need any protection, as your guides and helpers always protect you. Your spirit guide and doorkeeper protect you from harm, but they only protect you from the things that you are unable to protect yourself against, so protecting yourself from negative people and negative situations is your responsibility.

"Why don't they protect me?" I've heard people wail. The answer is that we humans have been given the gift of free will, so have a choice whether or not to protect ourselves. If your guide places the protection around you without being asked to do so, then your freedom of choice would be removed. The more steps you take to strengthen your natural defence system, the better.

Psychic protection is one of the most important and least taught lessons, and yet is vital to good health and well being. It diverts negative energies away from your body so they bounce off your aura, which ensures they cannot siphon off your much-needed energy. As well as placing your protection around you each day, as an extra safeguard, you can ask for assistance from your guides and helpers.

Rule Number 1 is: Always give your guides permission to protect your energy field from intruders. It is important to be very specific in your instruction. It makes a lot of sense to ask that this is done twenty-four hours a day, every day, so that you do not need to keep asking them to protect you. It also means that on the day when you are very busy and forget to put on your protection, you know your guides will take action.

Try to find a simple method of cleansing and protecting your aura, as methods that are time-consuming don't always get done. Keep it simple and always remain well-grounded. Positive thought is the best protection of all—when you are worried about picking up negative energy or thoughtforms, you attract them to you. The power of positive thought is very powerful—never doubt it.

The term "psychic protection" confuses many people who are new to the spiritual pathway, which is hardly surprising as it suggests a scene from a horror movie. With the *Harry Potter, Star Wars,* and *Lord of the Rings* movies being some of the most popular films shown, it's easy to think any talk of psychic protection is theatrical and unnecessary. This cloak of psychic protection is an invisible energy guard that each one of us can use to protect ourselves from a range of problems—plus the good news is that it's free. Your cloak of protection is always available, so you can pull it on as quickly as pulling on your outdoor coat. The main difference is that it is so much easier to put on your outdoor coat—remembering to put on your protection requires discipline.

Get around the problem of forgetting about protection, or being too busy and thinking you'll do it later, by placing large signs about to remind you to act now. It may sound a bit daft, but writing the word protection on a sign in large letters with a brightly coloured felt pen, then propping it on the bedside table catches your attention when getting out of bed. Place another sign on the kitchen table—if one sign fails to remind you to don your protection, then another will succeed. I had a problem recently when my house was on the market to be sold. I had to remember to hide the signs before a potential buyer came to view the house, as they would probably think I am a little strange.

Your Cloak of Protection

When you join a good psychic development circle, you will be taught the basics of protection and chakra awareness, as they are the foundation on which to build all spiritual work. Once you have been taught these important lessons, you realise you've gained a new confidence and are ready to learn how to link into the spirit world. When sitting in a development circle, to ensure complete protection, it is essential that you place your own protection around you and not rely on the circle leader's prayer for protection of those in the circle.

As you develop your awareness and become more sensitive to energies, you are always vulnerable to negative spirits, so it's sensible to get into the good habit of placing a protection around you each morning when you get out of bed. It only takes a few moments to put on your cloak of protection and it's a safeguard, both for your aura and your energy. This invisible energy guard is very subtle, so you will never be aware of it other than the confidence you gain from knowing you are protected from all negative eventualities. It's similar to the feeling of confidence you get from knowing you used a good deodorant!

Protection isn't simply about placing a cloak of protection around your body, as your entire energy field is vulnerable. Don't forget to place the protection around all seven levels of energy, so your aura is completely protected from all harmful invaders, whether fragments, thoughtforms, or spirits.

To put on your cloak of protection, you should first cleanse your body of negative energy, so sit down and relax. Now visualise a beam of White Light coming in through the crown of your head and sweeping all the negative energy from your body as it travels through your body and into the ground. Now take three deep breaths to relax, then begin to visualise your body filling up with bright White Light. See it coming down into your body through the crown of your head, directly from your Creator, until your body is filled with light and you are ready to don your protection. If you are short of time, you can quickly visualise yourself pulling a blanket of White Light around your body and under your feet.

When you don your cloak, its purpose is twofold:

1. It stops energy draining from your aura.

2. It stops negativity entering your aura.

You are effectively creating a safe and positive energy field around you, which is a natural defence against people's negative thoughts and any parasites looking for a home. Any time you're planning to attend a spiritual workshop, lecture, circle, shaman gathering, traveling on trains, tubes, etc, or visiting busy department stores or a cinema, you'll need your cloak. Check to be sure you are wearing it, as you are quite liable to meet an over-enthusiastic person who is not well earthed, or an energy vulture who will drain your energy.

Do you feel drained of energy after traveling home from work in the rush hour? It's not the crowd and the rush to catch the train, bus, or tube that depletes you, it is the negative energy given off by those around you, who've had a bad day at work and are tired or angry.

Equally it can affect you on the way to work, as you could be sitting next to someone who's just had a row with their wife, or has a bad hangover from heavy drinking, so wherever you go, you benefit from wearing your invisible protection.

Negative energy has the advantage of being invisible; it's a nasty unseen vibration, so unless you are very aware of energies, you will be unaware of its presence. It lurks in the most unexpected places, waiting for a vulnerable host or energy supply, so never underestimate the value of protection. It is a *must*. As well as placing a cloak around your body, you can also place a protection around your home, business, or car.

The Two-Ring Interlock Exercise

The two-ring exercise is a simple and quick way to acquire an instant protective barrier, as it can be done with your hands under the table or desk, so nobody in the room is aware that you have sensed negative energy and are taking evasive action to protect your energy field.

This method is popular with many mediums and therapists as it can be done without a patient suspecting you are doing anything unusual! To do this exercise, which will protect you from psychic attack or energy vultures, start by placing the tips of your middle fingers and your thumbs together to make a ring. Do this exercise with each hand so that you have two separate circles, one in each hand. Now interlock the circles together to make a chain effect. To make this tool effective, hold your hands in this ring-lock position, facing the direction of the attack, and believe it will protect you from negative energy. Remember the power of positive thought is very effective—do not doubt the power of this chain. Finish the exercise by placing a beam of pure White Light around you.

Don't ever feel self-conscious when doing this exercise—anyone watching you will probably assume you are making a pattern with your fingers. This interlocked ring can be done quickly at any time, in any place, when you feel the presence of any uncomfortable energy. Try experimenting with it now, so that you are familiar with it. When alarm bells ring and you instinctively know you need protection, you won't have to try frantically to remember how it's done!

The Golden Triple Protection

As an alternative to using White Light for protection, some people prefer to use the golden triple protection method that is equally effective. This etheric gold shield has three separate layers.

Layer 1. Visualise a fine layer of shining gold energy closely around your body.

Layer 2. Visualise the second layer as a very fine, shimmering gold mesh, the sort of thing worn by knights in days of old.

Layer 3. This final layer is a complete solid sheet of gold which entirely surrounds your body, acting as a complete seal.

This wonderful triple layer of protection will make you feel very secure from all forms of negative energy—the only energy capable of penetrating through this gold seal is the energy of pure love and healing. Does it all sound a bit elaborate and hard work? Don't be fooled, as once you have done this exercise a few times, you'll find it takes only seconds to complete.

Does This Cloak Really Work?

Whatever method you choose to use will work well, as the power of intent is positive; by intending your protection to work it will be effective. Don't ever worry if you forget to include a verse in your favourite protection prayer, as it will still work, due to the power of intent. Always place a protection around yourself any time you feel uneasy and sense the presence of negativity, or feel your space invaded. Try to do it as soon as you sense a problem approaching, rather than wait until you have been drained of energy. The really big benefit of putting protection around you each morning is that you then don't have to worry about meeting negative people or entities.

The Golden Rule is: *"Protect when you go to bed, and protect when you get out of bed in the morning,"* then you are constantly protected. As well as placing a light of protection around yourself, you can use the same principle to protect your children, your animals, or your car. Remember you have nothing to lose and a lot to gain, so it's worth making the effort to think "protect."

I automatically place a light of protection around my car as I leave home, and always when it is parked in a public place. This effort has been well rewarded, Many years ago I worked one day each week doing marketing for a small company whose office was in a quiet back street. Parking was a problem as the area had double yellow lines, but traffic wardens very seldom visited this little road so local business people always parked there.

As I had heavy boxes of files to carry to this office, I always parked on the forbidden lines and mentally asked for my car to be protected from wardens. All went well until one day I came out of the office and found my car had a parking ticket! When I realised every car on the road had a ticket, I thought spirit could not have done anything about my ticket, so when I got home I sent off a cheque for the parking fee and forgot about the matter.

You can imagine my amazement and delight a few days later, when I received my cheque and the parking ticket in the mail from the department, saying the traffic warden had omitted to put the time or date on my ticket, so it was invalid. I said several thank you's and have kept this ticket as a memory of my spirit protection.

I have always believed that if you are a giver and enjoy helping people, you will receive help from the spirit world, provided your demands are reasonable. One thing worth remembering is that the spirit world does not help, unless you request assistance. It goes back to the issue of free will—they can only help when asked, as they do not interfere with your life.

Never consider doing any spiritual work involving another dimension, whether it is releasing an earthbound spirit or giving healing or Reiki, until you've checked that your protection is in place. If you intend to remove an entity, then double-check and take strong precautions. For added protection when removing entities, I usually wear a cross and have a Holy Bible as part of my DIY kit, and I say a prayer of protection. It's all about positive thought and intent—when dealing with the very dark side these tools are positive energy.

It does not matter which tools you choose to use. The main thing is that they have good energy and give you extra confidence. Remember you are never entirely alone when doing this work as your guides and helpers are at your side, so should you encounter any difficulties, they are ready to join you.

A Protective Shield

Are you uneasy about being in the company of a very aggressive person? Try to visualise yourself pulling down a wall of thick steel between you and the person, pull a steel curtain across from floor to ceiling. Steel energy is very powerful and when reaching from ground level up to the sky can protect from bad energy in the surrounding area. This exercise, as well as offering you protection, can be used around your home or workplace and is an excellent tool for use in bed to separate you from the energies of a drunken or aggressive partner. Tell any of your friends who have boozing or violent husband problems about the protective shield; they'll be really grateful.

A technique useful when dealing with aggression is to visualise a protective battle shield over your solar plexus chakra, as this is the part of the body that is often directly hit by unpleasant verbal abuse or anger. Have you ever experienced the feeling similar to being punched in the stomach, which happens when you are at the receiving end of unpleasantness? If so, you'll appreciate the value of an invisible shield. You can design your shield so that it has your name and tools drawn on it or any symbols of strength, then it's available and ready for use when you need it. You may want to have it highly polished with a mirror effect to disperse any negativity that approaches you, so that it acts like a feng shui bagua mirror. The more personal your shield, the more positive energy impregnated on it.

Your Bubble of Protection—One That Won't Burst

Another tool to include in your protection is an affirmation that I will tell you about later. One of the simplest ways to wear protection is to visualise your body, including your aura and the space under your feet, in a bubble of light, surrounded by powerful White Light, so that you are in a complete ball of light. Visualising yourself going into a bubble filled with pure White Light is a popular form of protection used by many therapists and light workers. You simply visualise entering your bubble of light and closing the door or zipping it shut. This is a great tool to use when you want quick protection, as you literally visualise yourself jumping into the bubble and relaxing immediately.

Workers for spirit often personalise their bubble, choosing a favourite colour for the outside and a relaxing colour for the inside. The ideas are endless, so let your imagination have a field day, then you will feel familiar with it and treat it as a haven. Some will decorate their bubble and furnish it like a little shrine, with a large cross or Star of David on the door and a large angel or two on the outside wall. One friend of mine has an enormous, comfortable old armchair and she sees herself sitting safely curled up in this great chair while doing her work. The bubble is useful at all times and is not solely for rescue work.

If you live in a busy city or crowded town or an area of discontent and aggression, your bubble will keep you safe from negative vibes. You can use your bubble on a large scale to protect your home, simply by visualising a loving protective bubble, or to protect a psychic development group or rescue circle, as its uses are endless.

Once you become confident about using the bubble, you can put your children, partner, or pets in the bubble. It's a very good protection for your pet dog or cat if you live close to a busy main road, so put them in a bubble each morning when you are doing your own protection. Are you concerned about your child being bullied at school, or being influenced by other children into the joys of drugs? Then think "Bubble."

Your bubble is a protection against negative energy, but it will not work miracles or stop major accidents. We are often meant to learn from disasters and upsets. Most people say "it was a nightmare at the time, but we've come out of the experience much stronger. It has helped us learn to deal with life's blows."

On a lighter note, my proof that a bubble works came in October, 1996, when the south coast of Britain was hit by Hurricane Lili. The tail end of the hurricane lashed homes and gardens. I was living close to the beach, but my home was on the market for sale. I wanted my white rose tree to remain in bloom to impress prospective purchasers coming to view the house and garden, so when the winds started howling, I sat down and mentally put my rose tree with its beautiful blooms in a bubble, but did not think to put the rest of the garden in the bubble!

Next morning when I surveyed the storm damage, the garden shed, located one yard from the rose tree, had part of its roof ripped off, half the branches of a plum tree close by had been torn off, and the fence panel next to the rose tree had fallen down. When I looked at my white rose tree, I was overwhelmed with gratitude to see it completely intact. Not a single petal had fallen on the ground.

I could not have asked for more positive proof that the bubble of light, with the spirit world's assistance, was indeed positive proof of the power of protection. Here was confirmation that when we make a conscious effort to protect ourselves or our goods, outside help assists us. I will certainly never doubt the power of protection after Hurricane Lili.

The Energy Vultures

Your bubble is invaluable when you meet an energy vulture. It sounds horrific and conjures up a picture of a large vulture declaring attack, but in a sense, that's what happens. Energy vultures are people you meet in everyday life who literally take the energy from your body.

You must know some of these vultures or energy vampires, as some mediums call them. Most of us at one time have unwittingly fallen prey to a psychic vampire but didn't realise until too late that our energy had been pinched! Psychic vampires do not suck your blood, but they do syphon much-needed positive energy from your body. Sometimes it can be a chance encounter, when you meet someone in the street or at a party, but worse, it can be a member of your family, in-laws, or a work colleague. These vultures crop up in all sorts of places and hit when you least expect it, so how do you know when you've been a target? The usual sign is feeling emotionally drained for no apparent reason, but if your immune system is strong, you will bounce back quickly and probably forget the incident.

You may wonder why these vampires feel the need to steal your energy. The most common reason is that they are people who constantly feel inadequate and lack self-worth. Receiving a boost of good positive energy has the short-term effect of giving them a great surge of powerful energy. These are the people who are keen to have your company, and when you leave them, you feel absolutely drained of energy and you don't realise they are blatantly taking your energy. Some vampires themselves don't realise they are taking your energy, All they know is that they feel great after they have been in your company, so it's no wonder they are keen to be with you.

Because they get only a temporary lift, they soon drop down again to being their normal abysmal self, and it's time to look for another victim. If you regularly meet one of these energy-stealing vampires, either at home or work, then it is important to take precautions.

You must place a cloak of protection of your choice around yourself when you know you will be meeting an energy vampire. If it is an unexpected meeting, then quickly put a protective light around your aura. It does not matter whether you use a white or golden light, just enter a bubble of light, a ball of light, or visualise a solid wall of light between yourself and the vampire. In the end, it's all about positive thought and intent, so you will be protected whatever method you choose.

Another alternative is to programme a crystal to give you protection. Simply hold the crystal in your hand, mentally run a white light through the crystal to cleanse it of any negative energy, and then ask the crystal to please protect your aura from psychic vampires. Perhaps the biggest problem about recognising someone as a psychic vampire is that they appear to be perfectly normal and friendly people. Not surprisingly, the existence of psychic vampires is not yet accepted by many people, but in recent years I have been assured by several psychologists and hypnotherapists that there are vast numbers of these energy thieves among us, in many different forms. Dr. Joe H. Slate states in his book *Psychic Vampires*[1] that the American Psychological Association's recommended reading list for psychologists includes books on spiritualism. Many psychologists treat people with vampire symptoms or psychic attachments and find the ability to recognise and diagnose these problems helps to successfully speed up the treatment. A good friend of mine who is a psychotherapist has often told me how, by working with the spirit world, he is guided to ask the right questions and find the correct solutions.

I am often asked if psychic vampires are evil. The answer is no, as most of these energy predators are probably not even aware they are helping themselves to your much-needed energy. Another question often asked is if you need to be psychic to be a psychic vampire, but these individuals seldom have psychic or spiritual gifts and do not need to have supernatural powers, as they instinctively recognise people with good energy.

I have a couple of friends who belong in this group, so I have to wear my protection when we get together and I require a psychic bath to cleanse my energy field when I get home. If you have friends who exasperate or exhaust you, or who always succeed in depleting your energy, then think "protection." We all know people in this group—when we see them coming we think "Oh, no, how can I avoid being caught in a long conversation?"

Do not let people burden you with their troubles. Being sympathetic to someone who has family or work problems or has been bereaved is good, but avoid those who always want to tell you their problems. Have you ever noticed that they don't ask how you are feeling? All they want to do is talk about themselves. People in this group will keep you listening on the phone for an hour, talking about their day, or sit chatting over coffee for a couple of hours, without ever enquiring about how life is treating you.

Isn't it odd that this situation can go on for some time before one day it dawns on you that the person is really selfish by taking your energy and your time? Energy interaction is very subtle and the transfer of energy is a process that goes on quietly.

I experienced an example of leaching of my energy when I went to offer healing at a group meeting. After all the people waiting for healing had been treated, a young man came across to me and offered me healing. As I wanted to encourage his healing gift, I happily accepted, and sat down to enjoy the peaceful experience, but this was not to be!

This young man was a powerful vulture and I first began to feel uneasy when he commented that my energy was wonderful and very powerful. As the session progressed, I started to feel nauseated and faint, and certainly did not feel the presence of healing energy. I have been giving and receiving healing for many years and in all that time had never experienced a healer who was an energy thief. I asked him where he had learned to heal and he said he was self-taught, and had come up with this wonderful system of pulling out what he thought was negative energy from the person, to make her or him well. This technique may work on patients who are full of negativity, but what he was doing was pulling all my good positive energy from my body, picking it up to the extent that I was so weak I could hardly stand up.

I had put a cloak of protection around myself but as I had allowed him into my aura, I was in trouble. The upshot was that I then had to have a full session of healing from a friend to rebalance my energies, and an instant cleansing was needed. Afterward I felt angry with myself for being so stupid as to put myself in this situation, but perhaps it was a lesson to remind me that energy vultures do exist.

Are you, like me, sensitive to energies, and know instantly on entering a room if there has been anger, or if strong emotion is present? Are you quick to pick up people's feelings, and thoughts? Then, unless you are well protected, you are quite liable to absorb the negative emotions in a room or from a person.

If you fall into this category, think "protection" to remind yourself to put on your cloak each day. Do you know anyone who is psychic, but not well earthed—whose feet are not firmly on the ground as they are a dreamer? There are lots of these nice people around who float about, loving everyone, but who are living in a daydream.

Being Well Grounded Is a Must

This group, who are often new to the spiritual pathway, are vulnerable every time they walk out of their front door, so protection for them, and from them is a must. They've probably read some books or attended a few New Age workshops, but nobody has taught them the importance of being earthed and wearing protection, so they don't appreciate the necessity of regularly protecting or cleansing the energy field and being grounded.

What exactly does being well grounded mean? It means having a strong connection with the Earth. It is very important to be grounded when doing any spiritual work, particularly so when doing any form of rescue work. We are all born with an invisible link to the Earth, which runs from our Creator down through our bodies and into the Earth. This invisible link creates a balance of positive energy from the universe with the negative energy of the Earth.

There are two groups of people who don't have a good strong link with the Earth. The first are those who have been exposed to geopathic energy, powerful electromagnetic fields, or other negative energies. These people will often feel detached and distant, and complain of looking at jobs awaiting their attention, but they can't gather momentum to tackle the work, whether in the office or home, and are able to make only a half-hearted effort. They don't realise there is an energy link problem and assume their lethargic feeling is due to diet, pressure of work, or worry.

This is not the problem and for this group, the remedy is simple. Sit down and relax, then visualise a beam of White Light traveling down through your body, from the top of your head, through your feet and deep into the ground, where it sends out strong roots.

People who are sleeping over geopathic stress will find the problem returns until the ground has been cleared of GS. By moving your bed to another part of the room you can often move away from the GS line, but if there are several lines in the room you will need the assistance of an energy consultant.

The other group of people who often don't have a powerful Earth link are those dreamy, artistic, or vague people who seem to float along on a cloud. They should not do any spiritual work until they have strengthened their Earth link. They should make a strong effort to feel the ground under their feet, and visualise deep roots traveling far into the soil.

Learning to control their breathing helps to establish balance, so slow deep-breathing exercises are beneficial.

When doing rescue work you are in the driving seat, and you must be in command of the situation, otherwise you cannot hope to send powerful energy to help those stranded souls homeward. Doing this work can often mean dealing with sad and sickening events, so it's important that you are emotionally strong and your energy is rock steady. This also applies to everyone who does healing or other therapies.

Another alternative to pulling a White Light down through your body is to visualise an energy beam that connects you to your Creator. We are all connected to the universal energy by an invisible link, so when it is accidentally severed, you should visualise this energy beam, coming down through your head and body and deep into Mother Earth. Any time you feel a bit lightheaded or distant, pull this beam down. It is worth getting into the habit of doing this trick, as it's a quick way to help you remain well grounded.

If you have any relatives or friends whom you suspect may suffer from a weakened link, then you can dowse to confirm if they need to be more grounded, and if so, you can explain to them how to renew this important contact.

Grounding yourself is particularly important if you live or work in a high-rise block of flats and are several floors above ground level. Also, people whose bedroom is above a garage may need grounding, as there is an energy void below the room. A room above a garage is considered bad feng shui, as the room is not linked to the Earth; plus, if a car is parked in the garage, the negative energy from the metal mass will rise to the room above. In this type of room, you must visualise strong roots grounding through the floor of the bedroom, right down through the garage and deep into the ground. The same situation arises with flats built over an archway.

Do you find visualising an impossible skill? Then don't worry if you cannot see or feel the energy flowing through your body, as the power of your positive thought will make it work in spite of your difficulty. Perhaps you may find it easier to visualise yourself as a large tree with roots going into the ground. Experiment and find what feels right for you—the only thing that matters is to be grounded. Whichever method you use is unimportant, as the main thing is to be aware of the importance of being grounded at all times.

How to Cleanse Your Energies and Aura

Methods of cleansing the body's energy are many and varied, so take your choice!

Whichever way you choose to use White Light to cleanse, it will be effective. One useful and very quick way to cleanse your energies is to pull a beam of White Light down through the crown of your head, right through your body and out through your feet, into the ground. I do this quick exercise after I have given a patient healing, and after I have been in the company of anyone who is negative or stressed. It is done in a matter of seconds, so is a quick tool for an instant cleansing when there is no time to do a thorough one. One good thing about this exercise is that it can be done when you are standing or walking, as you do not need to sit down and concentrate.

Water—The Natural Cleanser

See yourself standing under a waterfall with the fresh water cascading down around you, and feel the fresh water cleanse your body and your aura. This method of cleansing your aura only takes a few seconds and can be done while standing in the supermarket, on public transport, or anywhere you feel your aura needs a quick cleanse, so be different—have a quick shower in the supermarket.

The Seven Breaths Exercise

There are times when you feel that your body's energies could do with a good spiritual bath, and for this treatment I recommend the "Seven Breaths" exercise. I was taught this method of cleansing the aura at a healing workshop, and use this tool when I feel that my energies need a good cleansing. The seven breaths is a particularly good exercise, if you have been doing rescue work with the black side, or been in a building where energy was heavy, or with people who were full of negativity. It's a tool for those times when you instinctively know your energies need a thorough spring cleaning.

Start by sitting quietly and taking a few deep breaths to relax, then take a very deep breath in, and on the inward breath visualise the breath sweeping up outside the front of your body from the ground, to the top of your head, then on the outward breath you see it sweeping the back of your body, from your head to the ground. Then repeat the breath, but this time take it from your feet, sweeping the aura on one side of your body, up to your head on the in breath, and on the out breath, you sweep the other side of the body. This exercise is repeated seven times for the back and front of your body and seven times for the sides of the body. Each time you start a new breath, you take it further from your body, so the aura is being swept clean for a distance from your body.

To summarise, your first breath is swept up close to your body and each successive one is taken further away, so you can see your energy being swept clean several yards' from your body. Remember the aura can extend several yards distance from your body, so giving the entire energy field a good bath is a treat for your body. When you have finished this exercise, relax and have a big stretch, and you'll be amazed how energised you feel.

The Power of Affirmation and Prayer

Saying an affirmation of protection with intent and positive thought will ensure it is effective. It does not matter what words you use in your affirmation—it is the saying it that is important. Something along the lines of the following words is ideal: *"Only positive energy can ever penetrate my protective shield as it protects me from negative energy and psychic attack."*

The Lord's Prayer is a very effective and powerful prayer, or you may prefer to say a verse of a favourite psalm. There are several psalms whose words offer the Lord's protection. It is a matter of choosing what feels right for you, so don't worry if others in your circle are using other methods of protection.

Energy Cleansing Tools and Methods

Smudge Sticks—A Fun Tool to Cleanse Energies

Several Eastern customs that help give the energies of a room a spring cleaning are becoming popular in the West. One of these is the use of a smudge stick, a favourite with the Shaman, which gives off a wonderful aroma and is similar to incense. I was first introduced to using a smudge stick (sage brush) many years ago at a Native American Indian group who met nearby.

I was completely ignorant of smudge sticks, and watched with interest and amusement as people took the stick and swept it around their body, from the ground up to the head and down the back of the body, then each side was cleansed. This method has become popular today, as it is one of the tools used by many feng shui consultants to cleanse the energy of houses, and is particularly good at lifting negative energy from corners. Smudge sticks can be found in many New Age shops and are fun to use and kids love them. It's a quick and effective way to lift the energies in a room after your lodger has moved out, or after a broken marriage. The sage brush is also beneficial when anyone in your home suffers from depression, frustration, anger, or is very unhappy, as it clears the heavy energy, and gives them a lift.

Try Clapping—It Breaks Up Negative Energy

Space clearing of all invisible energies has been an accepted practice in the East for many centuries and is always used to clear any negativity in a new home that may have been left by the previous owner or tenant. If your husband complains of the smell of the smudge stick, then perhaps you should try the "clapping trick." It doesn't leave any evidence.

A popular Eastern treatment of negative energy, clapping is fun and can involve the family, as children love to clap. You walk around each room in the building and clap close to the walls, starting at floor level and working up to the ceiling. The sound will rapidly lift negative energy (Sha) in the room, particularly in dark corners, and the great benefit of this tool is that it is fun and completely free.

Clapping can also be done around your body to remove unwanted negativity, so if you think a member of your family may have an attachment, then a hearty session of clapping will often move the minor entity on its way.

Have a Good Shake

Another fun way to cleanse your energy field is to have a good shake. Do you remember the childhood game when you danced in a circle and put your left leg or arm in the circle and gave it a good shake, and ended with great giggles as you put your whole self in, shook it a little, and turned yourself about? This was a great birthday party game and we were too young to realise the practical implications of a good shake, as we were far too busy enjoying ourselves.

When you shake your body, either a little or a lot, you dislodge negative energy that may be stuck on your body, so giving your body a regular shake is a great habit to acquire. It's a bit like having an energy bath, as it removes both stale energy and negativity that may have been picked up from passersby in the shopping centre or bus. There is nothing New Age or spooky about giving yourself a good shake. How often have you seen your dog enjoy a good shake?

A Good Stretch Dislodges Stuck Energy

Watch how often your cat or dog has a good stretch. Regularly giving your body a good stretch gets the energy flowing and gets rid of stuck energy. It helps your physical health and stops energies from becoming stagnant, which can happen when you spend too much time sitting in an armchair or lazing in bed. A good stretch will stimulate your metabolism and shake off unwanted negative energy, so follow your pet's example—we can learn a lot from our four-legged friends.

Your Candles Can Cleanse

Candles are a user-friendly tool to lift energies in a room, and come in a wonderful range of colours, shapes, and scents. It does not matter which colour candle you burn—by lighting the candle with the intention that it will lift the room's energy, the power of intent will make it happen. Don't go dashing out to buy pretty candles because you only have uninteresting white ones in the larder—save your money, as they will be just as effective as more ornamental ones.

Cleanse with an Incense Stick

Incense sticks are also delightful tools to cleanse the energy of a room, as they give off a relaxing fragrance that lingers, but again it is all about positive thought, lighting the incense stick with the intention will make the energies lighter. If anyone complains of this Eastern aroma, then wind chimes may be the right tool for your home!

Wind Chimes Can Move Energy

Wind chimes are particularly useful where you want to keep energies flowing in a hall or long room and keep them from coming to a halt, as stagnating energy will make you feel tired and flat. It does not matter what sort of chimes you hang, or what colour, size, or sound. These little chimes moving in a draft or breeze will stop all energy from becoming stuck in a room and around you. Any area where the energy feels sluggish and heavy will benefit from having a set of wind chimes, as their tinkling sound lifts the energy vibration. Don't worry if you are not sure where to hang them; ask mentally and you will be guided to the correct place to hang them.

Many teenagers buy wind chimes today to decorate their bedrooms without realising they offer beneficial gifts. Encourage any difficult child to have a wind chime in his or her room, as it will help to lift their moods. Why not invest in some delightfully dainty little bells, as used in feng shui? The bells lift the energy with their delicate sound, while always looking decorative.

Crystals—A Reliable Cleanser

Crystals are a very popular choice for protection and cleansing. They have very powerful energy, and can be used for cleansing either a room or a person. The secret is to programme the crystal to do the task you require. If you want your crystal to heal, protect, or cleanse, then hold the crystal in your hand, and mentally ask it to please cleanse your energy, or protect you from negative energy, etc.

There are a great many books on the different crystals and how to cleanse and programme them, and classes on crystals are being offered at many adult centres. Crystals are here to stay.

Should you decide to use a crystal for cleansing, please remember that crystals can absorb negativity and so it's important to cleanse them regularly to keep their energy clean. A quick way to cleanse your crystal is to soak it overnight in a cup of water and sea salt, or leave it outside on the windowsill in the moonlight. Even a new crystal needs to be cleansed as it will have picked up negative energy from people handling it in the shop where it was purchased.

Hang a crystal in the window to clear energies coming from a building opposite yours. If the room gets sunshine at any time of the day, enjoy the beautiful colours when the sunlight catches the crystal. An added bonus is that this effect is auspicious and beneficial to the energies in the room.

Crystals are made from a combination of silicone dioxide and water, and have the ability to vibrate at a very high frequency. Crystals always grow in a north/south direction, so their energies are running parallel to the poles.

Crystals originate in Nature and come from the bowels of the Earth. They are thrown out of molten rock, which then solidifies over a period of time, so crystals are part of the wonderful cycle of Mother Earth. All crystals have a different energy vibration so they are individuals, and for this reason it is important to buy the crystal you are drawn to, rather than one someone recommends. You will find that some crystals feel more friendly than others and there will always be one that feels as though it belongs to you. It will work well with you because its vibration is compatible to your energy vibration.

The Power of Sea Salt

The three most powerful tools in the world to clear negativity have been given to us by our Creator. One is the White Light that I have been talking about, the second is positive thought, and the third is sea salt, which is the oldest natural element known to man. When sea salt is combined with positive thought, it is a tool never to be underestimated.

Sea salt will disperse negative energy in either a person or a place. By visualising yourself sprinkling sea salt over a friend or relative whom you feel is full of negative energy, you will clear much of this unwanted energy from them. Unfortunately, if they are not protected, they will collect more negative energy when they are exposed to it.

The same applies to a building. Simply visualising yourself sprinkling sea salt over the building, with the thought that it will clear negative energies, guarantees it will work, although not on a permanent basis. The combination of sea salt and positive thought can be used on a much larger scale than our daily problems, as this tool is effective in countries at war.

By mentally seeing a country at war and sprinkling sea salt over the troubled land, you will help to disperse the negative energy, which is always present in war zones, as a blanket of dark energy hanging over war torn countries. Why not write sea salt on a postcard and prop it up in the kitchen, so that when it catches your eye, you can mentally sprinkle some sea salt over a country where fighting is in progress?

There are plenty of countries to choose from, as there is a lot of unrest in the world at the present time. You have nothing to lose by doing this little exercise—only takes a few seconds and a lot of people will benefit. It will help reduce the negative thoughts that fuel hatred in the part of the world that you are concerned with, so get sprinkling.

Sea salt can also be used as a tool to rescue earthbound spirits, so if you know of anyone who has recently died who was a strong disbeliever in an afterlife, and therefore liable to become earthbound, think of them and mentally sprinkle them with sea salt to disperse their negative thoughts and speed up their journey home.

Clearing the Clutter

Negative energy in your home can often be caused by clutter. Having a really big clearout of clutter frees the stuck energies and lets them flow, and I guarantee you will feel good after you've done the deed. Don't attempt to clear out things when you are feeling tired and flat, though, as you will find yourself lifting things out of the wardrobe or out of the cupboards, having a look at them and putting them back. Wait until you are in a positive mood, then it's all stations go. Take a realistic look at the contents of cupboards, and ask yourself if the space is more valuable than what it contains now. Get rid of things you have not used for years or clothes that are too tight, or out of fashion. It's so easy to think "I paid a lot for it so I will keep it," or else "I'll keep it in case I lose weight." Get rid of it, as it creates negative thoughts every time you remember that you are overweight!

My method of clearing out clothes is, I look at them and think "Would I like to meet a handsome man while wearing this?" If I know I would not like to be seen by anyone whose opinion matters, then out it goes. Clothes that stay in the wardrobe and are never worn collect negativity and smell dusty when you eventually inspect them, so get clearing. Charities shops are always grateful for your old clothes and knicknacks. The interesting fact is that I have never missed anything I cleared out and if asked a few days later, I would have great difficulty remembering what I had offloaded.

I find it helpful to keep a box in the garage for unwanted items. Each time I unearth an item I don't like or want, it goes in the box in the garage, until some kind soul comes collecting jumble or I take it to a local animal charity.

Emotional Clutter—More Fuel for Negativity

As well as material clutter, most of us carry around a lot of unwanted emotional clutter, which builds negative energy.

Do you have negative childhood memories from the past—perhaps schoolmates who called you names at primary school, a teacher who was unfair, or someone who stole your favourite pencil? Adult life brings lots of negative experiences: unfairness at work, a problem partner or flatmate, idle gossip, divorce, bereavement, or being discarded by the love of your life on your eighteenth birthday. The body is like a bucket—from the day you are born it holds all of life's experiences. Some experiences take up a lot of space in the bucket and it can almost overflow.

That's when it's very important to off-load some of the debris collected on life's pathway, as there's no advantage to carrying all this negative energy from these experiences around in your daily life. You will be amazed how much lighter you feel when your bucket has been emptied. This is particularly good for anyone who suffers depression or lack of self-esteem.

How do you empty your bucket? It's simple! Use a large ruled pad, and for three days leave it on the dining table or in your bedroom and start to write a list of everything negative you can remember that has happened to you in your life, from early childhood right up to today.

Once the emotional door is open, you will be amazed at the things you remember that you had completely forgotten about—little incidents that now, looking back, seem unimportant, but about which you remember at the time being upset or indignant. Now that the safety catch has been released, you will be quite astounded at the things you remember. By the third day you will have a great long list of events you are ready to discard and forget. Should any forgotten fact bubble to the surface that you feel is creating an emotional problem, this is the time to say good bye to hurt or sadness. It's time to have a final look at the list, mentally ask your Creator to take it all away, then strike a match and burn the list, so the clutter is gone forever from your life. Don't be surprised if you feel like jumping for joy. Don't worry that you will bring to the surface any issues that you cannot dismiss without causing emotional upset. The subconscious mind will usually only allow minor incidents that are taking up valuable space to come to the surface.

Another exercise that releases negative energy—this time caused by carrying guilty memories—is also much needed by most of us. We have all done things we later regretted. Although your crime was very minor and when you think about it, you probably laugh, because compared with today's violence, it seems unimportant, but you are still carrying the guilt of those years ago, so you must let go.

Like the previous exercise, write down the events you remember when you said something you knew was wrong, or things you should not have done. Your list will probably be very short, but it's surprising what bubbles to the surface over three days. When the list is complete, again ask the Creator to forgive you and to please take it away, then burn the list. Your bucket is now very empty and feels very light, as a lot of negative energy has been removed from your body. Having cleared your body, now it's time to look closely at your home and workplace.

Recognising Positive and Negative Energies

Energy is the source of absolutely everything in the entire universe in which we live a life in our material body. As you well know, it was all that existed at the beginning of time.

We are all made of energy and matter, which is a by-product of energy, so every living thing and every material object is energy and matter. Although the energy is completely invisible to our eye, it surrounds all of us all of the time—the main reason it is so important to keep our energy cleansed and balanced.

Our bodies are surrounded by several different energies: electromagnetic, magnetic, electrical, sub-atomic, and atomic. Some of these fields have a negative effect on us. Energy comes in many different frequencies, including light, sound, music, vibration, and our all-important brain waves are influenced by these frequencies. It's almost impossible for those of us who are not scientists to comprehend this energy frequency, which is everywhere. As well as surrounding all of us on Earth, this energy surrounds all those who have passed to spirit. Our human body is a very sensitive instrument and is accurately tuned into several different frequencies, so it is important that these are not disrupted, otherwise health problems occur.

Our eyes are tuned into the light energy input and are quick to warn us when the frequency is wrong. Our sense of smell relies on our nose and warns us of powerful energy from rotten food, gas, and other harmful smells. Our ears are tuned into sound, warning us when the sound vibration is wrong, and the human brain is a very important frequency as it sends messages to the organs in the body. The body is a highly sensitive and extremely intricate piece of natural machinery and is designed to enable us to tune into the invisible world on the other side of the veil.

Being aware of the importance of energy helps to keep you healthy and relaxed. Because every piece of furniture in our home is energy, it is important to maintain balance. If you sleep in a bed inherited from a deceased parent who suffered from serious illness, or perhaps the bed was given to you by a friend, or you bought it second-hand, then there's a strong chance that the energy of the bed badly needs cleansing of negativity. Check the energy of your bed—it is important to ensure it is positive as we spend roughly one third of our lives in our beds. The energy has a strong influence on our health and energy levels.

The same applies to a second-hand chair, table, or ornaments. They all hold the energy of the previous owner, so if you are a keen collector of antiques, it's time for a cleansing. In addition to cleansing any negativity clinging to our bodies from other people or places, we also need to clear negative energy collected from these natural and man-made energy fields.

Hotel Bedrooms

Are you a keen traveler? Do you regularly stay in hotels on business or pleasure? Then make a point of cleansing the bed in each hotel bedroom as it has been used by hundreds of people, and many of them will have had problems.

Some will be staying there to attend a funeral, others may be salesmen who have lost an important contract or are having an illicit affair. Lots of people using the rooms will be happy and well balanced, but as the bed holds energy from each of the hundreds of users, there will most certainly be enough negativity to justify a quick cleansing treatment. The other problem with hotels is that bedrooms are often off long corridors and as negative energy flows fast down the corridor, good energy does not enter the bedrooms.

Another problem with energy in hotel bedrooms is that the fire energy may be missing if the colours are pastel. If the window faces the door, any positive energy entering the room will go straight out of the window instead of circulating around the room. To a certain extent, the same problem applies to bedrooms in holiday cottages, caravans, cabins on a cruise liner, and other accommodations, so wherever you stay, think "cleanse," and protect your aura. If you are traveling by train, cleansing is a must.

Trains—Second-Hand Radiation

Some of us are more sensitive to negative energy than others, but most of us will admit we dread the person sitting down next to us on the train who proceeds to switch on his mobile phone and settles down to make a list of business calls.

Mobile phones give off electromagnetic energy, which is a negative energy and travels several feet in all directions from the phone, so affecting other passengers. Research done at Tohuku University in Japan has shown the EMFs from a mobile phone bounce off the metal structure of the train carriage. To add to the hazard, the windows are invariably closed, so the rays have nowhere to go, and keep bouncing off the carriage until they land on a passenger. The research also showed that electromagnetic energy from laptop computers behaves in the same manner

(Don Maisch. *EM Facts*),[2] so if you travel by train or bus and mobile phones are in use, remember your protection.

It's a good idea to get into the habit of thinking "protection" before boarding any public transport, as quite apart from the negativity from EMFs, there's also the chance you could easily sit beside someone who is feeling very negative because of a family dispute or work problems, and some of this negativity could land on your aura.

Your Aura

Some people talk about the aura as though it is simply some beautiful mystical rainbow of colour surrounding the head and shoulders of each one of us, and only seen by a chosen few! There's a lot more to the aura than many people realise, as this energy field has the ability to give away many of our secrets.

This special energy field is a well-designed interaction between every single feeling we experience, so whether our emotions are mental, physical, or spiritual, it all affects the colours and shape of the aura. Not only does this energy field surround all humans, it is also seen around all living things, whether an animal, bird, or plant, and is also seen around all solid material, so every piece of furniture, fittings, jewelry, etc., has an energy field. When people refer to their aura, it can sound a bit New Age, but there is no mystique about the aura. You couldn't live without it.

The aura is simply a force-field comprising several layers of energy mixed with esoteric substances, which is the body's protective shield against intrusion, so protecting it is essential. Always remember that these energy layers show your emotional state of health, as well as your unsuspected physical ones, since all health problems start in the aura, before being found in the body. This rainbow of colour gives an instant picture of any illness, which often shows as a fissure or jagged break when we have had an accident in the past.

The aura is an efficient piece of energy engineering, a complex energy field that shows all the day-to-day changes in our health.

When a person's health is unstable, the colours in the aura register the problem—instead of the aura being bright and evenly balanced, its colours will become dull. If doctors today had the ability to see the aura, it would make diagnosing problems easier and much more accurate. Of course they could always use Kirlian photography equipment.

Have you ever felt the presence of anyone when they were in your aura? Most of us have experienced a moment when we sense that someone is standing close behind us. You are unaware of their presence, and yet you know someone is there, although you cannot see or hear them. Your aura is a supersensitive, invisible energy field that acts as a protective shield, warning you what's going on around you, and it is the reason why you can sense when someone is standing behind you or a spirit is nearby.

As the aura is our Earth energy field, it's the energy that surrounds our bodies during this lifetime and is part of us in the moment. It is a combination of electromagnetic energy, our physical energy, and our sensitivity. When the aura is invaded, whether by a person standing too close to the body or if a negative spirit is present, you will get a warning bell ringing, as your aura warns you it is being invaded.

What Size Is the Aura?

The auric field is an area of pure energy and, when healthy, is free of all negative content, which makes it supersensitive to energy changes like intrusion. It warns you when a negative person or building is draining your energy, and when you enter an old church or place of great beauty and tranquillity, your energy field immediately picks up this uplifting energy and gives your body a sense of well being.

The size varies a great deal in depth, from person to person and from minute to minute, as this energy field is affected by feelings of anger, fear, misery, depression, joy, love, and exhilaration. The aura of the average person can range in size from a few inches to a couple of yards from the body. Although the aura of all humans is constantly changing in shape and colour, the aura of non-living material does not change, as the health and energy level of material things does not usually alter.

What Shape Is the Aura?

This rainbow-effect energy should flow in a smooth outline and follow the lines of the body when a person is healthy. When a person is physically or mentally ill, or on drugs or alcohol, it reflects on the aura, which then appears to have jagged edges with sharp dips in the outline shape. That's a sure sign of trouble, as energy cannot circulate smoothly around a jagged energy field.

Does Your Aura Leak?

A leaky aura, as the name suggests, is an auric field with gaps and cracks. These must be sealed, as gaps can allow some of the body's vital energy to leak out, or if a negative entity is attached, then the energy is drawn out intentionally. A gap in the aura will allow an uninvited negative entity to enter your body, so the shape and condition of your energy field is important, as this energy is the mirror of the body, which shows the true state of your health.

Colours of the Aura

The colours of the aura vary as every person has their individual field, and colours change depending on your state of health. Some books describe different meanings of the colours, so don't take the meaning of each colour too literally. *The all-important fact is that your aura should contain light and bright colours.*

YELLOW, which is the intellectual colour, also suggests peace within, and shows in most people's aura.

LAVENDER and shades of PURPLE are very spiritual colours and show strongly in the aura of those people who are on a spiritual pathway.

RED predominating in the aura indicates a person who often holds a lot of anger. This can be an inner anger that badly needs to be released, but red is also the colour of a very passionate person, who is often very materialistic.

ORANGE is a very spiritual colour, and usually suggests a strong person who can lead or take control, a positive person.

PINK, as you can guess, is the colour of love, so when pink shows in the aura, this person has a great deal of love to give to everyone.

WHITE in an aura does not suggest purity. This is an unhealthy non-colour, and shows up when there is lack of harmony in the body,

BLUE is a great colour to have in the aura as its one of Nature's colours, found in the sky, and is the sign of a stable person with a quiet, peaceful mind. When the blue is a more TURQUOISE colour, it suggests strength, stability, and a person who is a great organiser.

GREY/BLACK suggests a person with dark thoughts, perhaps prone to depression, or the presence of a negative entity.

Meditation is a great tool to improve a dull aura, as it stills the mind and gives the body help to heal itself. Again, please don't take these colour descriptions too literally, as their meaning can vary considerably, depending on shape, depth, and so forth.

Different aura readers will often have their own interpretation of colours, so do not be too influenced by what you are told about the colours of your aura. The all-important thing to remember is to keep your aura clean and bright. There is no such thing as a perfect aura, as everyone's aura is individual to that person, so don't be too impressed when people talk about their wonderful aura.

Seeing the Aura

Seeing auras is nothing new—they've been seen by certain people for many centuries. Old paintings of religious leaders like Jesus, Buddha, and others often feature a glowing halo of beautiful light, either around the figures or above their heads. Carbon-dated paintings, found in ancient caves, have also depicted figures with a halo or bright energy. To see an aura may take a bit of perseverance, unless you have a gift, so try taking your eyes into "daydream mode" while looking at a person. This way they are almost out of focus and the optic nerve is relaxed and free from tension.

An alternative way is to fix your gaze steadily on a person for several minutes with your eyes relaxed. It's a case of experimenting until you find a way that works for you. It is usually easier to see auras when in a room with other healers or spiritual people, as there is a high level of spiritual energy present to help you. One easy way to see what your aura looks like is to have a Kirlian photograph done of your aura. It's quick and painless!

Kirlian Photography of the Aura

It is impossible to hide your faults or health problems from anyone who is an experienced Kirlian photograph aura reader, as the facts are there for every reader to see—you have no secrets. You cannot fake your aura. It's an energy map of the body, showing the state of your health and any spirits or entities in your energy field.

Spirits Can Glide Through Your Aura!

Having Kirlian photography of your aura is an excellent way of confirming if you have an entity on board, as it will show up as a black blob in your aura. It is easy for a spirit or entity to join your aura as they can penetrate everything except White Light. Spirits are energy—they can glide through your aura with ease, just as they can also travel through buildings, doors, etc. The only thing that will deter them from going somewhere is powerful White Light or positive energy. Devious earthbound spirits or parasites can travel through all seven layers of a damaged aura, because when the immune system is low, the human physical vibration is not strong enough to act as a reliable safety barrier against the energy vibration of a very determined spirit. For this reason it is vital to keep your aura cleansed and well protected at all times. If you're in any doubt that your aura has been invaded, it's time to visit a Kirlian photographer.

Kirlian photography is a form of photography that can photograph a person's aura or biofields. It was invented by a Russian scientist nearly sixty years ago, and was a follow-up to the electrography photography of the late 1800s.

Today, thanks to the ingenuity of British scientist, Harry Oldfield,[3] who invented a PIP scan camera, which takes colour photographs of the entire body's energy, organs, and auric field, it's now possible to have a colour photograph of your aura, showing any energy blockages in the body. This fascinating photograph is a form of x-ray, which shows the organs and tissue of the body, but not the skeleton. The amazing photograph shows clearly where any energy blockages are present, so pinpoints any health problems before you are aware of them. The energy will show up as a bright red area wherever there is any inflammation in your body.

Although Harry Oldfield is based in England, he has a school where therapists of many nationalities are trained to use the PIP Scan, so this amazing scan is available in several countries around the world.

Have you ever visited a psychic fair and seen a Kirlian photography stand? These offer an instant photograph of your aura, which can be useful in confirming any of your suspicions that you have a health or energy problem. It's an interesting and fun thing to do and is always a good talking point, as family and friends are often keen to hear the explanation of this strange picture.

The Kirlian photography trade is doing a wonderful job of creating awareness of the importance of keeping the aura healthy, as we all need reminding to cleanse this energy field, particularly if you have a busy life. If you are concerned about your aura, you can ask a friend to dowse it to check for problems.

Dowsing—A Useful Tool

Have you discovered the wonderful world of dowsing? It's an invaluable gift given to us by our Creator, so most of us are able to dowse, and when you have learned about this skill, you'll wonder how you ever got on without its assistance. I can hear you thinking "Why are so few people aware of it?"

Dowsing Can Save Lives

If you ask the average person on the street the question: "What is dowsing?" they'd probably scratch their head and say "My friend's mother held a needle over her tummy to find the sex of the baby," so that gem of information, plus the fact that some people know farmers use it to find water, is the extent of many people's knowledge. This is your opportunity to learn to dowse and it will open up a whole new field of interest and can keep the children amused for hours!

Before telling you how dowsing can be used in everyday life, and to detect earthbound spirits, entities, a badly balanced aura, or health problems, let me explain the history of this well-respected tool.

Dowsing has a long history. Drawings of dowsers carbon dated as eight thousands years old were found on the walls of the ancient Caves of Tasseli, situated in the foothills of the Atlas Mountains.

Dowsing is used in many countries, and even ministries of agriculture employ dowsers. In Russia, dowsers work from aeroplanes to find lead strip deposits located several hundred feet under the ground. Dowsing is such a popular tool in Russia that programmes about it are regularly shown on television at peak viewing times. Russian industry recognises it as an important tool for scientific study, and it is possible to obtain a post-graduate place. It will be many decades before we in the West ever see industry accepting the value of a dowser.[4] Russia has always been a forward-thinking country, leading the way in research into microwaves and electromagnetic fields.

For several centuries dowsing has been unpopular with certain religions, but sixty years ago the Roman Catholic church decreed that it accepted dowsing when it was used for God's work and not for self-gain. Obviously, it is impossible to use dowsing for self-gain, otherwise we would all win the lottery or make a fortune on betting.

Dowsing has been used by governments during wars for many decades. The British government even used dowsers in World War II to find unexploded mines with delayed action fuses. These lethal bombs had sunk deep into the ground, so dowsers did a wonderful job in saving lives. One very well-known dowser was based in Portsmouth—his brief was to detect unexploded magnetic mines and he succeeded in finding a number of these bombs, thus avoiding many more casualties.

The American government recognises the benefits of dowsing, and during the Vietnam War trained several groups of Marine personnel to dowse, enabling them to find Vietcong tunnels, unexploded booby traps, and valuable ammunition stores.[5]

How Does Dowsing Work?

Nobody really knows how dowsing works, but there are two very separate schools of thought on this subject.

When we dowse, we use the left side of our brain, the artistic side. Many dowsers, particularly those with a scientific or engineering background, firmly believe the skill is linked to a change in muscle response and brain rhythm.

It sounds plausible, but what triggers these unexplainable muscle responses? Any hypnotherapist will confirm that one side of the human brain is dominant, and when a question has been asked, the dominant side switches off and allows the alternative side to switch on, to answer the question. For those who need a technical explanation, this is the only one available.

Do you believe in life after death? Then the other explanation will perhaps be more acceptable to you, as many dowsers, including myself, believe strongly that the skill is linked with the world of spirit and that a helper in spirit is giving the correct answers. Whatever you believe, you must admit that dowsing does a superb job of helping us to reach the intangible.

Today modern technology has moved forward at such speed that most of us have lost touch with Nature and with our basic gifts. We are being blinkered and blinded by modern equipment and no longer use our gifts. For most people, learning to dowse is a few minutes' exercise, which, once mastered, is a free tool for use on all sorts of subjects.

Learning to Dowse

To dowse you can use either a pendulum or a pair of dowsing rods. For beginners, I recommend the pendulum, as it is easily transported in your pocket or purse, and is simple to use. You can use anything as a pendulum, as long as it is heavy enough to swing. A front door key on a piece of string, a pendant, or a crystal on a chain—literally anything that will swing—can be used, but if you decide you'd like to become a serious dowser, you can purchase either a wood, metal, or stone pendulum from any New Age shop. Before you start to use your pendulum, cleanse its energy by passing healing energy through it or holding it under running water. It is also important to place protection around you, and make it a rule always to put on protection before you dowse.

Finding Your Yes and No Sign

To enable you to dowse, you must establish your "Yes," "No," and "Don't Know" signs. To find the directions of your signs, you must ask the pendulum to show them to you. Hold the pendulum cord between your first finger and thumb, or if that's not comfortable, then between your middle finger and thumb, and you are now ready to dowse.

Before starting, many dowsers mentally say "It will only be used for good." Serious dowsers ask:

1. May I have permission to dowse? (It could be the wrong time or conditions.)

2. Do I have the ability to dowse?

At times your energy link can be blocked.[6] Once you have received permission to dowse, it's time to learn your signs.

You then mentally ask the pendulum three separate questions:

1. Please show me my "Yes" sign. This can be clockwise, anti-clockwise, or back and forward. Once you have established your "Yes" sign, it's time to find your "No" sign.

2. Once again, hold the pendulum and ask to be shown your "No" sign, which may be clockwise, counterclockwise, or back and for-

ward. Once this is known, repeat the exercise to learn your "Don't Know" sign.

3. Again hold the pendulum and ask to be shown your "Don't Know" sign. This is used if you ask a question to which you should not know the answer, or if you phrased it wrongly

Phrasing the question correctly is all-important, otherwise you get the wrong answer. You always have freedom of choice, so if you start a question by saying "Should I do this or that?" it's liable to give the "Don't Know" sign, as you have the choice of "this or that," and you should make the choice. So instead of saying "Should I take some iron tablets," you ask if your body is short of iron, or ask if your health will benefit from a course of iron. Dowsing is now taught at many adult centres, so if you would like to learn more about this fascinating subject, you can enroll in a class.

Using the Rods

If you prefer to use dowsing rods, they can be made from metal coat hangers, or bought from dowsing groups or New Age shops. Many dowsers make their own rods, either from tree branches or by cutting the handle end off metal coat hangers, so they are left with an L shape, while serious dowsers will make their rods from branches of hazel, apple, or birch trees.

Once you feel confident to use your new dowsing skills, you can find the answers to many questions or get information on a wide range of subjects. The tool is particularly useful for health, energy, or spiritual questions.

Some Uses for Dowsing

Dowsing can provide you with answers to many typical questions:

- Locate geopathic stress lines in your home.
- Check for electromagnetic field effects from overhead power lines, radar beams, etc.

- Check your food for harmful substances such as salmonella bacteria or organophosphates.

- Find trapped spirits or entities.

- Check your aura for entities or attachments, dents and jagged edges, or cracks, if it is leaking energy.

- Cleanse the aura and show you the "Yes" sign when it is cleansed.

- Confirm if an earthbound spirit is present.

- Establish the sex and age of the earthbound spirit, and establish year and cause of death, i.e. illness, accident, murder.

- Reason the earthbound spirit has remained here—if they want to take anything with them or if they're trapped in a band of negative energy.

- Establish the number of earthbound spirits on the site.

- Is the spirit lost? Does the spirit know how to get to the Light? Would they like your assistance to go to the Light?

- Find out if powerful negative energy is present in a room, or in a building, or if the building is sited on a negative ley line.

- Find a missing object by establishing where to look by a process of elimination. You can narrow a search down considerably by dividing a room or other space into four quarters, then ask which quarter contains the missing object.

- Ask if a mischievous spirit has hidden the missing object, being specific about colour, so that the wrong item is not searched for.

- Trace electrical or mechanical faults in an object, simply by writing down a list of possibilities and asking each one in turn.

Dowse for the Most Effective Treatment

Save money, time, and suffering by dowsing for the most suitable treatment of pain or physical ailments by asking individual questions to establish the cause, and then dowse for treatments such as physiotherapy, massage, acupuncture, or healing, etc.

Geopathic Stress—The Hidden Enemy

There are many things between heaven and earth that man cannot begin to comprehend—both dowsing and geopathic stress (GS) fall into this category. The Chinese were the first nation to accept the existence of this negative energy, calling it the Belly of the Dragon. Geopathic stress is a negative energy that rises from underground water and rock cracks several hundred feet under ground. It is responsible for many spirits being earthbound and also for many health complaints. These negative rays of energy rise in a thin line or a spiral and on their way to the earth's surface are contaminated by natural disturbances and distorted electromagnetic faults.

There are many streams and rivers running at different depths, deep underground, so it's possible to find several streams running under your home. There could be three lines running parallel, or two crossing one another. Above a crossing point is the worst possible place to sleep, as there is double strength negativity on this spot and it has a severe effect on the immune system.

You will be able to find crossing points with the aid of a pendulum or rods. Geopathic stress is found in many homes and doesn't seem to have a preference for any particular type of soil or building. These rays do not affect your health if you walk or stand over it for a few moments. They will only affect the health of those who are exposed for several hours each day or night. We spend roughly one third of our life in bed, so the presence of geopathic stress in the bedroom is bad news.

You are as likely to be affected by geopathic stress if you live on the tenth floor of a building, as you are when living on the ground floor, as these rays rise from the foundations of a building to the roof and will affect everyone on all floor levels who is sleeping over the line.

I have found over the past decade that everyone who has come to me for healing of an illness, other than injury from an accident, has been sleeping over geopathic stress. It is the most common cause of immune system damage and this prime factor is not often recognised by the medical profession. Usually when I have cleared this energy from a building there is an almost instant improvement in the health of the patient. If you waken in the morning feeling tired and lacking energy it may be a sign of GS.

Geopathic Stress and Trapped Spirits

During the many years I have been clearing geopathic stress from buildings, I have found a great many earthbound spirits are stuck in these buildings. Houses with several GS lines have powerful negative energy, so are often a favourite place for negative entities to reside. These entities prey on people with a damaged aura and because sleeping over GS rays can severely damage the aura, the entities are quick to move into their aura.

Geopathic stress has been accepted in many parts of Europe since the 1920s, but is still not accepted by medicine and science in either the UK or the USA. There are a very few good books available on geopathic stress, but I recommend Rolf Gordon at Dulwich Health's excellent book, *Are You Sleeping in a Safe Place?*[7] and *Earth Radiation* by Kathe Bachler.[8] Find out more about this subject, as it could be affecting the health of a member of your family or friend.

Do you ever enter a building and feel the energy heavy and cold? As well as sometimes being a sign of spirit presence, it is often a sign of geopathic stress or black ley lines. Most of us are completely unaware of what goes on under our home and we don't give the matter any thought. When you purchase a new home, you don't usually ask the builder or previous owner if there are underground streams deep under the building! There are enough problems in life above ground, so we don't consider the possibility that there could also be problems present under our home. Don't worry, geopathic stress does not come from local streams running under your home, it comes from those that are several hundred feet underground. When dowsing outdoors for GS, most dowsers prefer to use rods, as they are not so easily affected by the wind. For inside use, the pendulum is the favourite.

Ask the following questions:

1. Ask the pendulum if there is geopathic stress in your home.
2. Then ask if any member of your family is sleeping over it.

3. Do you work over a GS line (several hours each day at a computer or desk sited over GS could be harmful to health).

4. Ask the number of GS lines rising under your home, and if they cross under your bedroom.

5. If you are really interested in finding our more about GS, you can dowse to establish the depth underground, with the following questions: (a) Is there underground water flowing more than 50 metres below the foundations? (b) is there water flowing more than 100 metres below the building, etc.? By asking a series of questions, you can acquire information about any GS in your home.

6. Do you or your family constantly feel below par since living in your home? Then dowse to ask if there are any black ley lines under your home.

Mystical Ley Lines

There's lots of mystery and mystique about ley lines, but what exactly are ley lines? You often hear people say proudly "Oh, my house is built on a local ley line" but do they know anything about the history or source of these ley lines? Leys are energy lines, and can be either negative or positive. Many old churches were built on ley lines, to take advantage of their positive energy, proving that our predecessors had a much greater understanding of earth energies than we have today.

More and more knowledge is being unearthed about the history of leys, and although the definition is vague, an opinion held by many people is that they are lines of energy created by people many years ago, when they walked a route to church or to a village. Regular use of the track allowed positive energy to build up in the ground. Another school of thought says that ley lines are not manmade. They are natural energy lines linked to the universal energy grid and are an important part of the Earth's energy system. Leys are found in many parts of the world, and a network of these lines are known to crisscross Great Britain. An excellent book by Hamish Miller and Paul Broadhurst is *The Sun and the Serpent* (Pendragon Press).[9] It is the story of two years' research of the

St. Michael ley line, which runs across the South of England, from Norfolk to Somerset. Scotland has some fine examples of leys. If you want to travel, South America is well worth a visit, as there are many to be found in Mexico, Peru, Lima and Bolivia.

Awareness of ley lines was first recorded by Alfred Watson many decades ago. Interest in the subject has grown over the years and today you can attend workshops or adult centres to learn more about the history of leys.

Black ley lines should be avoided at all cost. As the name suggests, they are black negative energy and not a healthy place to stay. Should you find there is a black ley under your home, it's advisable to call on the services of an earth geomancer to clear the energies of the ley. Any dowsing society or group will be able to give you the name of a local expert.

Ley Lines and Trapped Spirits

Feng shui masters have great respect for underground energies and accept that many ghosts and earthbound spirits are drawn to these lines, where they are held by the negative energy. There are many stories of hauntings on highways and local folklore telling eerie tales of strange sightings on ley paths. These are not just local fairy stories, handed down the generations, as there are too many coincidences.

Almost identical stories are told in other countries of similar ghost sightings on leys by peasants who have not heard rumours about ghosts on leys. There will always be sceptics, and there will always be ghosts, but more of us are becoming aware that a ghost who is always seen in the same area is not a spirit come down to visit a relative, but is either a spirit who is earthbound or is a memory imprint of an event that happened in the past.

Summary

Psychic protection is all about protecting your aura and your space from intrusion. This can be something as simple as meeting a friend who offloads all his or her problems onto you and leaves you feeling drained of energy. Negative energy can pass to you from a person who has had a bad day standing next to you in the supermarket, as their negativity can cling to your aura.

You may believe that you don't need to consciously place any form of protection around you, thinking your guides and helpers will always protect you, but this is not the case. Guides will only protect you when you have asked them to do so, and even then they do not protect against everyday issues like negative energy clinging to your aura.

Whether you use a cloak of White Light, a steel shield, a bubble of Light or Gold Light, it is all an invaluable addition to your body's natural defence system and is effective, due to your intent and positive thought.

Whatever form of protection you use will work, as long as you never doubt its effectiveness. Remember you are in the driving seat, so you are in control of the protection of your aura and of ensuring it is kept clean. You do not know when you will be exposed to negative entities in a building, or to an earthbound spirit who is ready to alight on an unsuspecting body, so think "protection."

Your aura needs regular cleansing as well as protection, so get into the good habit of cleansing your aura everyday. It is important to cleanse it each time you have been in contact with anyone who has been very negative, or whom you feel has drained your energy. You will be amazed how much better you feel after your aura has had a bath, as you will feel rejuvenated and energised!

Each and every one of us is on a slightly different vibration and this sensitive vibration can often act as a protection against intruders, as a person whose aura vibrates on a high frequency is impervious to those negative earthbound spirits or entities from the lower Earth plane, as they are on a lower vibration. It is still better to be safe than sorry, so get into the habit of thinking "protection," as getting rid of an attachment is no easy matter.

You are responsible for looking after your aura, so get into the habit of checking your protection each morning and at bedtime, as protection is a good habit.

Notes

1. Joe H. Slate PhD. *Psychic Vampires.* Llewellyn Publications, 2004.

2. Don Maisch. EM Facts Consultancy. "Trains Trap Mobile Phone Radiation." *BBC Online Health,* May 1, 2002.

3. Harry Oldfield. Oldfield Systems Ltd.

4. Rodney Davies. *Discover Your Psychic Power.* Aquarian/Thorson.

5. Christopher Bird, "Divining." *The Observer* for US forces 13.3.67.

6. T. Edward Ross and Richard D. Wright. *The Divining Mind: A Guide to Dowsing and Self Development.*

7. Rolf Gordon. Dulwich Health, London. *Are You Sleeping in a Safe Place.*

8. Kathe Bachler. *Earth Radiation.* Wordmaster Ltd.

9. Hamish Miller and Paul Broadhurst. *The Sun and the Serpent.* Pendragon Press.

chapter nine

Negative Entities Galore/Exorcism

●

Do you ever hear words of communications that you sense come from a guardian angel or guide? Beware, as the dark side is very cunning and devious, and is always looking for an opportunity to enter our thoughts. The human mind must always be aware that there are two very separate airwave frequencies. Either of these frequencies can tune into the mind, but they are completely the opposite of each other. This means that the thoughts they express to us are either good or bad, depending on the airwave.

The first frequency is the Light channel. The signals sent by this frequency often appear as a very faint message, so that it may seem like intuition or a very distant voice that says the minimum words. These faint messages say words that are often an invaluable help, but are sometimes difficult to hear and the words are not usually repeated.

Thoughts manifesting directly from the frequencies of the satanic dark side channel are usually crystal clear and very positive, leaving the person in no doubt that they have heard a message. This message can appear logical and convincing, but it may tell the person to make some unpleasant comments or urge them to do a violent or dishonest deed.

The voice is so authentic that the receiver believes it has come from a guide or relative but, in fact, it is the dark side's devious way to feed the mind and the ego.

How can we possibly know instinctively which thoughts come from the good source and which come from the dark side? Here are some hints:

Rule 1. If the thought is very clear and given in a firm tone, encouraging you to respond in a positive or aggressive way to a situation, then it has most probably come from the dark side.

People who are very negative will be more likely to receive communications from this side, as it is easier for the dark side to communicate when there is negative energy present. In a sense, negative people unintentionally leave the door open for the wrong messages.

Rule 2. When the thought you receive is so distant that it is barely audible, to the extent that you may think you have imagined it, but it feels right, then this is usually a genuine message from the Light side. Messages from your guardian angel, guide, or helper, usually also come through the same side of your head, or in the same ear. By thinking positively and being reasonably free from negative thoughts, you put up a barrier of positive light so the dark side will find it much more difficult to influence your thoughts. Each time you receive a sudden flash of intuition or knowing, it should never be ignored, unless your gut feeling tells you it is wrong.

Should you be in any doubt about the source of a message, ask the spirit world for a sign of confirmation. They may show you a picture of any one of a wide range of things—one time it may be a door key, another time a star, crown, rainbow, or a signal that means something to you. If you have not yet developed your psychic ability, and don't see or hear things, ask for a word of confirmation and you will be given a word, but don't strain too hard to listen for it, as you could miss it by being too tense!

The rules are: (1) Always remember when working with the dark side to check the source of any message, as they are artists in the art of deception; and (2) Always trust your feeling as it is usually correct—never ignore this inner voice.

Dealing with the Dark Side

Dealing with dark entities and negative earthbound spirits is very different work from rescuing a lost or trapped earthbound spirit who is grateful for your compassion. It is wise to have a partner when working with the negative side, if you are not experienced in this work.

Dark energies may be either powerful negative parasites who have never incarnated on earth, or objectionable, negative earthbound spirits. Both groups are very much more common than most of us realise. Spirit release workers report these entities seem to be present in a high percentage of people suffering from psychological or behavioral problems. This fact is confirmed by Dr. Irene Hickman in her book *Remote Depossession.*[1] She suggests that a very high number of people with addiction to drugs, alcohol, or tobacco have at least one attachment. You will often notice a change in a person's behavior pattern when an entity has jumped on board.

More confirmation comes from Dr. Edith Fiore in her excellent book *The Unquiet Dead.*[2] Dr. Fiore states that a great many of her patients who request psychological counselling have some form of attachment. These findings are confirmed by other doctors specialising in this work, so it's time to create awareness that this escalating problem requires specialist treatment.

A large number of people do not realise they have an attachment. It is not surprising to find these beings in people with certain types of emotional problems, but therapists have also found them in nurses, therapists, and Reiki healers, who all seemed to be fairly normal but were vulnerable due to illness or lack of protection and were unaware that at least one entity was sharing their body.

Recognising the Symptoms

When a powerful entity is present, the person will sometimes do things that are totally out of character, perhaps become very rude or hurtful and then feel terrible remorse. People who are hosts to parasites will often complain they are being drained of their energy by an invisible feeling that affects decision making, and makes their head and thoughts feel blurred and very fuzzy. It's as if they cannot coordinate thoughts and are incapable of making a positive decision.

How often do you hear someone say "I can't think what possessed me to do that?" or else they look confused and say "Whatever has got into me today?" Other folks will shake their head in puzzlement and say "I don't seem to be myself today!" This can simply be a case of someone being preoccupied and making an error, but if it happens frequently it can also signal the presence of an entity. When a person has an attachment that is influencing their behaviour, they are often aware something is not right, but can't put their finger on the problem. Please recognise there is a possible entity presence when they are upset, confused, and do things that are out of character, as they could be influenced by an unknown invisible force.

Hear a big warning bell if someone acts out of character by having sudden impulses, overeating, or becomes rebellious or disruptive. Anyone who behaves strangely without explanation could possibly have an unwelcome attachment. These can affect people in several different ways, as some people are completely drained of energy, while others suffer severe depression and mood swings, so watch out for these clues that uninvited spirits or entities may have joined the person's energy field.

Other serious signs are when a person complains of hearing voices, or has unexplained cravings for drugs, cigarettes, or alcohol, when they normally dislike them. In extreme cases when a person has been taken over by several attachments, they may develop multiple personality problems, so seek expert advice.

When a person has had an attachment for several years, the nasty side of their nature is nothing new, so think back a few years and ask yourself if the person was always unpleasant. Did an upsetting or traumatic event occur in the past, perhaps an accident or serious illness? This would have weakened the immune system and allowed an entity to enter their aura.

If you sit in a psychic development circle, watch out for any person who shakes uncontrollably when channelling in trance, as this is often a sign that their guide is trying to get through but being blocked by an entity in the person's energy field.

It is time for modern medicine to accept that there are basic natural laws of good and evil that create balance, and these should always be considered when certain emotional symptoms of illness are present. The possible presence of entities in a patient is seldom considered by the medical profession in the Western world, but long accepted in the East.

The ayurvedic medicine practised in India includes entities in its diagnosis, which perhaps explains why so many eastern people living in the UK are so receptive to alternative medicine, healing, and psychic surgery.

There are a great many cases of mental illness where modern medicine and technology fail to relieve the symptoms, so it is important that doctors think "entity," and learn to explore this avenue of discarnate beings, which is still very much a taboo subject.

It is ironic that medical science is so desperately limited in its ability to successfully treat patients with serious behavioural illnesses, when all that's often needed to get to the root of the problem, whether schizophrenia, manic depression, or other mental problems, is to reduce medication and remove entities.

More and more doctors and therapists are attending depossession courses, so we should soon start to see improvements in this area of medicine.

Listen to Your Body's Warning Signs

If you are sensitive to energies, your body may give you a warning sign when you are in the company of anyone who has a powerful negative entity onboard or whose energies are very negative. You may also get a warning if you are in a building that has very negative or black energy. Some people feel an uneasy tingling on the back of their neck or an icy chill as a cold shiver runs down their spine, while others report they experience goose pimples warning them of a presence; another group will experience an uneasy feeling for no obvious reason.

Any time I meet a person who has an entity attached to them, the outside of my upper arms develop a tingling feeling, so I know to be on the alert and ensure my protection is around me. The same warning feelings appear when visiting a building where geopathic stress or entities are present.

Always listen to your body's warning signs—whether it's a strong feeling in your solar plexus or a cold shiver, it is trying to tell you something! How often have you heard someone say, "My gut feeling was telling me that and I should have listened!"

What Is a Negative Entity?

What do negative entities look like? How do you recognise them? These are very commonly asked questions and it's hard to find information, as very few books have been written giving details of entities, although lots of hair-raising stories have been written and told about fantasy demons and negative beings.

The term "negative entity" refers only to nonphysical beings who act as parasites when attached to human beings. Entities who have never reincarnated on this planet are very often found to be the root cause of antisocial symptoms, eating disorders, or various mental, physical, or emotional problems, often linked to behavioural problems.

One of the big differences between negative entities and good human beings is that we have opposite beliefs! Whereas we believe in our Creator, the world of spirit, good, and love, and abhor evil in all its forms, these parasites strongly oppose love and light, which is completely unknown to them, as they have never incarnated on this planet to experience these feelings.

Entities come in a range of shapes, sizes, and power; they do not have a physical body, but this does not seem to hinder them. These beings from the dark side fall into two separate types, the major and the minor entities. Each type includes many variations in size, power, and shape. Their appearance goes from one extreme to another, depending on the strength of their desire to frighten the rescuer.

The variety of shapes are often grotesque and can include reptiles, scorpions, large lizards, snakes, or large black birds. Should you ever see one of these beings, have a close look at their eyes, as they may be red or an icy-cold black colour. Many spirit release workers report meeting beings who snarl or make a loud hissing noise at the rescuer, but it is all show, and as long as the release therapist is well protected, they can laugh at the being, showing they are not impressed by its antics. Let me remind you again that these beings have never been human, and they are not simply a spirit who has lost its way and needs our help. Always treat all entities with respect, but never underestimate them.

When Is the Most Common Time
for an Entity to Attach to a Human?

An entity is always watching for an opportunity to attach to a person, so will attach to any vulnerable child or adult, and some research by psychologists suggests they can attach in the womb. They can seize their opportunity if a person has had an accident and their aura has been damaged, or if they have been seriously ill, causing their aura to be se- verely weakened. People who suffer from lack of self-esteem or are full of negative thoughts are a prime target, as the weakness shows in the aura, announcing to the entities that this is an ideal host.

These unwelcome entities can stay with a person for several years and quickly integrate with their unsuspecting host, sharing their joys and fears, and day-to-day thoughts. The strange thing is that although friends or family may notice a subtle change in the person's behaviour, they themselves are often unaware they have an attachment.

Many mediums and therapists have commented to me about the number of entities they have seen in hospital wards. As well as attaching to patients whose health is below par, they can also attach to nurses and other medical staff, as most of those in this profession feel great compassion for their patients so open their chakras, which leaves them vulnerable.

It's no joke having a major lodger, as love and joy are unknown feelings to them so they can disrupt family relationships, destroy a career, or encourage their host to make wrong decisions. The meanest of this group, the multiple parasites, take up residence in folks they can control—usually those people suffering unexplained anxiety attacks or manic depression.

Just as the earthbound spirit's mind stays alive and clear after death, so do cravings. Thus a drug addict, after death, will often attach to another addict to feed his craving for drugs. If you enjoy the challenge of doing battle with the enemy, find yourself a partner and get involved in this satisfying and very different ball game from rescuing lonely trapped spirits.

Benefits from Removing Negative Entities

This side of rescue work is truly satisfying as the difference in a person's personality and appearance, after these parasites have been removed, is quite amazing. Often all signs of stress and anger have gone and their long-lost gentle smile returns when the entities have been taken away to be cleansed, healed, and educated by Archangel Michael and his warriors.

Who Is Archangel Michael?

Archangel Michael, who works within the Universal Spirit Law, and whose energies are on a very high vibration, is one of the seven main archangels and his job is overseeing the fight against the dark side. In the spirit world, as on Earth, there is a police force who control law and order, and Archangel Michael commands the spirit army of Light Warriors, the Light police, whose job it is to stand firm against all dark forces.

People often ask why he does not remove all entities from people? There are two answers: First, there should always be some negative entities in the universe to create balance, as there must be evil as well as good, like yin and yang. Otherwise, we would not learn the difference between good and evil. The second answer is that neither Archangel Michael and his warriors or any other powerful spirit helpers are allowed to do this work until they have been asked by us, as they respect our free will.

We have all been given the gift of free will as part of the Universal Spirit Law, so we have a right to choose whether or not to remove entities. The spirit world cannot remove an entity from a person or balance their energies unless the victim asks for their assistance. When you are doing spirit release work, if you ask for their assistance, the spirit world will instantly surround all negative entities with pure light and deal with the situation.

Always call on the help of Archangel Michael when working against a large group of entities or when faced with a particularly viscous dark entity. As well as asking him to bring his army of light workers, I also ask him to call in the assistance of light workers from other planets when I am faced with a very large-scale battle.

Removing these parasites from people is nothing new, as it has been practised for many centuries. If you look in the Bible, you'll find plenty of references to "unclean spirits being cast out by Jesus," during healing treatments, so nothing has changed. He did tell us to do as he does, so we should continue to cast out these evil spirits as he directed us to do.

Be Aware

Don't try to remove an entity from a friend or relative unless you have experience of this work, as entities are a devious bunch and it is virtually impossible to remove them by visualising they have gone and filling the space with love.

If you believe the entity has gone after your visualisation or conversation, check again later as it may have gone into hiding. Thoughts travel at the speed of light, so the entity is well aware of your intention, and is taking evasive action. It is possible to remove some of the weaker entities with gentle persuasion, but certain groups of entities have very powerful energy, and will seldom respond to gentle persuasion. Attempting to talk them into leaving a person is unlikely to be successful unless you bombard them with White Light as you talk, and call in the troops.

Some hypnotherapists and psychotherapists can release entities from their patient by regressing the person and helping them to search for the entity in their body or aura. Once they have found it, they can remove it, but this is a job for only the experienced therapist.

Remember all entities are there because they want to be there, as they enjoy influencing a person's behaviour. These dark force entities are very defiant and hostile little beings who are intent on disruption. The more powerful of these entities will arouse strong feelings of greed, power, lust, or even bullying in their host. They intend to stay, so have no intention of leaving unless defeated. Bombarding them with White Light seems to be the most effective treatment, and Samuel Sagan M.D., in his book *Entity Possession,*[3] states it is unlikely that entities will be removed solely by psychotherapy. Here are a few facts about these parasites that are responsible for some health problems and disruption in our lives.

The Minor Parasites—Black Clingers

Black parasites come in a variety of shapes, the most basic group are known by mediums as little black clingers, and these hangers-on type of parasite cling tightly to the human aura. They are the least harmful of all parasites and are content to live in the aura of any unsuspecting person, as they are only intent on soaking up energy from their host. Some appear as a solid blob, while others can be a fluid energy that can change shape.

I was recently asked by a scientist friend who walks a spiritual pathway, "What are these little 'black blobs' I keep seeing attached to people?" He explained that he regularly sees these attachments on people when walking in the town, or in a local supermarket, and was mystified about their source and purpose.

Off-putting and a bit scary you'll agree, particularly as most people are unaware of their attachments. When they cling to your aura, they can continue to drain your energy for years by disrupting the smooth flow of universal life force energy, so that you feel drained both physically and emotionally, for no apparent reason. To make matters worse, these mini-nuisances have the ability to divide and multiply. Once they move into the aura, their numbers can increase, a most unwelcome lodger!

These little blobs are not of the demonic category. They do not have a brain, and only minimal awareness; thus, they keep a very low profile when they become firmly attached to your aura, and use your body's energy to their advantage. I say "lodger," but in fact they are scavengers, and many people have a large number of scavenging lodgers attached.

I have often cleared eight or ten from one person. It's quite common for them to bring their friends along—anyone who has a weak immune system, or is depressed or a drug addict, is a haven for these unwelcome parasites.

Each of these little blobs possesses a magnetic force of attraction. When one becomes attached to the aura, this force acts as a magnet and will draw others to the aura, so it is important to regularly cleanse your aura to discourage these energy thieves. You are probably wondering why these minute parasites need to attach to the human aura. The answer is that they attach to the human aura because they are too weak to incarnate on their own, so are looking for a free ride and a free meal.

Clearing Minor Parasites

These minor blobs are easily cleared as they are weak and do not have enough strength to withstand a strong blast of White Light, so if you are concerned that they may be attached to the aura of a friend or relative, then you can dowse to confirm their presence. If the answer is positive, then sit down and place a cloak of protection around you before attempting to remove them. Once you are confident your protection is on, simply channel White Light to the person in the same way as you would channel healing energy, and ask the assistance of the spirit world to deal with these blobs. After you have channelled the energy for a few minutes, dowse to ask if the parasites have gone from their aura.

Armies of Demons

We often quote the phrase "as above so below," and this is the case with the dark side, as they have a structured tier system consisting of the most powerful demons at the top who control the lesser entities, and at the bottom of the pecking order are the minor entities.

Although it is hard to believe, demons often form an army of minors and these small entities are trained to work in battalions. These beings have only sufficient intelligence to carry out orders and are devoid of fear or any other emotions, so they obey their leaders without question.

Theatrical though it sounds, many spirit rescuers have been told by entities that their great ambition is to eventually control the world's population, so it is in their favour that so few people are aware of their existence. They are responsible for some of today's lack of respect for authority, use of drugs, and irrational, impulsive antisocial behaviour.

It is all difficult to believe, but while living at my previous home, I had firsthand experience of fighting these armies of minors and enjoyed several battles. Existence of armies of entities and other facts are confirmed in *The Diary of Lucifer* by Dr. Irene Hickman.[4]

When you move into the work of clearing entities, be aware that you will come across armies of minors who are controlled by major entities. When engaged in a battle to clear an area of these pests, you will find they call in other battalions to assist them. Don't be alarmed; it is a bit nerve-racking the first time you tackle this scale of battle, but you should call in Archangel Michael and his team of warriors to join the battle and assist in removing these groups.

What Exactly Are Major Entities?

The major entities are either black, grey, or a dark shade, and are much more cunning and intelligent than their little brothers, the clingers, and their removal creates a far greater challenge for Light Workers. The Law of the Universe states that no being should ever impose itself on another being, as we are all given free will by our Creator. Perhaps Lucifer forgot to tell his entities that any attachment affects our free will and can influence our decisions—for this reason alone, it is vital to remove attachments from all human beings.

Nonphysical parasites or beings consist of electromagnetic energy. As well as being attracted to people with weak immune systems, they are drawn to those who use the Ouija board. I'll talk later about the dangers of using this board.

These attachments are unenlightened, uninvited, low-level spirits. They are parasites who have come from their den in a lower energy plane. They are from the dark side, and the sole purpose of these mini-evils is to create disruption.

This group seems to be very aware of what is going on around them and chooses carefully those to inhabit—the more negative the person, the more they can feed off their energy.

The major entities cause by far the most trouble, and are often just one jump ahead of us. They know beforehand when they are going to be attacked, so are prepared to take evasive action. How do they know when they are about to be attacked? They are not psychic, but thought travels at the speed of light. As soon as a rescue worker decides to remove an entity, it has received the message. This makes their removal harder, as they jump off their host until the attack has been carried out, then hop back on.

I have trained myself to get around this problem simply by extending my thought, and in the instant that I think I will do the work, I place a net around them so they are trapped. They have another trick up their sleeves, adding to the difficulties of the battle—they have the advantage of being able to split their energy into parts, which fooled me the first time I saw it happen.

These entities feed on the energy of their victim, whose energy levels may be very negative due to disappointments in life, worry about finances, or marriage problems. Alternately, their victim could be living or working in a building that is situated on a black ley line, or have excess electromagnetic energy from electronic equipment, i.e. mobile phones, pylons, computers, etc. The fabric of buildings, such as window frames, doors, curtains, and furniture, all hold negative energy. A building that has not had its energies cleared for several years is a powerful source of negative energy. Our atmosphere today is contaminated by manmade electromagnetic fields and pollution, so we all live and breathe in a sea of negative energy, which means no shortage of food for parasites.

When a really powerful dark entity moves into a person's body, it will continue to live and grow inside a person, and throw out seeds that land on unsuspecting, vulnerable passersby until its presence is recognised. These powerful parasites take great pleasure in moving into the human energy of their hosts. They feel good when attached to this energy field, hardly surprising, as they are able to draw all this wonderful free energy, so it is no wonder that they put up a strong fight to stay there.

Major entities come in a range of sizes and never incarnate. They can work either alone or in groups, thus any unfortunate person can have several of these menaces attached at any one time, and as I mentioned earlier, they have the ability to plant ideas in the person's mind, so you will sometimes hear a person say "I don't know why I committed that offence."

Ironically, the person really does not know why they threw a brick through a window or shoplifted, or did some other deed that was totally out of character, but it's difficult to get anyone to believe their story. These hostile beings are defiant and intent on causing disruption. They can create negative feelings of greed, a desire to bully or torment and a lust for control and power. While one person may have one of these parasites, another may be host to several of these beings.

Negative Earthbound Spirits Pounce on the Weak

Another group of negative entities who cause serious problems are the negative earthbound spirits, who, in their lifetime on earth, were drunkards, child molesters, or extremely cruel or vicious people. As they still have the cravings, they will often attach themselves to people with similar behaviour, or to weak people whom they can influence to indulge in antisocial habits. Some of these spirits have been lurking in the dark realms and are caught in a web of negativity, so it's essential that their presence is recognised, the energy lightened, and they are banished from the person's aura to a place where they can be cleansed and healed. Today there are many techniques taught to recognise these entities and enable us to remove them, so at last we have declared war on these "nasties" and now their numbers will decrease.

To summarise, we are talking about three separate groups of entities.

1. First are the minor clingers who are energy thieves; they attach themselves to a person and stay there, so everywhere the person goes, the clinger goes too. They stay until they are removed by a medium or healer.

2. The second group are the powerful major entities who attach to people or buildings and stay until removed, so may have been

there for many years. Also in this group are the drifters who float around, looking for areas in which to cause trouble.

3. The third group are the negative earthbound spirits, who in life were unpleasant people. These disembodied spirits are intent on carrying on as they behaved on Earth, and get their kicks from their hosts.

Any of these groups of entities can be present in mental hospitals. When a person has a serious illness or mental problems, cracks appear in their energy field, allowing these entities to enter. This can cause mental suffering and anguish, but these symptoms can be dramatically reduced when a medical doctor accepts the presence of these phenomena.

Parasites are crafty—as well as attaching to patients with emotional problems, they have been known to attach themselves to a patient who is under general anaesthetic, while going through a low period in their life. Many therapists report patients stating they were almost certain that the attachment had joined them when they were in a hospital having an operation, or recovering from an accident, as that is when the symptoms first appeared. Understandably, this is one problem that hospital staff do not recognise and they would be horrified to learn of the existence of entities in hospital wards!

Any person who has had an attachment removed will tell you they are feeling so much lighter, and describe a feeling of joy that the voices have gone away or the tension of being aware of constant mental influences has completely disappeared. Those people who are sensitive to energy will often say that they were aware of the presence being lifted from their body.

Once the person has been cleared, it is important that they realise the importance of protecting their aura. This entity was not an isolated incident—more of these parasites are always awaiting their opportunity to take up residence in an unsuspecting host. The power of negative energy can take over susceptible people and create this unstable mental state, but fortunately, healthy people do not usually suffer from these symptoms.

Don't confuse good earthbound spirits with disharmonious energies. It's natural to be frightened by the unexpected sight of a spirit or ghost, particularly if the spirit shows itself as a dark shape. You can jump to the wrong conclusion and instinctively assume that it is an evil spirit or demon, as it's easy to think the worst. There are very few really evil spirits around and these groups do not often show themselves to people—99 percent of earthbound spirits are friendly, so unless you happen to be in a building where black arts have been practised, or hard drugs used, you can safely assume the ghost means no harm to you and is probably lonely and afraid.

Things to Remember When Removing Negative Entities

Rescue mediums have a violent fight on their hands when clearing a group of powerful negative black entities, as it takes a lot of bombarding with White Light to get rid of them. It's a wise move to keep your aura cleansed to discourage them from moving in to your energy field. It is so easy to get an attachment and so difficult to get it removed.

Never forget that when you think of releasing the entities you are about to bombard, the little devils have picked up the thought, are warned of attack, and are ready for the invasion. They know in that split second when we think about attack and may retaliate, so always make sure you don your protective cloak.

War Games

Negative entities come in a range of shapes and different levels of nastiness. They are an unsavoury bunch and of very low energy. Meeting them is a bit like something you'd see in a horror movie, as some of the darker ones will snarl, moan, groan, struggle, and wriggle, as they try to avoid capture. Part of the challenge of Light work is that every case is different, so there is no set of rules to follow. You have to change your technique depending on the type of entity and it's weakness. It's a bit like playing war games, as you have to work out your strategy to win the battle.

I work with my guides and helpers when I do this work. Distance is no object as it is as easy to remove an entity attached to a person on the other side of the world, as it is to remove one from a person sitting opposite me in this room. Remember that as soon as you think about any entities, they know your thoughts, so can prepare. Recently I was involved in a large scale battle to remove a group of entities from an estate, so was glad of a friend's extra power in this fight, as this group of major entities had been resident in the house for many years and had a strong hold in the building.

When we bombarded them with Light, we saw a hilarious sight, as they had been well aware we were about to attack and were hiding behind an enormous barricade, so we could hardly work for laughing at the antics of this devious group who were not going to give in easily. It took us twenty minutes, with the aid of Archangel Michael and his team of warriors, for them to be weakened sufficiently to be taken away.

I had an example of how an entity can change a person's personality recently when I was asked to treat a doctor who was behaving oddly and his concerned family had contacted me to request healing. He would not allow any member of his family to visit his home and he shut the door on their faces when they called to ensure he was well. As he did not respond to absent healing, I looked further to find the root of his behaviour problem and went through the usual routine of balancing his chakras, polarity, earth link, ions, etc., and found no form of physical illness, so was convinced the problems were created by an entity.

This medical doctor was not normally an eccentric, antisocial type of person, so it was noticeable that his behaviour was strange and out of character. Sure enough, I found the culprits, six nasty entities who were firmly attached, so much so that it became a real battle to release them. The treatment worked well and I heaved a sigh of relief when they left. As usual, I asked my helpers to show me a sign confirming that they had left my patient's body. I was highly amused when I heard a helper shout in my ear, "It's a goal!" and was shown a football flying through the air. The spirit world has a great sense of humour and enjoys a joke.

Hide and seek is not only played by children, as entities are expert at this game, so don't be surprised when clearing a person, if you find one or two of these devious entities are hiding somewhere in the body. Some therapists state entities only live in the base chakra area, but I have found them on the crown of the head, ovaries, spine, and other areas of the body. Perhaps you'll find them behind the pelvis or an organ, and the crafty ones will leap out of the person's body when they know you are declaring war.

I am not exaggerating when I say it becomes like a sport, only it's one-sided, as the good team always wins. Never feel guilty, or that you have failed in the task, if you have to ask assistance of Archangel Michael. The spirit world is always very grateful for any assistance we can give them in their fight against the dark side.

Collecting the Fragments

When we suffer severe shock, sadness, or injury, it is possible for small pieces of our personality to break off and float about in space, so it is important for therapists to dowse to ask if your patient has any fragments missing, as it is so beneficial to return the missing fragments. This can be done by taking the patient on a spiritual journey and asking their higher self to collect the missing pieces and reattach them. As missing fragments are seldom talked about, the patient is most probably unaware that fragments can go missing.

I had some work done recently on me to check for missing fragments and was quite astonished to find that I had eight pieces missing, although I felt perfectly fit, so it is easy to be unaware you have fragments missing. If you'd like to learn more about fragments, I recommend *Psychic Vampires* by Joe H. Slate PhD.[5]

When you collect the missing fragments, usually with the assistance of the patient's higher self, it is important to balance and cleanse the energy of the fragments, so they are again on the right vibration to be compatible with the body before they are reunited with your patient. Collecting fragments is also known in certain communities and by shamans as soul hunting. This can involve rituals, trance dancing, and drumming, which help the patient to get into the right energy vibration to make contact with the missing pieces.

The astral body shatters and separates from the human body after death, as it is no longer needed. When a person who had an addiction, whether for alcohol, drugs, sex, or gambling dies, it can attach to another person. It is possible that a fragment of their personality that contains the craving can break off from their astral body and float into the astral plane to find a home with a like-minded human.

When checking the health of a patient who has addiction problems, consider that the source of the addiction could be a fragment that has attached to the patient. This is not an entity, simply a fragment, so removing it is much easier than removing an entity.

Basic Rules to Follow When Removing Entities

1. Check or dowse for fragments.
2. When possible, always work with your spirit guides and helpers.
3. Ask the guides for any helpful information on the being.
4. Say a descriptive prayer of protection before starting work.
5. Cleanse the patient of negative energy.
6. Fill the patient with White Light.
7. Cleanse the patient's aura of negative energy and seal cracks.
8. Remove negative entities.
9. Check for any remaining seeds, implants, curses, or karmic oaths.

How to Remove Negative Entities

The first thing to establish is how many entities are attached to the patient's energy field—unless you know how many to remove, it is easy to leave one behind. You can dowse to confirm the correct number of entities on the person and also dowse to confirm they have all been removed.

Remember to throw a net of White Light around them as soon as you think of removing them. Once they are trapped in this position, you can start cleansing and balancing the victim's energy. By clearing the victim of negative energy, you are effectively removing their source of food. Start by clearing the person's body of all negative energy and filling it with White Light, then cleanse and balance their aura, and heal any cracks so the door is closed to other entities.

Then it is time to clear both the person and their home of geopathic stress, the negative energy from underground water. Also check that they are not sleeping over a black ley line. A large number of buildings with geopathic stress are home to many parasites, as they have an affinity to this ongoing source of negative energy.

Once the energies have been balanced, it is time to renew the patient's Earth link. We all have an invisible link with the Earth, which can be accidentally severed when exposed to powerful electromagnetic fields, geopathic stress, or the presence of parasites. A symptom of the presence of strong geopathic stress rays is when a person constantly wakes up feeling tired, feels a bit distant and detached, and has difficulty getting their momentum to work.

Next, the body's level of positive and negative ions should be checked and the body's polarity, and then it's time to balance the chakra system, as these are the body's power points.

Each chakra is responsible for the smooth working of an area of the body. If one or two chakras are blocked, it can affect both health and emotions. When this treatment has been completed, it's time to say a final good bye to the bad guys, so bombard them with pure White Light and call in the assistance of Archangel Michael to take the entities away to be cleansed and healed. Some rescuers visualise the entities being arrested and taken away by powerful white helpers, or placing a fish bowl over them, while others place a "No Parking" sign across the person.

No matter how angry you may feel about the disruption a parasite has caused to a person's life, never treat negative or evil spirits with threats or anger, as threats are negative energy and you are feeding them more fodder. The only way to weaken them is with love—remember, good always wins over evil.

Distance Depossession

Spirit release work can be done as effectively at a distance as when the patient is present, so here are some of the great benefits to working from a distance,

1. Both traveling time and energy are saved.

2. It's useful when the person lives in an inaccessible area.

3. You avoid being close to the entity.

4. It is less upsetting for the patient.

5. The patient does not need to know when you are doing the work.

6. It resolves the difficulty when a patient refuses to visit a therapist.

7. When you have been asked by a person to remove an entity from a patient who is adamant that they do not have an entity, you can get permission from their guide to do the work and avoid upsetting them.

It is understandable that some people are upset and indignant at the idea that there could possibly be a parasite attached to them, so distance work resolves this situation. Most of the work I do is from a distance, as I can choose my time to carry out the release and don't need to worry about driving in bad weather. So how does all this magic work? It is all about intent and positive thought.

The Power of Positive Thought

Intention is a field of very powerful invisible energy, which is in and around all of us and can be tapped into at any time. This energy of intent is a wonderfully powerful tool that is a gift from our Creator, the source of all beings, and is always around us. Remember we are all made of energy and this invisible power tool is available twenty-four hours a day, so have faith in this power as it is there to be used, and it does make things happen. This amazing power of intent is in every one of us and every living thing, so use it.

The Silent Minute

Perhaps the finest example of positive thought was displayed in 1942, during World War II, when Britain was losing the war against Germany and a miracle was needed to turn the battle in our favour. That's when

Wellesley Tudor Pope introduced the Silent Minute. At 9:00 every evening, many millions of citizens prayed for the safety of the nation and observed this dedicated minute on land, sea, and air. It was also practised in air raid shelters, hospitals, battlefields, prison camps, as well as almost every home, both rich and poor, in the nation.[6]

BBC Radio observed the Silent Minute in both their home and overseas service every evening until the end of the war, and the introduction of this powerful wave of positive energy created by the mass participation was the turning point in the war. Almost immediately after the introduction of this indestructible tool, the course of the war changed dramatically in Britain's favour.

What we are talking about here is the power of collective thought, which can be used to create good or bad, so this free tool should be used wisely. Random generated numbers (RGN) suggest there is an energy field around each one of us that responds to our every thought, whether negative or positive, so that we influence energy around us. If enough people send out love and positive thoughts, it will create a powerful field of positive energy that will dispel negativity. This tool can be used on a large scale to solve some of the problems in the world today, simply by enough people sending out love to the areas where there is hatred and bloodshed. The power of positive thought is more than a tool to be used to protect our aura—it can also be used to protect our future.

Poltergeist on the Warpath

Perhaps the most frightening and irrational category of powerful spirits is the poltergeist. These require firm handling from an experienced rescuer. The name "poltergeist" brings fear to most of us, as we visualise images of violence and anger, with heavy furniture being thrown around a room. Sometimes a poltergeist will have a really crashing time, sending much loved items from one end of the room to the other, and it's quite common when a poltergeist is in full flow to see books, tape recorders, chairs, and other objects flying across a room. The energy in the room will feel so heavy and angry that even the most insensitive person cannot fail to be aware of this violent energy.

The name comes from the German word *poltern,* meaning "creates disturbance," and *geist,* meaning "ghost." *The Concise Oxford Dictionary*[7] description is "a noisy mischievous spirit, or one manifesting physical damage," and that description sums it up accurately.

Fortunately, poltergeists seldom make their presence known. These earthbound spirits are often angry and very baffled by their situation and so behave in a violent manner from the sheer frustration of not being recognised. They are making a frantic effort to attract attention to their plight.

Some experts believe the poltergeist is person-centred, rather than site-centred. In other words, they believe the energy of a person in the building is responsible, probably that of a disturbed adolescent, or a depressed person—an interesting thought, but this does not explain why poltergeist attacks are short term, usually lasting weeks or months.

One explanation given by some experts is that a child or teenager in the house has been possessed by a negative entity, which is responsible for the poltergeist activity. Other experts firmly believe this phenomena is linked to electromagnetic hotspots, where there is a strong surge of energy, either from a nearby overhead power cable, pole, radar station, etc. These could be the explanation for light bulbs constantly blowing, or video or TV set malfunctioning, but is this energy capable of picking up a vase of flowers and throwing it across the room? If you are concerned about a poltergeist in your home, contact someone who uses a field meter. They can measure the levels of EMFs in the home and establish if electromagnetic rays are the cause of the poltergeist-type activity.

The big question all honest sceptics must ask themselves is: "Why do poltergeist activities usually cease permanently after an angry spirit has been rescued?"

When a murder has been committed, the site holds very negative energy, which can stay there for a very long time. If the spirit of the murdered person has become stuck in the site, the poltergeist's violent action can be their "enough is enough" cry, as they are desperate to move on.

The event may have happened over a hundred years ago, but the negative energy remaining there can have a serious effect, as it is imprinted on the land.

Another poltergeist can be an angry previous resident who objects to the person living in the home, or disapproves of alterations, or sometimes it can be a deceased jealous relative or partner. Usually a medium has no difficulty finding the identity of the culprit responsible for the chaos—once that is known, it's easy to placate the spirit, and help them to the Light.

It takes a brave person to deal with a poltergeist, as they are very determined to make noise. It is vital to ignore the noisy, angry, negative energy and speak gently to them, while bombarding them with White Light to weaken the negative energy. It can be a truly unpleasant and frightening experience—most certainly a tale that will be told to friends and get handed down in the family for many years.

Very Angry Spirits

As well as the poltergeist, there are angry spirits who are genuinely upset because their beloved fireplace or cooker has been discarded and replaced by modern equipment or their old coal shed has become a bright sun lounge extension. Most of us have known a few people who in life were self-opinionated and did not like change, so on death have refused to move on, wanting to stay nearby and keep an eye on things. This is quite common as a person's personality does not change on death—they make their presence felt to register their disapproval by annoying tricks.

Thoughtforms—Little Poison Arrows!

From poltergeist to another nuisance. Have you ever heard of negative thoughtforms? As the name suggests, these are negative thoughts sent to people, sometimes known as poison arrows, and can have a similar effect on the recipient as the presence of a clinger does. These negative thoughtforms are caused by an intensity of emotions and powerful thoughts, and can be caused either intentionally or unintentionally. Regularly sending out bad thoughts to a person or having recurring, angry, and negative mental arguments will create a thoughtform.

Most of us don't realise that it is possible to charge our thoughts or words with negative energy that is sufficiently powerful to take on a life of its own. Thought and prayer are very powerful—this type of form is an example of the power of negative thought. They cling to the person's energy field, and the more curses, negative things said, or bad thoughts sent to them, the more build-up of negative energy, as thought is a very powerful and much-underrated weapon. Although these negative thoughts change to become negative energy forms, they will never have a soul or consciousness and will remain a negative energy.

It is possible that if thoughts are sent out with hate and vengeance, in a few cases the thoughts may be strong enough to become parasites. This will have the effect on you of making you very tired and drained of energy.

You can protect yourself from thoughtforms aimed by a jealous or negative person simply by making a conscious effort to put a cloak of protection around your body each day, and to regularly cleanse your aura. These invisible arrows can be removed by a powerful healer or by asking the spirit world to work through a pendulum, so don't assume they are attached to you for evermore.

The power of prayer is very positive, and can reverse the effect of negative thoughts, which is wonderful. The very powerful energy of prayer is a combination of love and positive thought, capable of canceling negativity attached to a person.

Black magic is a powerful form of thoughts and should be avoided at all cost. I believe strongly that everything you give out, you get back tenfold. Those getting their kicks from sending out this form of magic have a bad time coming.

Psychic Attack Is Very Real

Whereas everybody is well aware when they are being drained by a psychic vampire, or bombarded by a poltergeist, psychic attack is a very different form of bombardment, as it is usually planned by a person who is either jealous or bears a grudge against you. It silently attacks from behind you, so you don't realise you are being attacked until you are a victim of this silent war.

Negative bombardment is a common problem, whether it's a jealous ex-partner or a business competitor, and many people believe the correct way to deal with attacks is to send the negative beam straight back to the sender. This is wrong. It is not the wise way to cope with this problem—it is essential that each time you are aware of nasty thoughts or attack being directed at you, you must send out loving energy to the person to deplete their power.

If you retaliate and send back their negativity, you are giving them more power, so although it is probably the last thing you feel like doing at that moment, send love to them! The best way to declare war on them is to weaken their energy by sending lots of love, as they will not appreciate this invasion of positive energy.

In *Practical Psychic Self Defence,*[8] Robert Bruce writes that psychic attack can be broken instantly by walking across a water main or garden hose. Other options he suggests are taking a shower or sitting down quietly and doing a visualisation of walking over water. What he is really saying is that by visualising water or taking action to cross over it, the positive thought and the power of intent will work to make it effective.

How Do You Recognise a Psychic Attack?

Here are some of the symptoms often felt, varying from person to person:

- A very sharp pain in your head or back, almost as though a knife or arrow has stabbed you.
- An unexplained ache in your head, back, or neck.
- An unaccountable lack of energy.
- Feeling afraid, sad, or deflated for no apparent reason.
- Unpleasant nightmares, disrupted sleep pattern.
- An uneasy feeling that you are being invaded or attacked.
- Certain symptoms appearing at the same time each day, for no obvious reason.

This happens when the attacker sits down at the same time each day or evening with intent to do the deadly deed. Often an attacker relies on their victim's fear and weakness to make the attack more effective. It's a really alarming feeling to know that you are under psychic attack and you can find yourself almost waiting for it to happen. You can become so unnerved that you imagine an attack is responsible for every little twinge or tiredness you experience.

Are you worried about being attacked? Then hang a little eight-sided bagua mirror on the outside wall of your home, facing the direction you feel an attack may come from. The bagua mirror is an effective feng shui tool that diverts all negative energy approaching your home, whether from a telegraph pole, cemetery, or unpleasant neighbour. These unobtrusive little mirrors are inexpensive, and can be purchased in most New Age shops.

Spirit Possession Does Happen

Psychic attack is a fight against an invisible enemy. Another equally awful experience is when a person is possessed by an earthbound spirit. Being possessed by a spirit is most people's worst nightmare. It's not simply something from a horror movie—this situation really does happen in real life.

The rule when working with a spirit possession patient or an earthbound spirit who has practised witchcraft or black arts is to always put on protection before starting to help the person and ask for assistance from our Creator and his team of helpers. Don't ever be too proud to call in the troops to assist in the battle and never underestimate the situation, as it can be a real battle, with them as determined as you to win.

Spirit possession is the final insult! Think about the implications of possession, and you will realise it is the ultimate invasion of your body. As your every thought is influenced, you can say good bye to your right to have any sort of privacy.

The spirit that is resident in the patient is not simply attached to the aura. This spirit has actually taken up residence in the patient's body and will very likely attempt to make the host as dependent as possible on them in many ways, so that they will not be evicted. This is no joke.

In certain cases, a possessed person will complain that the spirit has a sexual hold over them by causing them to sustain amazing sexual experiences, such as they have never known. They may be loathe to give up this new-found pleasure. The problem arises when the person becomes exhausted and cannot keep up this regular nightly romp, and as they are also emotionally exhausted, they do not have the energy or determination to get rid of the interloper.

Categories of Spirit Possession

The first type of earthbound spirits are those who may not have accepted that they have died and have taken the opportunity to move into another person's body, after drifting along in the in-between worlds area until they saw their opportunity to attach to a person, often someone with a weak immune system.

The second type can occur when a person has been killed in an accident and their organs donated to a recipient. You have probably heard of cases where a transplant patient who has always been a nonsmoker complains of an unaccountable desire to smoke a pipe, or the patient who is thirsty for a glass of whiskey when they have never drunk spirits. Others report a desire for a big fry-up with lots of sauce when they have always hated the smell of sauce and have never eaten this type of food. These symptoms are often a sign that an earthbound spirit is still attached to the organ and so has joined the recipient.

The third type is the nonhuman, negative entity who is responsible for a change in a person's behaviour. Once this nuisance has been removed, it is essential that the subject learns to place protection around themselves each day to ensure that another entity does not move in.

Should you ever become aware of being possessed or a member of your family becomes a victim to this nightmare situation, then I advise calling for assistance from Archangel Michael and his army of warriors. As with negative entities, the spirit world is also on duty twenty-four hours a day and specialises in fighting the black side, so can be there at your side in a split second, as they travel in the speed of your thought.

Recognise the Signs of Negative Entity Possession

These are often symptoms of a person who is unwillingly the host to an unpleasant lodger.

- Does the person intentionally break things or get pleasure from destroying them?

- Do their eyes look different than usual? Is there a cold chill or glint in their eyes that makes you shiver or feel uneasy?

- Do their eyes sometimes look a bit wild, or have a strange expression?

- Are they constantly detached, never seeming to be really switched on to conversation and what's going on around them? Do they experience unexplained memory loss?

Help Is at Hand—The Depossession Groups

Clearing this type of possession is a job for a specialist, and the Hickman Academy (Depossession Institute) in both the US and UK offers courses on clearance of unwelcome attachments.

Spirit possession can be one of several different forms of attachment. It can be an earthbound spirit, an extra terrestrial, or a dark entity. Any of these very unwelcome and uninvited attachments can play havoc by creating strong anger, fear, etc. Both the Hickman Academy and the Spirit Release Foundation have for several years taught methods of spirit release to deal with these unwanted guests.

The method of rescue work involves rescuers working in pairs. While they converse with the discarnate entity, they scan the person's body and aura to establish both the number and type of parasites present. Sometimes they will call on angels to help remove offending entities, and lead them safely to the Light. Hickman rescuers work both directly with the person and from a distance.

The Spirit Release Foundation was formed in 1999 in the UK by a group of very aware medical and complementary practitioners who realised the services of rescue workers was much needed, as attached entities and earthbound spirits are an ever-growing problem today, and associated with an increase in cases of behavioural problems. The SRF links with countries all around the world and is a nondenominational association, not associated with any specific religion. Spirit release therapy is taught by the SRF's accredited tutors, and a certificated course is available to practitioners. The association's aims are as follows:

1. To spread awareness of the subject of entity attachment among the medical health profession, mental health workers, complementary therapists, and members of the general public.

2. To offer a strong support service to spirit release therapists and their patients.

3. To organise conferences, workshops, and weekend diploma courses.

Both the Hickman Academy and the Spirit Release Foundation have been filling a tremendous gap in this field until recently, as practitioners have experienced great difficulty finding accurate information about spirit attachment. Until these organisations were formed, it was an almost impossible task to find information to treat a patient who had an attachment or was possessed by a spirit, as there were no medical guidelines to explain in simple terms how to release the offending lodger. For this reason, many medical people are attending workshops run by SRF, and also depossession classes taught by the Hickman Academy. These organisations are doing a great job of spreading awareness of attachments, a subject seldom covered by the media.

Remote Spirit Therapy to the Rescue

Distance is no problem. Spirit release or rescue work can be done from a distance and many specialists are now offering this service. I work only from a distance and find it easier to link with the problem, as this avoids the energies from other members of the family confusing things. The patient can sometimes be aware of their loved one's anxiety, and energies build up, so it's often much easier to conduct the rescue from a distance. One advantage of working from a distance is that the patient is not aware of the time when the work is being done, so is not tense or ill at ease—in the case of someone who is not aware of their predicament, they do not erect a barrier.

Remote rescue therapy is non-invasive so there are a great many advantages, particularly the fact that therapists are not confused or influenced by other energies in the building. When you work on site, it's easy to get involved in an emotional situation, so I recommend remote rescue, as the rescuer is not vulnerable to outside influences.

Patients usually report that after an entity or attachment has been released from them or from their home, they feel so much lighter, have more energy, and find their sleep pattern has improved greatly. Good news, but it is important to make everyone concerned well aware of how the attachment happened—when they understand the facts, they can take positive steps to avoid a repeat experience.

An excellent book that describes in great detail the battles between the spirit world and the evil black side found on the lower astral plane, is Stephen Turoff's book *Seven Steps to Eternity.*[9]

Don't Be Fooled by the Ouija Board

Why do mediums and most experienced rescue workers throw up their hands in absolute horror when you mention this board and warn you to not on any account use the Ouija board? They know only too well that when you use this exciting board, you are very effectively opening the door to any mischievous or negative spirits, as well as good spirits, to communicate with you, so here are the big questions:

1. How does the Ouija board allow evil spirits to communicate?
2. Can you become possessed of an evil entity by using this board?
3. Is this board simply an innocent game that allows our imagination to run riot?

If you are aware that your immune system is low or your aura is damaged, then be aware that the dark side will be attracted to you, and remember that a recognised source of entity presence is the famous Ouija board.

The fascinating Ouija board has long been known as a great source of fun, but it is also a known source of trouble, as it works on the low energies—anyone using it is vulnerable to entities and earthbound spirits. It seems like an exciting way to spend an evening with friends, but many people have a tale to tell of the unpleasant effects from allowing these unenlightened spirits into their home. The boards have been used for over a hundred years by hundreds of thousands of people as a tool to communicate with their deceased family, not realising they could be heading for big trouble from negative entities.

There is no doubt in many mediums' minds that this board will enable you to make contact with other dimensions, but are we really sure that these are the ones we want to contact? What is the mystery surrounding this board? Does it somehow act as a doorway or portal to the spirit world? We all know that symbols are very powerful, so is it possible that the original layout was used to contact demonic energies? Then this board would represent negative energy and this energy would be carried down over the years and so these negative energies could be implanted on the design of the board. It would also apply to boards made at home with pieces of paper—all a bit far-fetched, but never underestimate the power of negative energy.

When using this talking board, there are almost certainly spirits present in the room. You may feel confirmation of their presence by a draft of cold air or a chill in the room. Should your body shiver and you feel goose pimples covering your entire body, don't shrug it off, thinking it's probably due to excitement and apprehension. It is most likely your intuition (gut feeling) warning you that an entity is nearby.

Who are these unenlightened spirits? They are negative energy spirits who are on a low vibration, and are constantly looking for ways to create mischief. Using the Ouija board opens the front door, inviting these low level forms into your living room. Anyone who has used a board will tell you that these low level spirits give an unbelievably convincing performance on the board. The answers are so realistic that it fools even the strongest sceptics. Many of the answers to questions are 100 percent what you want to hear, so are confirmation of your doubts, yet few are the truth and, ironically, it's often some time later before you realise you have been cheated, as the answers were a fraud.

I had a couple of medium friends who sat together every Sunday for several hours, asking the board questions. These women, who were well aware of their guides and helpers and before using the board, always said a prayer of protection to bypass negative entities, which protected them from attachments, but did not stop the spirits from telling them a whole load of absolute nonsense!

One of the women was having an affair and was so smitten with the man that she was seriously considering leaving her husband and family. This was great fodder for the Ouija board, as it spun her an amazing tale that she would live happily ever after with this man and that her loving husband, who was in his forties, would die within a year, leaving her free to marry this man and bear his child, a beautiful, healthy son. That was ten years ago. The husband is still very fit and well; the lover dumped her for someone who was free, and almost all the guidance given by the board was nonsense. They were facts geared to cause disruption in her life, and certainly not to bring her happiness.

If you must use a Ouija board, don't trust any of the information given and say a prayer of protection before starting the activity. Other than the excitement from getting a message, there is no useful advantage to the Ouija board, but there is no point in banning them, as users will make their own boards.

Magazines could do a good job of warning young people of the dangers, so they are not tempted to make their own cards, but perhaps a warning would make them more of a temptation. Most people simply don't realise how easy it is to acquire a spirit attachment from this form of entertainment, and how difficult it is to get rid of it. When it has moved into your aura, it is often there for a long time before its presence is discovered, so please avoid the Ouija board unless you are very confident your aura is well protected, so that you won't need the services of an exorcist.

I was recently a guest on a phone-in programme for a local radio station and was appalled to find a Ouija board sitting on the desk in front of me. The presenter proudly told me that the previous week he had tried to contact John Lennon on the Ouija board during a programme.

Mediums cannot choose which spirit speaks through their channel. They have to wait for the spirit to come if they choose, so there is no way you can ask this board to communicate with your loved one, as it involves a lot of energy and unless the spirit is in the habit of coming through, then it is much more likely that the message is from a mischievous spirit.

Exorcism Is in Big Demand

Exorcism is a method of clearing negative or evil spirits from a building or from a person and is a service offered by many churches. It can be a long and slow business, as malevolent spirits are not easily moved by prayer, particularly as they have probably never been in a church and had no religious beliefs. The power of prayer is very powerful, as it is positive energy and love, which cancel out some of the negativity, but we must always remember that everyone, whether alive or dead, has a free will, and will decide for themselves when they are ready to move onward.

This free will is the root of the problem, as it often requires devious tactics to move a determined spirit to the Light. When dealing with a strong militant energy, it is important to be in control of the situation, not a job for the faint-hearted, as this unpleasant character won't have changed for the better on death—he'll still have his unpleasant ways.

When exorcism involves a powerful demonic being, it is advisable to work with a partner, as it can be a long battle of wits and you can support one another. Whatever the level of negative beings, it is wise to double-check the energy of the building and fill it with Light before starting to deal with the spirit, as it is very important to use every tool possible to deplete their energy sources.

After bombarding them with love and White Light, if you know the problem is a spirit who had an addiction for alcohol or sex, then try to tempt them with a promise of lots of whiskey, beer, or sex waiting for them at the Light. Surprisingly, this often works.

During the past ten years, there has been an enormous increase in demand for exorcists, so much so that Chicago has a full-time exorcist. He is an evangelist preacher and author who is very experienced in this field of work, and works with a team of forty exorcists throughout the ministry in America.

The Roman Catholic Church in the US reports that they now have ten exorcists, whereas only one was required ten years ago. As well as exorcism, they find an increase in demands for spiritual cleansing ceremonies.[10]

Many bishops and priests carry out exorcisms, and the International Association of Exorcists claims to have carried out over 3,000 exorcisms in the past fourteen years.

Perhaps the most famous person to carry out this distressing task was the late Pope, who is reported to have conducted an exorcism in the Vatican on a young woman who yelled obscenities and spoke in tongues. Fortunately, this powerful leader of the Roman Catholic Church succeeded in releasing the cause of her suffering.[11]

The Vatican's Courses in Exorcism

The need for an enormous increase in the number of trained exorcists has been recognised in Rome, so the Roman Catholic Church has taken positive action in announcing that a Vatican-sponsored college is launching a new course for exorcists. The two-month university course will include some practical lessons on the history of Satanism, psychology, and the law.

The news about exorcism is not simply media overreaction, dramatising a situation to make interesting reading—the problem is real. There are those out there who work with the dark side and who enjoy dabbling in satanic rituals.

The Vatican's new attention to this problem derives from the recognition that there is an urgent need to cast out devils in those who are possessed. It is a serious business as those who experiment with this satanic cult-type entertainment often do not realise that not only are they a danger unto themselves, they are also a threat to the community.[12]

Speaking in Tongues

What is speaking in tongues? Many are impressed by this ability, others are uneasy about it, and so they should be, as it says in the Bible that one should not speak in any tongue in church, unless those present understand what you are saying, which does seem very sensible. Speaking in tongues comes in two separate forms. The first is known as *Xenoglossia*, when the person speaks in a strange tongue recognised by listeners but unknown to the speaker. You've possibly heard of a person who, when in trance, can speak fluent French or German, but when in a normal state, cannot speak or understand a word of the language.

Be on your guard if you are ever in the presence of a person who goes into trance, starts to shake violently, and is struggling very hard to speak, but seems unable to control his voice. This is almost certainly a sign that the spirit guide of the person in trance is struggling to channel a message to the group, and the entity is blocking the energy.

The second type is *Glossolalia*, which is speaking in tongues with a totally unrecognisable language. It can be a babble, or totally lack sense, as though the person has no control over the actions of their mouth. This can be a sign of possession.

Ghosts and evil spirits have become much more fashionable since people were reminded of the subject in the film *The Exorcist,* as this film created great awareness of demons, Satan, and possession. Perhaps this film did us all a big favour, as these enemies have always been present, but most of us were unaware of them. Now that we are more aware, we can get rid of them.

The subject is talked about openly today and people accept the existence of mischievous spirits and entities, and realise help is available, whereas, many years ago, people would not have admitted there was a problem for fear of being placed in a mental institution. It is hardly surprising that this subject was very taboo half a century ago, although demons and malevolent spirits are nothing new, as exorcism goes back in history a very long time. The Bible details several cases of exorcism, so the need is an age-old problem, and cannot be completely blamed on alcohol, drugs, and other modern-day problems. Whatever the cause, it's nice to know that help is available to control this nightmare situation.

Recognise the Power of a Negative Presence

Never underestimate the power of negative energy as it can be found in the most unexpected places and is capable of doing the most amazing things. I recently taught dowsing to a class at an adult centre, and witnessed just how powerful this energy can be. The class had been underway for an hour, and all sixteen students had succeeded in learning to dowse by getting their pendulums to give them correct answers to the exercises.

Suddenly the classroom door opened and a cold chill came into the air as a young girl entered the room, dressed all in black and carrying an enormous number of plastic carrier bags. She sat down with the other pupils and then abruptly arose from her chair, and started to walk very slowly around the room with her head down as though looking for something. I asked her if she had lost something and, to my surprise, she replied that she was looking for the black energy.

The other students were beginning to get a little uneasy as they sensed something strange had occurred in the room and their suspicions were correct, for to the astonishment of all of us, every pendulum in the room ceased to work. At this stage, I realised there was a serious problem so called the security guard to escort the girl from the classroom, as she had not registered for this lesson and should not have been in the room. I later learned that this sad young woman suffered from a serious mental health problem and that she had that morning left the local hospital for mentally ill patients. She also had a powerful negative attachment, which may have been the cause of some of her health problems.

There was so much power from the negative attachments that it had changed the energy in this large classroom, so I had to collect my thoughts quickly and cleanse the room of all negative energy. Next I needed to cleanse each pendulum individually, so that the class could continue to enjoy the dowsing exercises.

I have always treated the dark side with great respect, but until then, I had never realised that the negative power of one person could completely change the energy in a room. This remarkable demonstration was a powerful lesson to everyone in the class that we must never underestimate this invisible, silent enemy.

The Law of Karma

We often hear someone say "Oh, it's karma," as an explanation for something happening to a person, and perhaps it is. The basis of karma is creating balance, so when a person intentionally hurts another person, or is cruel to an animal, then a karmic debt is outstanding in the person's karma bank. Like any other bank, it is not good to be overdrawn, and eventually the books must balance!

The following quotes all sound as though they were written with karma in mind, as we are often told: "What you give out, you get back tenfold," and "As ye sow, so shall ye reap." "An eye for an eye and a tooth for a tooth" also belongs in this category.

Karma is all about balancing your "give and take department," so the first rule of karma is: "Only ever do unto others as you would have them do unto you." If you are ever tempted to do a bad deed or hurt another human being, then stop and remind yourself of the Law of Karma, and think whether you would like to be at the receiving end of the treatment.

If more awareness of the effect of karma can be created, then perhaps we can reduce the number of wars and level of strife in the world. If you have serious concerns about karma or encounters with the dark side, then relax, as you can insure against certain paranormal experiences.

Insurance Against Paranormal Phenomena

The world of insurance is changing with the times, and one enterprising London firm of insurance brokers is actually offering insurance coverage to anyone who is concerned about poltergeist attack, problems with vampires, or alien abduction.

Are you wondering if there is any demand for this type of coverage? The answer is yes—the first week this coverage was offered, the company, whose policy is underwritten by Lloyd's, received over 1,000 enquiries.

So there are some worried people out there. *Psychic News* reported that the following situations are covered by the policy:

1. Attack by Dark Entities.
2. Impregnation by Aliens.
3. Abduction by Aliens.
4. Accidental Death due to Paranormal Forces.
5. Conversion to Vampire or Werewolf.[13]

Experiencing any of the above nightmares could be very lucrative, as compensation ranges from £100,000 to £1million, so it's not surprising that, in the United States, around 200,000 people have purchased this type of policy. Are you reassured to know that this type of insurance exists against the probability of it happening to you?[13]

A branch of Russia's state insurance administration offers a policy against being kidnapped by extraterrestrials. The only catch is that your heirs must present "irrefutable evidence" of those other-world forces. This department can't lose (*Neotic Science Review*).[14]

Summary

I have tried to create awareness in this chapter of the importance of recognising the presence of negative energy and negative entities. Many people ask "Why does God allow negative entities to exist?" and "Why does he allow negative spirits to possess a person?" The answer is that if there was only good in the world, we would never learn about evil. The Creator has given us free will so we must learn to choose whether we want to be in the good camp or the evil one.

Psychic attack, spirit possession, dark entities, and low-level spirits all thrive on negative energy, so it is important to avoid negative situations in your life, as anger and hate create food for the bad guys.

When dealing with dark entities, it is essential to remember never to underestimate them and try to be one jump ahead, as this devious bunch are always ready for action. They come in a variety of different shapes and levels of power, and turn up in the most unexpected places, so it is important that we are aware of them, and know how to get rid of them. Distance is no problem as spirit release work can be done remotely, and is effective whether on the other side of the world or in the same room. The advantage of working at a distance is that it avoids the presence of the entity in your home or therapy room, and it can be done at a time convenient to you.

Perhaps the most important things to remember when in the presence of a negative entity are to always trust your gut feeling and always listen to your body. If you ever feel a negative presence, or the energy in the room seems dark or evil and you feel concerned or frightened, then don't delay, call for the assistance of Archangel Michael.

The power of prayer and White Light are both powerful weapons to be used against any dark situations. Any time you feel threatened by a negative person or negative spirit, use prayer and White Light to diffuse this energy.

Always remember to regularly cleanse your aura of negative energy and fill your body with White Light, as this acts as a deterrent. Make sure you place a cloak of protection around your aura each day, definitely when you expect to be in the presence of negative people, so you will be safe from invasion.

Have a look at the list of symptoms of possession and if you sense that a relative or work colleague has an attachment, perhaps you can mention the possibility of an attachment. It is difficult to raise this sensitive subject, but the person may be aware something is not quite right, and can't put their finger on the problem.

They will be relieved when you suggest it is worth visiting a spirit release therapist and will be forever grateful for your advice. An easy way around the problem is to leave this book in a prominent place so that they will see it and ask questions, so giving you the opportunity to talk about it.

We have talked about poltergeists and the possible different causes of this strange happening, how to deal with this powerful display of psychic energy, and discussed the Ouija board and the harmful effects of using this device, which encourages energies from the lower Earth plane to come into your home. Don't be tempted to use it, and warn your family and friends of the dangers.

I have tried to give you an insight into the enormous subject of negative entities, and if you would like to learn more about this fascinating dark world, then have a look at the books listed below in the notes.

Today I received very unpleasant proof that the dark side does exist, as I received an email from the publisher requesting a new disc of this book as they were experiencing difficulties formatting it. Feeling mystified, I switched on my computer to investigate the problem and all was revealed as, to my horror, I found that the section on earthbound spirits had been very effectively corrupted, and was so scrambled that it was unrecognisable. Part of the print was in red ink and part in black ink, all words had a line scored through them, and a black line running down the side of each page. To make matters worse, some facts had been removed from several chapters and mixed together, so the negative energy or malicious spirit who was trying to delay the publishing of this book did an excellent job.

I called for the assistance of a computer consultant who said he had never seen anything like it before, and could not offer an explanation. As a last resort, a qualified Microsoft technician was called to assist, but he also said he could not offer any logical explanation for this malicious destruction of my work. Fortunately, I had a copy so all was not lost, but it certainly demonstrated the power of the dark side and the evil intent of low level spirits. I always put on a cloak of protection when doing this work, but from now on I will have to also place a protection around my computer.

Notes

1. Irene Hickman D.O. *Remote Possession. Diary of Lucifer.* The Hickman Academy for Spirit Release & Healing. June 2004, Issue 18.
2. Edith Fiore, *The Unquiet Dead.* Ballantine, 1995.
3. Samuel Sagan MD. *Entity Possession.* Destiny Books.
4. Hickman (2004).
5. Joe H. Slate PhD. *Psychic Vampires.* Llewellyn Publications.

6. *Planetary Connection.* Spring 94. "Writing on the Ground."

7. *The Concise Oxford Dictionary.*

8. Robert Bruce, *Practical Psychic Self Defence*. Hampton Roads.

9. Stephen Turoff. *Seven Steps to Eternity.* Elmore-Chard. London.

10. *Rod and Pendulum.* No. 16. Jan. 2001. *New York Times.* 28 Nov. 2000. John W. Fountain, "Exorcists and Exorcism Proliferate Across USA." Jonathon Petre. *The Daily Telegraph*, London. 26 Nov. 2000.

11. Society News. *The Times* (via Drudge) Richard Owen. PDT by Gritty. "Exorcism Pope cast out demons in the Vatican." http://www.freepublic.com/forum/a39bc43c71c4f.htm

12. BBC News, World Edition. 17 Feb. 2005. "Rome Priests get Exorcism Lessons" by Mark Duff. BBC News, Milan. http://www.bbc.co.uk/2/hi/europe/4272689.stm

13. *Psychic News.* Stanstead Essex. UK. "Insurance Offer Paranormal Policies."

14. *Planetary Connection.* Spring 94. "Beam Me Up I'm Insured." *Neotic Science Review.*

chapter ten

Let's Talk About Death and Dying

———————————————●———————————————

Perhaps now is the time to change our perception of death—so many of us today seem to neglect the all-important subject of death. We prepare for our life by constantly learning new skills, we also prepare for childbirth, but most of us have not made any serious effort to prepare for our death. Perhaps it's time for an enterprising person to introduce "Preparing for Death" classes. We are all able to transform death into a lovely reality, instead of a grey wilderness.

It is our outlook and our way of life that controls our journey. Death is inevitable but it is not final. When we all accept that it is an important part of a long journey, we will reduce the number of trapped spirits and eliminate the fear that surrounds death.

Why do so many people in the Western world find the subject of death difficult to handle?

Why do neighbours and friends become tongue-tied and uncomfortable when you have lost a loved one? Why do they quite noticeably avoid meeting you? A friend recently told me how upset she had been by the behavior of neighbours whom she had known for many years, but who more or less ignored her when her husband died.

Death is very much a part of the natural living process. It is a continuation of life, and those of us who are able to accept it as a part of the cycle are guaranteed a wonderful transition to the next stage of life. It is time for the media and the churches to help spread the word to help everyone to realise there's more to death than simply dying and being buried.

Birth and death are the two most traumatic happenings in our life and although we don't realise it at the time, each event is opening a door to a whole new experience. Both are an equally important part of the natural universal law that governs the never-ending cycle of human creation.

Our death is not the end of our souls, nor is it a huge black void of unfriendly emptiness waiting to envelop us in its energy—it should never be shrouded in a cloak of mystery, fear, and confusion. Death leads to the new beginning and to being reborn, so death is rebirth—it is a necessary incident and is a part of the Law of Life. It is inevitable and necessary as it is required to allow us to move on to the spiritual dimension to continue learning.

Although we call it "death," those on the other side call it "reawakening." Within a split second of death, we again become a spirit, and as every spirit consists of a fluid energy, it allows us to float around in space.

The physical body is a spiritual shell that houses the body only in this life. In each incarnation, you receive a new body, but always retain the same spirit, as your spirit never leaves you. It is immortal. We are all energy, and our bodies and our spirits are on slightly different frequencies. Upon death, the body reverts back to dust as Nature recycles it, but never doubt the spirit lives on. Very little of life is permanent, although to all of us it seems real, and our earthly bodies are not as they seem to us. Scientists tell us it is really only a mix of electrons, protons, and neurons.

Our bodies are composed of a life force field and an electrostatic field, the experts tell us. It is a simple plan that has worked smoothly since the beginning of time, whereby energy keeps on shaping and moulding our bodies at such a high speed that it is invisible to the naked eye. It does sound very far-fetched and extremely difficult to comprehend, but the system works. One of the easiest ways to describe death and the move of the spirit to the next world is to compare it with a caterpillar that leaves its cocoon when it is time to move on to the next phase of its development. That is exactly what happens to the spirit on death—it moves on to the next stage of development.

To add to the confusion, each one of us has two bodies, the one you see and feel, which is your physical body, and the other body that is invisible and a mass of subatomic particles that move on a much finer energy vibration. When we pass to the world of spirit, we leave absolutely everything behind except the memory. The mind lives on after death.

It is eternal, so we take all of life's experiences with us to the next phase of development.

There is proof that the mind is everlasting, as many accurate communications have come from the deceased. Those in spirit can have a sensible conversation with us, whether about scientific research in a previous century, or the ingredients for their favourite cake. This sort of information proves the mind lives on long after the body has decomposed. When you accept this fact, your life becomes easier, and you feel lighter, with the realisation that life is eternal. Death is not the permanent end of life—it is simply a big step forward in our development. The mind is like a kernel, a nucleus and the centre of information, registering every detail of our life. This is taken to the next stage of our journey.

The amazing power of the mind is a gift from our Creator; it is everlasting as it is the power at the centre of the soul. The brain's job is to act as a go-between for facts to pass from the mind to the person, so the brain is responsible for amplifying our every thought.

All of these thoughts originate in the mind and not in the brain, as the mind is the source of all information.

As soon as we die, several important things occur. First, the invisible silver thread that links our physical body to our etheric body is cut— some people claim to have seen this cord leave a person's body on death. The next thing to happen is that the memory of everything we have learned during our lifetime on Earth is transferred to the soul, which holds all knowledge of our experiences.

When a person is lying in a hospital bed, pronounced dead after an accident or illness, the mind is still in perfect working order, although the body appears to be dead. Sir Oliver Lodge said "Everything material is temporary, but the forces of the world of the mind are permanent."[1] Yes, it is an ongoing process of life after death, and death after life, until our soul has learned all its lessons and is complete. This fact is even confirmed in Tarot cards, as the Death card in a reading is a sign of a new beginning and not usually of a death, although this card worries a great many people.

Messages from mediums tell us that death is a moving on into the Light, leaving your body, which is the outer skin. Like many things, natural wear and tear has taken place, and the time has come to discard the Earth body as it is no longer needed. Our current life on this planet is only a very small part of the gigantic life we all experience. When we say good bye to our life on Earth, we start the all-important spiritual process of letting go of Earth ties, of saying farewell to those nearest and dearest, and remembering we will meet them again at a later date. This is not always easy.

Carl Jung taught us that death is a new form of life. It is simply a transition, but many people argue that we have only other people's word that there's a good time waiting for us on the other side!

Over the past few decades, many messages and books have been channelled, and many near death experiences reported. All consistently tell of the amazing feeling of love. Do you know anyone who has had a near death experience? These are very common and are reported by all ages from young children to the elderly, but all have the same story to tell. The story must be correct as young children who have died suddenly in an accident and been resuscitated have no idea about death and have not been influenced by others, yet all tell of very similar feelings.

These words from an old spiritualist hymn ring very true: "What men call death is but a simple crossing over life's river to the other side."[2]

This parking zone is there for those of us who want to linger, before moving on to the next phase of our development.

The universe is infinite. It is endless, so life is a wonderful continuous process of evolving. It is a slow process as it goes on for thousands of years, while we continue to learn and evolve to a higher vibration.

If someone could supply each one of us with a simple handbook of instructions and guidelines, life would be so much easier, and fear of death would be banished forever. We would know it is a part of life's cycle. As they near death, so many people ask "What is the purpose of life?" and "Where have I come from, and where am I going?" Death is only a doorway leading to the next phase of our life on the astral plane, which is all around us. There is no concrete proof, no technical proof from science, but plenty of reliable circumstantial evidence, all pretty convincing, that life is continuous after the body dies. When you talk about death, you have to talk about the soul, as the subjects are interlinked

The Soul Is the Boss

The soul is our life force. It is the indestructible direct link with our Creator. I have been taught that the soul is like an orange, which has many segments. Each segment is like a life on Earth or another planet where we learn many lessons. In each life, we learn completely different lessons until we have learned all our lessons and the soul is complete.

Souls usually reincarnate in groups, so there is an affinity between people who knew each other in previous lives. For this reason, you sometimes find when you meet a person for the first time that you feel you already know them very well. Their mannerisms and turn of phrase are so familiar and yet you *know* you have never met them before and don't even know anyone who is very similar who could remind you of them. How many people have you heard talk about this type of experience?

The very seed of our being is our soul and it grows with every experience. It is nondenominational so is not favoured solely by any one religion, nor is it linked to any specific skin colour, as every person on this planet has a soul and each soul can incarnate in a selection of countries over the centuries. The soul is completely separate from the brain and the body. Its job is to hold a record of your experiences and ensure you learn all of life's lessons to become a complete soul. All souls are different as every human being is different—even identical twins are not identical, as they may not have been twins in previous incarnations. Each soul holds a record of all of each life's experiences. Carl Jung describes the soul as "the living thing in man which lives of itself, and is the cause of life."[3]

Many people present at a death will report seeing a strong light leave the body at the moment of death, but what is this light, and where is it going? This is the soul leaving the body on its journey back to the source. The soul is the boss, it has the final say when it will leave the body and it chooses the next incarnation. In each incarnation the soul learns more lessons to develop a higher consciousness.

There are many different levels in the spirit world, so learning important lessons helps the soul to rise to a higher vibration. The magnitude of this fascinating subject is difficult to comprehend.

Each one of us is a very self-aware being with our own destiny, each with our own soul, and each of us is individually connected by an invisible link to the vast field of consciousness and our Creator. All that any of us know for certain is that the facts about our soul and the unexplainable process of nature, birth, and death will finally be revealed to us when we move to the other side of the veil. Our Creator is an intangible spirit, responsible for all life in the universe. This force of love is ever present around us, whatever our beliefs or religion.

What Happens at a Spiritualist Church?

Are you uneasy about visiting a Spiritualist church? The first time I attended, I was a little apprehensive. A friend had invited me to go along to a service at the local church and I remember wondering what strange happenings would occur, but my fears were quickly squashed, as we were made welcome by some very friendly ladies.

The service, like any other church, used several hymns and prayers, and on that day the first hymn was "The Lord Is My Shepherd," sung to the old tune, which had always been a favourite of mine from schooldays. I felt I had made the right decision to attend, as I was very aware of the peaceful energy in this little church service, which was held at the local scout hut—very basic, but it had a wonderful energy. Since that day, I have visited many Spiritualist churches and always found the same welcoming energy. This religion was formed over a hundred years ago and offers a unique help line for people who have suffered bereavement and need a little reassurance that their relatives are safe and happy on the other side.

The church does not have a resident priest or minister; it has a president who chairs the service, which is taken by a visiting medium. After the sermon, a clairvoyance is given. Because a different medium takes the service each week, there is variety and this church is never boring. It's very unusual for anyone to fall asleep.

The very simple service includes an interesting talk on philosophy, followed by healing being sent to those in need. The most popular part of the service comes next, when the medium gives the clairvoyant messages to those present from loved ones in the spirit world. These messages are always personal and often relate to current worries. The people who receive the messages are usually experiencing worry from family or job-related problems, or else it's a relative who simply wants to say hello and give a word of encouragement. Some messages are sad and some are funny.

One evening at my local church, the medium gave a message to a young man who was sitting at the front of the church. She said "Your grandmother is here and she is asking you to please get your car taxed and insured." Yes, his face went red.

On another occasion I visited a church service where the medium gave a message to a gentleman, saying "Your mother is here and says it's time you finished decorating the hall; it's over a year since you started"! His wife, who was sitting next to him, was smiling and nodding her head. There are no secrets from spirit. Clairvoyant messages are usually very specific, so the person receiving the message instantly recognises the person and their mannerisms being described.

Obviously, the quality and style of mediumship varies—some mediums will give names and places, while others may give less personal information. No matter how people may scoff at this type of church service, the clairvoyance given brings great peace and reassurance that the departed loved one is always close. A simple message from a loved one saying they like the person's new hairdo or the colour of their new three-piece furniture suite is the proof the person needs to reassure them their loved one is happy in the next world. This type of clairvoyance is proof of survival, which is the belief of spiritualism.

Sceptics will always say it's guess work and the message could be made to suit anyone, but some of the information is very specific and there's no way the medium could know any details about the person, as many of the mediums have traveled a considerable distance to come to the church. As well as traveling in the circuit of churches, they also travel to other parts of the country and several travel abroad to do workshops and clairvoyant demonstrations.

It doesn't really make any difference whether the medium knows the person or not, as the medium receives the message direct from spirit and is only acting as a channel to pass the message. She will describe the words she hears and whatever she sees, giving a detailed description of what the spirit looked like while living on the earth plane. A good medium will usually give a message that is 90 percent reliable. You have to make a small allowance for error, as the spirit who is sending the message is not always clear what they want to say—they can be emotional when passing messages to loved ones.

When I was fairly new to the spiritual pathway, I attended a local spiritualist church and the medium, a gentleman from London, gave me the last message of the service.

He addressed me, and in a loud voice said: "Young lady at the back, you who have everything." He was referring to my spiritual gifts, but in my ignorance, I though he was referring to my new Lapidus suit that had cost a lot of money! I wondered how he knew my suit was expensive, since I was sitting in the back row! It was only afterward that I realised he was not talking about material wealth.

Mediums work on different spiritual levels, so some will give messages relating to everyday life, while others will give wonderful spiritual messages from guides and helpers about the person's spiritual journey. Remember, we are all on different pathways.

In addition to their Sunday service, most Spiritualist churches have a healing service once or twice each week, when any member of the public can attend to receive healing. Healers in the church take at least a two-year training, which has strict guidelines set up by the Spiritualist National Union. The training is similar to that of the NFSH, which is nondenominational and the largest healing organisation in the world.

Religious Trends Are Changing

Today more seats than ever are vacant in a great many churches. This is confirmed by a survey done on Christianity, incorporating all denominations. The survey found a mere 8 percent of the population regularly attend a Sunday church service. If this decline continues for the next two decades, attendance figures will be down to 2 percent. Within the past ten years, attendance figures have dropped by 22 percent, which seems to suggest there is a change in attitude toward religion.[4]

The number of active churches is dropping steadily. In the UK, 1,900 new churches were opened, but this was cancelled out by the fact that 2,800 were closed.

Today, attitudes to religion have changed, as people discover the more spiritual side of life through yoga classes and meditation, etc., and religion's attitude toward communicating with spirit has softened.

The Vatican Okays Contacting Spirit

A great many Roman Catholics believe very firmly that their church disapproves strongly of the idea of any contact with spirits of the dead, but this is not the case. The Vatican newspaper, *L'Obsservatore Romano*, reports the Rev. Gino Concetti, chief theological commentator to the newspaper and the Vatican's most authoritative spokesman, stated positively that the church accepts the feasibility of a communication with the departed.

He says "Communication is possible between those passed to be in an eternal state of repose, whether that be in Heaven or purgatory."[5]

The Roman Catholic Church, much to their members' surprise, accepts that deceased relatives can trigger inspiration and have the ability to prompt impulses. The new Catholic Catechism states that deceased spirits can intercede on Earth.

Concetti quoted the wonderful words of the dying St. Dominic: "Do not weep for I shall be more use to you after death and I shall help you then, more effectively than during my lifetime."[6] The new catechism will reassure those members who for many years have suffered feelings of guilt while they secretly visited mediums to make contact with a loved one.

This change in the attitude of the Catholic religion toward communication with spirits is great news, but how many local priests have told their congregations about the update? Is the average member of the Catholic Church aware that the pope has okayed a visit to the local medium?

In a recent speech, the late pope told Catholics that Heaven is not up in the sky. This is, of course, the modern-day realisation, as we become more *au fait* with the ways of the spirit world. This announcement was followed a week later by a talk explaining there is no Hell, that such a place does not exist.

The Pope said "Hell is a state of mind for those spirits who turn their back on the Creator." He also stated that God is not an old man with a white beard, but has a male and female side.[7] This makes sense as it creates balance, i.e., yin and yang, negative and positive, male and female.

This church still teaches that all souls go to purgatory, where poor souls must serve time for the sins they have committed. Views have been reassessed by the church regarding the devil. The church now states this entity should not be thought of as a beast with a tail and pitchfork or a demonic figure who possessed people, but more as a persuasive force, with the ability to trick people.

Many Catholics must be rejoicing at the update of their religion's outlook, for the church has taken a monumental step forward by updating some of their old and outdated religious teachings, so modern-thinking members will find it easier to accept the new views.

A Funeral That was Out of this World!

Perhaps the most unusual and lonely burial of all times took place recently, planned with precision. It was completely void of music, prayer, and kind words! This was the strange choice of a geologist killed in a road accident in Australia, who chose to have his remains sent to the moon inside a Lunar Prospector spacecraft.[8]

Other men and women may have died on the moon in the name of research, but this is the first gentleman to have his ashes sent there, to be placed on the surface of the moon. The spaceship, which acted as a hearse, was on a NASA mission to search over the shadowed area to find water. The geologist's ashes certainly did not make a graceful landing on the moon, as the casket landed with an enormous crash, equivalent to a two-ton car traveling at 1,100 miles per hour—not a dignified landing, but he did get his last wish.

Summary

In some ways, death is very final, as it is the end of a life on earth, but life carries on in another dimension, so death is really a new beginning, an important part in the cycle of spiritual development.

Birth and death are by far the two most traumatic experiences in our life and each is a new beginning, although when you have been bereaved, it is not always easy to accept the fact that life is an ongoing cycle and is a vital part of the universal law of natural progression.

Today there is proof that life does not end on death—anyone visiting a Spiritualist church or a medium will receive confirmation that their loved one is enjoying life on a different dimension. They will often give words of advice on a certain family problem, proving that they are always near us and aware of what is going on in our life.

In an ideal world, we would all be aware that the human mind is everlasting, death is a necessary happening, and as Carl Jung wrote, "Death is a new form of life."[7] When death is understood, the fear surrounding this event will be eliminated and the number of earthbound spirits will be reduced.

When a new concept of death evolves, it may change the format of funerals—instead of being a sad event, we may see them becoming a celebration of the person's life, and more people requesting original or uplifting ideas for the scattering of their ashes, like the geologist whose ashes were scattered on the moon. Today ashes are sprinkled on favorite sites including a certain hole on their local golf course or on a cliff top where they had regularly stopped to enjoy the view.

Sir Oliver Lodge said "Everything material is temporary but the forces of the world of the mind are permanent. Now we are in the new century, attitudes are changing towards death and many people are beginning to accept that it is indeed a new beginning."[9] Stories have been handed down from generation to generation of the Grim Reaper standing at the end of the bed, waiting to take the deceased to some mysterious place. It is now time to say a very final good bye to tales of this ghostly figure, and banish his image forever from modern-day life.

In today's fast-moving world of technology and genetic changes, it seems rather ironic that, here in the West, an important subject like death is still veiled in mystery. In this chapter you've learned that the physical body on death is recycled and the soul moves on. Your body is simply the outer shell and in each life you receive a new body. People who have been born crippled or deformed will have a new body in their next incarnation, but will have the same soul.

Your soul is your life force and is with you for each lifetime, until all lessons have been learned. The soul is the seed of your being and the direct link with your maker, so never underestimate the importance of your soul. It is very separate from your brain and from your body. Souls incarnate in groups, so folks you know and love in this lifetime will meet again in another life. It seems such a long time ahead, but it will happen, as death is not the end.

Notes

1. Raymond Smith.
2. *Spiritualist National Union Hymn Book.*

3. *Nexus New Times*. Vol. 9. No. 3. May 2002. Dr. Andrew Powell. Jung 159:26. "Archetypes of the Collective Unconsciousness." *The Collective Works*. Vol. 9. Routledge & Kegan Paul, 1959.

4. *Life and Soul*. No. 19. July 1999. Roy Stemman. Karma Publishing Ltd. "Churchgoing Declines."

5. *Life and Soul*. No. 18. Nov. 1999, "No Heaven, No Hell & God is Feminine" *Daily Telegraph*.

6. Ibid.

7. *Nexus New Times*. Vol. 9. No. 3.

8. *Life and Soul*. No. 18.

9. Raymond Smith.

Conclusion

———————————————————●———————————————————

Welcome to the joys and rewards of spirit rescue. I hope in these pages I have succeeded in inspiring you to attempt to help any earthbound spirits you meet. Should you ever happen to be in a building where one or more of these spirits are trapped, please remember they will usually welcome your kind words, so don't panic! Try to tell yourself that you are helping the lost spirit of a person to find their way home. Imagine the feeling of trying to find your home on a thick, foggy night—that's how they feel, as they can't see their way home.

I have touched on the subject of dowsing and I can almost guarantee that if you do not already dowse, when you discover you have mastered this art it will open up a whole new world to you, and you will find yourself dowsing for answers to all sorts of questions. If you find that you have an affinity to your pendulum, then contact The American Society of Dowsers as they may have a group near your home. As well as using dowsing as a tool to find out information about an earthbound spirit, you'll find it useful to diagnose illness and determine which treatments are most beneficial.

If you have never done any healing work, now is a good time to explore this gift. Simply hold your hands out in front of you and mentally ask to be used as a healing channel. After a few minutes you will start to feel the energy channelling through your hands. Alternatively, if you are not confident to give healing to a sick person, perhaps you'd like to ask the pendulum to channel the healing energy to the patient or to any earthbound spirit.

Remember that you are never alone when you are rescuing a spirit, giving healing, or astral traveling, as your spirit guides and helpers are only a split second away. Should you ever be concerned about a situation, all you need to do is call on their assistance.

I have tried to impress upon you the importance of placing some form of protection around your body each day, so your aura is always protected from energy vultures and negative energy. There are several excellent books available on the many methods of protection, so if you would like to learn more about protection, visit your local bookstore.

Are you new to the spiritual pathway? Then think about joining a development circle or group and attend local workshops. Once you allow yourself to open up to the spirit world, you'll find that you are often guided to *what* is right for you, so go with your gut feeling as it will be correct and will lead you on your spiritual journey.

Good luck and blessings on your pathway.

Resources

———————————————●———————————————

Bachler, Kathe. *Earth Radiation*. Manchester, UK: Wordmaster Ltd., 1989.

BBC News, World Edition, 17 Feb. 2005, by Duff Mark, *BBC News,* Milan. Rome. "Priests get Exorcism Lesson." http://news.bbc.co.uk/2/hi/europe/42726589.stm

Bird, Christopher. *Divining Hand, "The Observer for US Forces"* USA 13.3.67, New Age Press Inc., 1989.

Bruce, Robert. *Practical Self Defence*. UK: Hampton Roads Publishing Co. Inc., 2000.

Clamp, John. *The Truth Campaign*. March 1997, quoted from *Beyond Death's Doors*, by Elisabeth Kübler-Ross. First published in *Kindred Spirit Magazine.* Vol. 3. No. 7. June/August 1995.

The Concise English Dictionary, seventh ed. UK: Oxford University Press.

Cooper, Diana. *A Little Light on Angels*. UK: Findhorn Press, 1997.

Davies, Rodney. *Discover Your Psychic Powers*. UK: The Aquarian Press, 1991.

Edwards, Sherry, M., ed. "Decloaking Pathogens with Sound." *Nexus New Times.* Vol. 7. No. 6. November 2000.

Findlay, Arthur. *Looking Back*. UK: Spiritualist National Union.

Fiore, Dr. Edith. *The Unquiet Dead: A Psychologist Treats Spiritual Possession*. New York: Ballantine Books, 1995.

Gordon, Rolf. *Are You Sleeping in a Safe Place*. London: Dulwich Health.

Hickman, Irene, D.O. *Remote Possession, a Diary of Lucifer.* UK: The Hickman Academy, June 2004. Issue 18.

Horizon Research Foundation. Research on Near Death Experiences. Southampton General Hospital, England. *http://www.horizon-research.co.uk*

IANDS. The International Assoc. for Near Death Studies, Inc. Local groups worldwide. Devoted exclusively to the study of near death experiences. http://www.iands.org

IIPC International Institute of Projectology & Conscientology. http://www.iipc.org *"You Outside of Your Body."*

Jack, Michael. *Dowsing Today.* UK: The British Society of Dowsers, 1996.

Life & Soul. "Animals Have Souls Too says Christian Professor"; "Buddist View of Karma." Andrew Linzey, Prof., Mansfield College. Oxford, UK; "Testing Telepathy," Matthew Smith, Consciousness & Transpersonal Research Unit, John Moores University. Liverpool, UK. No. 16. March 1999. Roy Stemman. Karma Publishing Ltd.

———. "Are Animals Psychic." Dr. Rupert Sheldrake. Hutchinsons, UK; "No Heaven, No Hell & God is Feminine." Source: *Daily Telegraph.* No. 18. November 1999.

———. "Dialogue With the Dead is Feasible Says Rome"; "Churchgoing Declines"; "Shirley MacLaine Claims She was Charlemagne's Lover." No. 19. Summer 2000.

———. "Psychic Research Enjoying a Revival at Nine UK Universities"; "Boy Reminds His Widow of Buried Treasure." No. 17. July 1999.

Maisch, Don. EM Facts Consultancy. www.emfacts.com Reports available on electromagnetic radiation and health issues linked to mobile phones and powerlines. "Trains Trap Mobile Phone Radiation," *BBC Online, Health.* 1 May 2002.

Malik, Yvonne. "The Memory Box." Wray. *Lancashire Magazine.* Lancashire. March/April 1994.

Miller, Hamish, and Paul Broadhurst. *The Sun and the Serpent.* Cornwall. England: Pendragon Press, 1989.

The Natural Death Centre. England. A charitable project to improve quality of dying, it provides information on environmentally friendly funerals.

Oldfield, Harry. Oldfield Systems Ltd. South Ruislip, Middlesex, England.

Owen, Richard. "Exorcist Pope Casts Out Demons in the Vatican." Freerepublic.com pdt by Gritty. A Conservative News Forum. Forum/a39bc43c71c4f.htm. *The Times.* 11.9.2000.

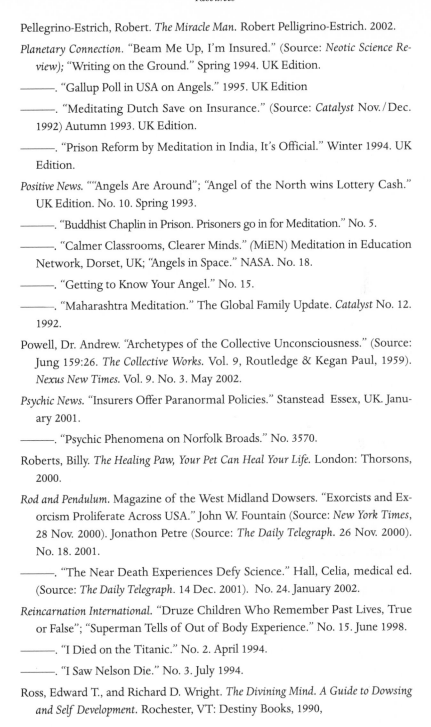

Pellegrino-Estrich, Robert. *The Miracle Man.* Robert Pelligrino-Estrich. 2002.

Planetary Connection. "Beam Me Up, I'm Insured." (Source: *Neotic Science Review);* "Writing on the Ground." Spring 1994. UK Edition.

———. "Gallup Poll in USA on Angels." 1995. UK Edition

———. "Meditating Dutch Save on Insurance." (Source: *Catalyst* Nov./Dec. 1992) Autumn 1993. UK Edition.

———. "Prison Reform by Meditation in India, It's Official." Winter 1994. UK Edition.

Positive News. ""Angels Are Around"; "Angel of the North wins Lottery Cash." UK Edition. No. 10. Spring 1993.

———. "Buddhist Chaplin in Prison. Prisoners go in for Meditation." No. 5.

———. "Calmer Classrooms, Clearer Minds." (MiEN) Meditation in Education Network, Dorset, UK; "Angels in Space." NASA. No. 18.

———. "Getting to Know Your Angel." No. 15.

———. "Maharashtra Meditation." The Global Family Update. *Catalyst* No. 12. 1992.

Powell, Dr. Andrew. "Archetypes of the Collective Unconsciousness." (Source: Jung 159:26. *The Collective Works.* Vol. 9, Routledge & Kegan Paul, 1959). *Nexus New Times.* Vol. 9. No. 3. May 2002.

Psychic News. "Insurers Offer Paranormal Policies." Stanstead Essex, UK. January 2001.

———. "Psychic Phenomena on Norfolk Broads." No. 3570.

Roberts, Billy. *The Healing Paw, Your Pet Can Heal Your Life.* London: Thorsons, 2000.

Rod and Pendulum. Magazine of the West Midland Dowsers. "Exorcists and Exorcism Proliferate Across USA." John W. Fountain (Source: *New York Times,* 28 Nov. 2000). Jonathon Petre (Source: *The Daily Telegraph.* 26 Nov. 2000). No. 18. 2001.

———. "The Near Death Experiences Defy Science." Hall, Celia, medical ed. (Source: *The Daily Telegraph.* 14 Dec. 2001). No. 24. January 2002.

Reincarnation International. "Druze Children Who Remember Past Lives, True or False"; "Superman Tells of Out of Body Experience." No. 15. June 1998.

———. "I Died on the Titanic." No. 2. April 1994.

———. "I Saw Nelson Die." No. 3. July 1994.

Ross, Edward T., and Richard D. Wright. *The Divining Mind. A Guide to Dowsing and Self Development.* Rochester, VT: Destiny Books, 1990,

Sagan, Samuel, M.D. *Entity Possession.* Rochester, VT: Destiny Books, 1997.

Scientific & Medical Network. Isle of Wight, UK. March 2001.

Slate, Joe H. PhD. *Psychic Vampires.* St. Paul, MN: Llewellyn Publications, 2004.

Spiritualist National Union (SNU) *Hymn Book.* Stanstead, Essex, England.

Smith, Raymond. *For Those Who are Willing to Listen.* UK: ConPsy Publications.

Taylor, Allegra. *Acquainted With the Night: A Year in the Frontier of Death.* Fontana/Collins, 1989.

Turoff, Stephen. *Seven Steps to Eternity.* London: Elmore-Chard.

Wiseman, Dr. Richard, Hereford University, *Rod & Pendulum,* July 2001. *Daily Mail.* 18 April 2001. James Chapman.

Zammit, Victor. "A Lawyer Presents the Case for the Afterlife." www.victorzammit.com.

————. Book 2. "Respected Scientists Who Investigated."

————. Book 3. "Electronic Voice Phenomena EVP." Source: Colin Smyth.

————. Book 8. "Scientific Observations of a Medium: Looking Back." Source: Arthur Findlay (Findlay 1955:350).

————. Book 12. "The Direct Voice Mediumship of Lesley Flint, Voices From the Dead." 1971. Source: Arthur Findlay. *Voices On the Edge of the Etheric."* Rider & Co., 1931.

————. Book 16. *"Out of Body Experiences."* Sources: (a) Inglis: 30–35. (b) Lazarus 1977:167. (c) Inglis 1977: 131.

————. Book 17. "Remote Viewing." Sources: Major David A. Morehouse. *The Psychic Warrior. True Story of the CIA'S Paranormal Espionage Program,* 1996; Joseph McMoneagle. *Remote Viewing Secrets,* Hampton Roads Publishing Co., 2000; Paul Dong and E.Thomas Rafill. *China's Super Psychics.* Marlowe & Co., 1997.

————. Book 20. "Electronic Voice Phenomena (EVP)." Sources: Dr. Karlios Osis of the American Society of Psychical Research and Sir William Crookes.

Index